Praise for the Previous Editions of
Get Clients Now!™

"Too many entrepreneurs think the Internet will somehow solve all their marketing problems by magic. *Get Clients Now!* provides a marketing plan that seamlessly integrates online and offline promotion in an easy-to-follow system. It's the perfect tool for the savvy business owner to achieve sales and marketing success."

> —Mitch Meyerson, author of *Guerrilla Marketing on the Internet* and *Mastering Online Marketing*

"If you've been waiting for the phone to ring, you're better off reading *Get Clients Now!* C.J. Hayden manages to cover the beginner's guide to marketing in an easy-to-follow, methodical plan that every new consultant should absorb."

> —Alan Weiss, Ph.D., bestselling author of *Million Dollar Consulting*

"*Get Clients Now!* proves that successful self-promotion does not have to be pushy, selfish, or manipulative. The newest edition of C.J. Hayden's bestseller will help you create a marketing plan based on building authentic relationships, being of service to others, and marketing techniques that fit your own personality."

> —Caterina Rando, author of *Learn to Power Think* and co-author of *Incredible Business*

". . . presents the two most important elements for a successful marketing program for consultants: an easy, yet structured process to follow, and the motivation to get started and keep at it."

> —Rick Freedman, author of *Building the IT Consulting Practice*

"This is a system that works. C.J. Hayden has taken the mystery out of marketing. She has written a book that is easy to read; easy to understand; and most important, easy to follow. . . . In the first 28 days, I added $5,000 to my bottom line! The focus and clarity this program creates is amazing. Anyone trying to grow a business without this book is doing it the hard way."

> —Rachelle Disbennett-Lee, Ph.D., Master Certified Coach and author of 365 *Days of Coaching*

"*Get Clients Now!* pioneered the idea of a simple, action-oriented system for professional services marketing. The updated edition provides an even more effective, proven model for 'non-marketers' to get—and stay—in action and build a sustainable business."

> —Steven Van Yoder, PR strategist and author of *Get Slightly Famous*

"It's a perfect way to get in gear . . . a formula that is right on and uncovers every aspect that needs attention. . . ."

> —Josiane Feigon, author of *Smart Selling on the Phone and Online*

"If you want your business to have shameless success, you need *Get Clients Now!* C.J. Hayden's comprehensive guide to marketing provides all the essential tools a self-employed professional needs to attract an endless stream of clients."

—Debbie Allen, author of *Confessions of Shameless Self-Promoters*

"It's no secret. A successful business requires marketing and self-promotion. If you want a serious dose of marketing medicine, this book is it."

—Bernard Kamoroff, author of *Small Time Operator: How to Start Your Own Business, Keep Your Books, Pay Your Taxes, and Stay Out of Trouble*

"Advice that seems simple is actually the most brilliant and C.J.'s advice *is* brilliant. She has taken the mystification out of marketing and has truly given you the 'magic formula' in the context of a 28-day program that anyone can follow. Whatever field you're in, if you want more clients—this is the book for you."

—Susan Harrow, media coach and author of *Sell Yourself without Selling Your Soul*

"All too often, I come across business professionals who have great ideas or products but don't have a clue about how to market themselves or sell their products. This is a wonderfully practical handbook that solves the problem . . . an excellent tool for anyone who is interested in expanding their client base with consistent, easy-to-follow steps. I highly recommend it!"

—Tony Alessandra, PhD, author of *Collaborative Selling* and *The Platinum Rule for Sales Mastery*

". . . a fantastic book that takes common marketing knowledge to new heights. The simple step-by-step marketing strategies are designed to help any and every small business succeed. Hayden takes you through each step, and helps you develop a plan that is right for you and your business! Excellent!"

—Alyice Edrich, editor-in-chief of *The Dabbling Mum*

"I have been using C.J. Hayden's *Get Clients Now!* system for years, and I know that I wouldn't be where I am today without it. I actually have a waiting list for clients! If you want to attract more clients with less effort, I urge you to buy this book now!"

—Rich Fettke, Master Certified Coach and author of *Extreme Success*

"Read this book NOW! Follow C.J. Hayden's program and see your business expand immediately. Her system works!"

—Jill Lublin, author of *Guerrilla Publicity* and *Get Noticed . . . Get Referrals*

"A brilliant and effective 28-day marketing program for professionals and consultants . . . offering tools that readers can inject into their marketing efforts with renewed energy and fresh enthusiasm, utilize to design enhanced plans of marketing action, and dramatically increase their client base no matter what their area of consultative practice."

—Bookwatch

"... a powerful resource that has helped me develop successful strategies to get more clients. C.J. Hayden's book opened up a whole new set of possibilities to connect with potential new clients. . . . it's a blueprint that can work for anyone."

—Adria Richards, technology consultant and trainer

"I have just completed working the *Get Clients Now!* program. . . . I got four new clients, lined up five workshops and two speaking engagements, and had an article written about me in the local paper!"

—Tifin Kutch Dillon, life coach and educator

"The *Get Clients Now!* format is the most time-efficient, productive program I have ever seen. . . . Instead of a production of $4,000 a month, I have been able to produce $8,000 and $10,000. . . . I will become a Mary Kay Sales Director August 1, being in the top 2% of the company worldwide."

—Sharon Richman, Mary Kay beauty consultant

"I can't begin tell you how excited I am about the Get Clients Now! program; it absolutely ROCKS! As a professional business coach, I am constantly looking for the best tools and systems to support my clients in building successful practices. By adding *Get Clients Now!* to my toolbox, my practice has absolutely exploded!"

—Travis Greenlee, internet marketing and business development consultant

"*Get Clients Now!* is a must-own book. . . . Long before I finished reading it as a whole, I had been introduced to ideas that were not so hidden but had never occurred to me as approaches. . . . like the pieces of a puzzle after it is assembled, the author takes the confusion out of marketing and provides fuel for success. I highly recommend this book to those seeking an intelligent marketing plan."

—Edward Harris, web designer

"... one of the most practical books I have ever seen in my entire life. Really nicely paced with all the forms right there, with a good balance of encouragement and insistence. Superb job! I'm using it already, today was my first day, and a prospect e-mailed me back unsolicited to call me in for an assignment next week. Just as you promised, once we start marketing with commitment, the work just flows in!"

—Gordon Graham, marketing consultant

"In a very readable style, C.J. Hayden presents a well-structured method for building up your marketing. The book is aimed at the self-employed and small businesses, and Ms. Hayden shows a good understanding of the difficulties we face in marketing ourselves. . . . This is the best small-business marketing plan I have seen."

—Ross Maynard, process improvement consultant

"Get Clients Now! has been the single most powerful success ingredient in my business. In eight months I have seen a four-fold increase in business, have a pipe-line that is overflowing, and a cadre of referral partners and strategic alliances that support my business efforts. I went from stuck-and-stymied to committed-and-cashing because the GCN program taught me how. . . ."

—Kathy Sullivan, web designer

". . . gives you a step-by-step, day-by-day action plan that you can tailor make to suit your personality. You don't have to do things you don't like doing, but you can see where all the activities you like doing fit in terms of effectiveness. I have attracted six new clients since starting the 28-day program, and I'm only halfway through. Fantastic!"

—Nicola Cairncross, financial intelligence coach

". . . easy to read, well-written, well-organized, and even usability tested. What I mean by that is that it seems like you have gotten a lot of feedback from real users of your system and then incorporated that feedback to improve the book. To me, as a computer guy, this is the highest compliment I can give."

—Peter Linde, information technology consultant

"I heard C.J. speak and bought Get Clients Now! . . . Within one year, following C.J.'s marketing and selling advice, I doubled the size of my coaching practice (and I couldn't handle any more work). I recommend C.J.'s book and program to other coaches. Just be careful who you loan her book to—you may not get it back!"

—Ron Paxton, career coach

"Get Clients Now! has been life changing. The program was so powerful that . . . I filled my practice for the next six months. . . . I can't say enough about the simplicity of the program and the results."

—Lia Allen, business development specialist

"I like the Get Clients Now! program because it's simple, straightforward, and it works. GCN has distilled marketing for professionals down to a science. I recommend that everyone who's either a solo practitioner or a small business owner read the book and get with the program!"

—Andrew Finkelstein, salon and spa business expert

"Get Clients Now! is practical, easy to implement, and best of all, gets results. C.J. takes you step by step though the why and more important the HOW of marketing a service business. I believe I have used it with at least 50 or more clients, and to a person, they say it has been incredibly helpful . . . and best of all, they are making more money as a result!"

—Louise Abbott, business coach

"When I started my business, I had no idea how to market, and floundered for months. . . . I bought the book and have developed many tools that I didn't have before that make marketing more systematic, less stressful, and more productive. This book has really helped me turn things around."

—Suzanne Guess, business communications specialist

"This is a 'must have' book if you are seeking to build your business and gain more clients. C.J. makes it so easy by giving a recipe of actionable items that move you towards your business goals. . . . She identifies the marketing strategies, and a daily action plan ensures that you are working on the marketing strategy success ingredients that will get you profitable results!"

—Maria Elena Duron, personal buzz agent and marketing coach

"I love the Get Clients Now! program. It is very easy to use and assists in defining clear direction for each step of the way. It is amazing how something so simple can be so profound. This is an excellent tool for the beginner and the advanced marketer alike."

—Carla Kroger, business productivity specialist

"Coming from a technical profession, sales and marketing have always been a mystery to me. The Get Clients Now! program was a terrific starting point for understanding how to attract clients, and how to balance working the business with working on the business. The book is a resource I pick up often, and each time I walk away with a deeper understanding of how to make this business work."

—Susan Penny Brown, principal consultant, Interim Technical Management, Inc.

"This is truly the sales-and-marketing bible for consultants, coaches, and all service business professionals. . . . Using C.J.'s reader-friendly 'build-your-own' approach, tons of straightforward tips, and specific marketing techniques, you can't help but boost your small business success. A five-star book all the way and one that you'll dog-ear, highlight, and refer back to again and again."

—David Newman, professional services marketing expert

"If you love what you do, but aren't sure how to go about getting more clients, this book is for you! You'll learn a sure-fire system to market your professional service business that you can use over and over again. The Get Clients Now! system will keep you focused, motivated, and in action. Plus, you'll get all the clients you want without struggle. If you only read one marketing book this year, this is the one!"

—Rosalie Marcus, business coach

"Without a doubt, the Get Clients Now! book and system has made the single biggest difference in the growth of BilCom Group. Not only did it provide a very methodical approach to marketing that did not require much of a budget, but it also helped us understand where we had been falling short in the past. . . . the program inspired us to set and meet aggressive goals, and gave us the confidence to slowly rise as an expert voice in the industry."

—Patricia Rivera, translation agency owner

"C.J. Hayden has produced what is for my money the best marketing system for consultants and coaches I've ever seen. . . . By following her 28-day plan, you put into place a lead-generating system matched to your personal skills and inclinations.

. . . Once you get started and rolling, you'll find that getting clients is a lot easier than you ever thought it could be."

—Michael Knowles, business consultant

"Prior to starting the program, I had a shotgun approach to fishing for clients. . . . The way the book systematically lays out the to-dos helps me in a business where I have to make too many decisions in a day. Your book is the business owner's secret little helper."

—Andrea Featherston-Rossi, advisor to equestrian entrepreneurs

Get Clients Now!™

THIRD EDITION

A 28-Day Marketing Program for
Professionals, Consultants, and Coaches

C. J. Hayden

AMACOM

American Management Association

New York • Atlanta • Brussels • Chicago • Mexico City • San Francisco
Shanghai • Tokyo • Toronto • Washington, D.C.

"Get Clients Now!™" is a trademark of C.J. Hayden, San Francisco, California.

Library of Congress Cataloging-in-Publication Data
    Hayden, C. J.
Get clients now! : a 28-day marketing program for professionals, consultants, and coaches / C. J. Hayden.—Third Edition.
        pages   cm
    Includes bibliographical references and index.
    ISBN-13: 978-0-8144-3245-7
    ISBN-10: 0-8144-3245-X
1. Marketing—Study and teaching.   I. Title.
HF5415.H296   2013
658.8—dc23

                                        2012040655

About AMA

American Management Association (www.amanet.org) is a world leader in talent development, advancing the skills of individuals to drive business success. Our mission is to support the goals of individuals and organizations through a complete range of products and services, including classroom and virtual seminars, webcasts, webinars, podcasts, conferences, corporate and government solutions, business books and research. AMA's approach to improving performance combines experiential learning—learning through doing—with opportunities for ongoing professional growth at every step of one's career journey.

Printing number

10 9 8 7 6 5 4 3 2 1

To my clients,
who taught me all I know

Contents

PART III: THE STRATEGIES   125

Foreword

THE PROSPECT OF GETTING CLIENTS—NOW!—is a delightful concept. It's a noble endeavor for any business; it's a desired pot of gold at the end of your rainbow.

It is also a tough job, a baffling and daunting task, and a goal not easily reached by the majority of businesses.

For those reasons, it is absolutely crucial that you pursue that goal with all the chips stacked in your favor. In this new third edition of *Get Clients Now!*, C. J. Hayden has stacked those chips for you. They are neatly and generously provided in the upcoming pages—each chip worth far more than its weight in gold.

Unlike the chips in a poker game, these chips entail no risk for you, and if you bet them, you're certain of winning—assured of victory in the game of obtaining clients. Is it easy to win that game? It is not. Is it the fast track to financial success? Often, no. But if you apply the easy-to-follow advice presented here, getting those clients will become a certainty.

Calling a spade a spade, author Hayden starts right out by telling you exactly why you don't have enough clients right now. You may wince when you read her words, but you won't be able to refute them because you'll know in your heart that they are true.

That's the bad news. The good news is that when you complete this book—and even while you're reading it—you'll see how you can reverse this situation and develop a roster of satisfied, long-term, profitable clients.

Sounds good, but where do you start? You'll get the answer to that question pronto. What should you do right this minute to get clients? That, too, is answered in a way that will bestow you with instant enlightenment.

The complex chore of amassing an abundant list of clients is made simple and attainable with the step-by-step plan the author has in store for you. Where were those steps when I was first starting out? They weren't in any books that I read, nor in the advice given to me by well-meaning friends and even mentors.

But here they are, along with exercises to help you establish the momentum you'll need, and a worksheet that will serve as an infallible guide in your quest for clients right now.

C. J. Hayden has created a clear and effective system for you so that your efforts are not helter-skelter. Along with her system, she gives you a veritable treasury of practical ideas and proven tactics—while stomping on the toes of conventional wisdom that may have led you up the garden path to nowhere until now.

As she reveals a new world of glowing possibilities for your business, she shines a light upon many ugly realities which may have been hindering your progress. But you will be impeded no more. You will no longer suffer from a dearth of clients. Your questions will be answered and your path will be illuminated.

Get Clients Now! makes a promise in its title, then gives you the reward of living up to it.

Jay Conrad Levinson
The Father of Guerrilla Marketing
DeBary, Florida

Acknowledgments

THERE ARE FOUR SOULS WITHOUT WHOSE HELP this book could not have been written: my life partner "Friendly Dave" Herninko, who provided endless good humor, hot meals, and loving reassurance so I could keep writing; my feline companions Seabiscuit and KimChee, who leapt on my keyboard, spun my writing chair in circles, and otherwise reminded me not to take myself too seriously; and the late Laura Whitworth, coaching godmother, who gave me the original idea that led to this book.

I wish to also extend my heartfelt thanks to the following people for their generous assistance: the readers of the first and second editions, who sent me their compliments, complaints, and inspired suggestions; the coaches, consultants, and trainers who have used this system with their clients over the past seventeen years; my amazing team of supporters at Get Clients Now!—Donna Feldman, Frank Traditi, Joan Friedlander, Grace Durfee, Angee Robertson, and Annelise Zamula; Barbara McDonald of Native Design for her superb illustrations; marketing guru Jay Conrad Levinson for his early and continued encouragement; the marketing and motivation experts who contributed their words of wisdom for the sidebars in this book; literary agent Sheryl Fullerton and AMACOM editor Ellen Kadin for their ongoing support; and all the gang at Come 'n' Get It—you know who you are.

"The significant problems we face cannot be solved at the level of thinking that created them."

—ALBERT EINSTEIN

Introduction

IF YOU ARE READY TO GET CLIENTS *NOW,* you have come to the right place. Get Clients Now! is a complete marketing and sales system for consultants, coaches, and anyone who markets a professional services business. This book contains a 28-day program for sales and marketing success that has been road-tested by readers since 1999, and delivered by over 300 licensed facilitators around the world. The Get Clients Now! system has all the tools you need to get your marketing efforts unstuck, make an effective action plan, and start getting more clients.

In this new, third edition, you'll find the latest marketing approaches for independent professionals, including social media marketing, Internet marketing, prospecting and networking online, and integrating your online and offline marketing tactics. You'll also find an even stronger emphasis on building high-touch relationships in our high-tech world; new ideas for dealing with fear, resistance, and procrastination; fresh contributions from experts in marketing and motivation; and numerous improvements suggested by the thousands of readers who have made *Get Clients Now!* their sales and marketing bible.

It's easy to think that there is some hidden secret to successful marketing and sales. When you consider all the books you could read, seminars you could take, or consultants you could hire, it makes the process of learning how to market yourself seem huge, mysterious, or even terrifying. But in fact there is a simple answer to all your marketing and sales problems, and it's right here in this book: *The magic formula for professional services marketing and sales is choosing a set of simple, effective things to do, and doing them consistently.* The Get Clients Now! system will enable you to do just that.

WHO SHOULD USE THIS BOOK

Get Clients Now! is the ideal sales and marketing tool for almost any professional services provider. Some of the many professionals who will benefit are: accountants, architects, attorneys, bodyworkers, chiropractors, coaches, computer professionals, consultants, counselors, designers, engineers, financial planners, freelancers, health practitioners, insurance and investment brokers, photographers, real estate agents, recruiters, speakers, therapists, trainers, and writers. Whether you are a professional marketing your own services or you have business development responsibilities for your firm, this book will provide you with a proven system for finding clients.

The Get Clients Now! system is designed to help you market and sell professional services to either businesses and organizations or individual consumers. If your service business also markets tangible products, e-products, or classes and seminars, this book may not be a complete solution. You may need other references to help answer questions about which marketing approaches are best for the product or seminar component of your business. But for creating a customized marketing plan to sell your professional services or those of your firm, you won't need to look beyond this book.

HOW TO USE THIS BOOK

Get Clients Now! uses a cookbook model to help you create a sales and marketing action plan. First, you will discover the Success Ingredients that are missing from your current marketing and sales activities. Then you will choose from the Action Plan Menu the specific courses of action you should take. Detailed recipes for the recommended tactics and tools are provided to help you successfully implement your plan.

You will get the most value from this book if you commit from the outset to completing the exercises as you go. Just reading the information presented here will be helpful, but where marketing is concerned, more learning is rarely enough to do the trick. You need to choose a direction, take action, and keep moving forward in order to succeed.

Once your action plan is designed, the 28-day program will put your ideas into action immediately. Many people who have used the program report improved results within just a few days. You can use the program quite successfully by yourself; or to make it even more powerful, team up with a business buddy, action group, or business coach. And you can repeat the program as often as you like to continue improving your results.

Throughout the book, you'll find references to specific services, software, devices, or websites you might find useful. This information can change quickly as communication technology and business products continue to evolve. Keep in mind that the basic principles of marketing don't change as quickly as technology and products do. The ideas and approaches behind the Get Clients Now! system will continue to be valid for years to come, no matter what new paths marketing or communications may take.

For additional resources on any of the topics discussed in the book, updates to the book's content, to download copies of the Get Clients Now! worksheets, or to find a buddy, group, or coach to help you work the program, please visit the book's companion website at www.getclientsnow.com.

C. J. Hayden, MCC
San Francisco, California

"Here is Edward Bear coming downstairs now, bump, bump, bump on the back of his head behind Christopher Robin. It is, as far as he knows, the only way of coming down stairs, but sometimes he feels that there really is another way, if only he could stop bumping for a moment and think of it."

—A.A. MILNE, *Winnie-the-Pooh*

PART I

The Setup

CHAPTER 1

What Really Works?

Effective Marketing Strategies

MARKETING MADE SIMPLE

Marketing is telling people what you do, over and over. There are many ways of telling people—in person, by phone, in writing, on the Web, through the media—but you do have to *tell* them. You can't just wait for the phone to start ringing. You have to tell them over and over. Studies estimate that the typical urban citizen is exposed to thousands of marketing messages per day. Where is your message in all that communication? What will make others remember you if they hear about you only once?

Getting prospective clients to pay attention to what you have to offer and remember you until they need your services can seem like an enormous challenge. So how do people in your line of work—consulting, coaching, and other professional services—get clients? Ask any successful businessperson that question, and this is what you will hear: "Referrals." "Networking." "Making contacts and following up." "Word of mouth."

It's simple stuff; you probably already knew these answers. So why don't you have all the clients you need? If you're like most other first-time users of the Get Clients Now! system, one or all of the following reasons will sound familiar:

> ▶ **You can't decide where to begin.** Marketing your business seems like an overwhelming project. There are so many ideas to consider

and so many choices to make, and you want to make sure you are doing it right. So you worry about how best to spend your time and money. Struck by "analysis paralysis," you start and stop, sit and stew, or just do nothing.

▶ **You aren't sure how to put the pieces together.** You think you should be making phone calls but wonder if you need to finish your website first. You suspect it might be time to identify some new prospects, but what about those follow-up e-mails you've been meaning to send? You wonder if all the networking will ever pay off, and whether that speaking engagement will really generate any clients. You don't have a system, a program, or a plan.

▶ **You can't stay motivated.** Even when you know exactly what you need to do, often you just don't do it. With no boss looking over your shoulder, it's too easy to avoid marketing and sales. When you don't see immediate results, you get discouraged. When someone rejects your sales pitch, it's hard not to take it personally. It's so tempting just to wait for the phone to ring, and blame your lack of business on the economy, the competition, or the time of year.

If any or all of these obstacles have stopped you in your tracks, you are not alone. People who market professional services rarely fail due to lack of information about effective sales and marketing techniques. They fail because they don't make use of the information that is right at their fingertips. This is why the Get Clients Now! system works; it provides both a structure and a tool kit to turn your marketing goals and ideas into productive action—and it helps eliminate the roadblocks.

Marketing Is a System, Not an Event
John Jantsch, www.ducttapemarketing.com

"Small business marketers love the chase," declares John Jantsch, a marketing coach and author of *Duct Tape Marketing*. Jantsch explains,

> They love a newfangled way to make the phone ring. But they often think of a marketing promotion as a single event. It's precisely this view of marketing that holds most small businesses back. They fall prey to the "marketing idea of the week" and never fully explore what it takes to create and build a completely functioning, consistently performing, marketing system.

Small business owners have no problem thinking systems when it comes to say, accounting or hiring. When it comes to marketing though, all bets are off. It's as if they are waiting for magic fairy dust to fall upon them with the next great marketing innovation.

Effective marketing is little more than creating and operating an effective marketing system. When I use the word system I mean several things: (1) the system is documented; you can't have a system unless you write it down, (2) the system is built on sound marketing principles, and (3) you constantly measure, innovate, and refine the system.

Once you have spent the time and energy to create a plan, you need to commit your plan to a marketing calendar and then allocate the money it will take to implement your plan. When you create a calendar it is much more likely that you will look at the tasks like a "to-do" list. So, instead of worrying that you should do more marketing, you simply scratch each item off your list and plan for the next. It's an amazingly simple but effective device.

HOW THE PROGRAM WORKS

Get Clients Now! breaks down the marketing and sales process into a series of simple steps so you will know exactly where to begin to get clients today. It organizes the steps into a proven system built around three powerful elements: effective, personalized marketing strategies; an action-oriented, 28-day program; and approaches for managing the fear, resistance, and procrastination that may hinder your marketing efforts. The program shows you how all the pieces of the sales and marketing puzzle fit together: what to do, when to do it, and how to measure your results.

Designing and implementing a successful sales and marketing campaign is a lot like cooking a nutritious meal. When you are cooking, you need to decide what's on the menu, shop for ingredients, and make sure your food choices combine to make a healthful diet. In the first five chapters of this book, you will be guided to select a regular menu of marketing activities that fit your personal tastes, prepare the essential ingredients for sales and marketing success, and evaluate your choices to create a balanced marketing approach.

When your personal marketing action plan is ready for consumption, you'll begin the 28-day program. You'll start each day with a specific list of things to do, and get daily advice for working through internal and external barriers to effective action.

To make the best use of this program, you should read Chapters 1 through 5 in sequence, completing the exercises as you go. When you are ready to begin the 28-day program, start reading Chapter 6, one section per day. Two rest days per week are built into the program. Chapters 7 through 10 contain essential marketing "recipes." You can use these for reference while you are designing your action plan, or for help in implementing your plan as you go. Each of these chapters covers one stage of the Universal Marketing Cycle that you will learn about in Chapter 2. You will choose a single stage to focus on during the program and will need to read only the chapter that pertains to the stage you select.

Since this a 28-day program, does that mean you will find all the clients you need in twenty-eight days? In some cases, yes. Since 1995, when this program first became available, many Get Clients Now! participants have landed as many clients as they could handle in less than twenty-eight days. But because everyone's situation and starting place is different, your immediate results may produce fewer clients than the total you want. You may choose to keep going with the program for a second twenty-eight days, or more, to further improve your sales. That's okay; the program is designed with this intention.

After completing the program, you may choose to repeat it using the same action plan for another twenty-eight days, or begin again starting in Chapter 2 to design a revised plan. Either way, you will continue to benefit from the improved strategy, focus, and motivation that the system provides.

Key Components of the Program

The Get Clients Now! Action Worksheet is the principal planning tool for designing your personal 28-day program. (See the Completed Action Worksheet in Figure 1-1.) Here are the six components of the program included on the worksheet:

1. **Marketing Strategies**—the two to four strategies you will be using during the twenty-eight days of the program.

2. **Marketing Stage**—the stage of the Universal Marketing Cycle where you are stuck or on which you need more work.

3. **Program Goal**—the goal of your program; that is, the results you plan to achieve in the next twenty-eight days. You will set this goal in Chapter 3.

Figure 1-1: Completed Action Worksheet

GET CLIENTS NOW!™ Action Worksheet

What strategies will you use?

DIRECT CONTACT & FOLLOW-UP	NETWORKING & REFERRAL BUILDING	PUBLIC SPEAKING	WRITING & PUBLICITY	PROMOTIONAL EVENTS	ADVERTISING
☑	☑	☐	☐	☐	☐

Where are you stuck or what needs the most work?

☑ Filling the pipeline ☐ Following up ☐ Having sales conversations ☐ Closing sales

How much business do you have now? __11 clients__

How much business do you *really* want? __20 clients__

What would that get you? __pay off my credit cards, take a vacation, feel less stressed__

What is your program goal? __4 new clients by the end of the program__

What will be your reward? __go out to dinner and a movie__

Success Ingredients	Target Date
1. market niche definition	03/06/13
2. 10-second introduction	03/08/13
3. 3 live networking venues	03/15/13

Daily Actions

1. Spend 1/2 hour each day on my Success Ingredient projects
2. Send letters or e-mails to 5 new people each week
3. Place warm calls to 2 prospects per day
4. Go to 1 live networking event each week
5. Contact 3 new potential referral partners each week
6. Have lunch or coffee with a colleague once per week
7. Spend 15 minutes interacting with my online network daily
8. Send an item of interest to 3 colleagues per week
9. Ask for a referral once per day
10. Visualize success daily

Special Permission __I give myself permission to have enough time for everything__

4. **Success Ingredients**—the missing ingredients you need to be successful in your marketing and that you plan to create during the program. You will discover these in Chapter 4.

5. **Daily Actions**—ten specific steps you plan to take on a daily or weekly basis during the program. You will choose these in Chapter 5.

6. **Special Permission**—the permission you need to grant yourself to be successful in areas where you may have failed in the past. There is more about this in Chapter 5 also.

Getting Help to Make It Happen

By using this program, you are going to add a new level of focus, strategy, and structure to your marketing that will substantially increase your likelihood of success. But you can stack the odds even more in your favor by adding some outside help. Here are some of the additional aids that can make your sales and marketing efforts more effective and less stressful:

▶ **Accountability.** Have someone other than yourself to who you are accountable—someone who will ask you once or twice a week what you have done so far, and what's next.

▶ **Perspective.** Get a different point of view on your progress or your challenges. Just hearing your problem restated by another person can give you insight that will help you find a solution. When you are feeling low because you haven't reached your goal yet, it's also great to have someone point out that you are more than halfway there.

▶ **Support.** It's helpful to have someone else to complain to or celebrate out loud with, someone who cares about your progress. If you are up against a roadblock, grousing about it for a few minutes may be all you need to get back into action. And having someone to share your success with can make it much sweeter.

You could use your spouse, best friend, or business partner to provide this extra help, but the individuals closest to you may not be the best choice. The people in your personal life will not always be thrilled that you plan to spend more time on marketing, and your business associates may tend to sidetrack you with immediate problems or day-to-day management tasks. You may find it more helpful to look for accountability, perspective, and support from someone with more detachment, yet who clearly understands the importance you are placing this month on achieving your marketing goals. The best way to get this extra advantage is from a business buddy, action group, or business coach.

A *business buddy* is a friend or colleague who also wants help to get into action and stay on track. The two of you assist each other in reaching your goals by setting up a regular check-in, with each of you reporting on progress, announcing successes, stating challenges, and committing to next steps. The buddy's job is to listen, celebrate, commiserate, ask clarifying questions, and be a brainstorming partner.

Action groups serve the same function for a group of people who wish to work together. You may be able to find an existing group with a business or marketing focus (sometimes called success teams or mastermind groups) through local business organizations, or by networking online. If you would like to be part of a group whose members are all using the Get Clients Now! program, you can find a group to join via the book's companion website, www.getclientsnow.com. Some groups have a professional leader, while others have each member take turns leading.

You can also hire your own *business coach*, a professional who is trained in assisting businesspeople to achieve goals and increase their effectiveness. Some coaches specialize in working with entrepreneurs or sales and marketing issues. They may call themselves business coaches, marketing coaches, or sales coaches. You might also choose to work with a life coach, executive coach, or success coach. Ask your friends and colleagues if they have worked with a coach to who they could refer you, or get a list of coaches familiar with this program from the Get Clients Now! website.

Keep in mind that support from a buddy, group, or coach does not have to involve in-person meetings and travel time. Many groups meet via telephone conference lines or live online chats, and your buddy or coach can work with you by phone or e-mail.

Say It and You'll Do It
Laura Whitworth, MCC, CPCC; 1947–2007

"Coaching works for many reasons that overlap and intertwine, but one of the strongest threads in this weave is accountability," contended the late Laura Whitworth, co-founder of The Coaches Training Institute, and co-author of *Co-Active Coaching*. Whitworth maintained,

> It is often the accountability alone that draws people to coaching. They may be competent and successful in many phases of their lives, but there is one

area where they have found they cannot make the changes they want to make alone. They're just not getting it done, and they want the structure of a partnership to help them do the thing that is hard to do.

How many times in your life have you said you were going to do something, and then not done it because nobody else would know the difference? Just the simple act of telling your plan to another person raises the stakes. On a freezing January morning, you might pull the covers back over your head rather than go to the health club alone. But if you've promised to meet someone there at 7:00 A.M., there is a much better chance you'll actually get your chilly butt out of bed and go.

WHAT WORKS AND WHAT DOESN'T?

In the Introduction, you learned the first secret of successful professional services marketing: Choose a set of simple, effective things to do, and do them consistently. Here is the second secret: *Marketing a service business is not the same as marketing a product.* Products are tangible; you can see them, touch them, maybe even taste them before you buy. Services are intangible. You can't see them until they are demonstrated. They can't be touched or tasted. Because a service is intangible, until it is performed for you, you have no idea how it will turn out, whether you will like it, or whether it will work for your problem, situation, or opportunity.

Therefore, when clients purchase a service for the first time, they must rely on their judgment about the person or organization delivering it. There is an old saying in sales and marketing: "People do business with people they know, like, and trust." If a potential client gets to know you, learns to like you, and believes that he or she can trust you, you probably have a sale. Without your having at least one of those factors in place, getting the business will be an almost impossible task.

Keep this crucial rule in mind as you look at Figure 1-2, "Marketing Strategies for Professional Services." This diagram operates on three levels simultaneously. First, it shows the six sales and marketing *strategies* that service providers can use. Second, it rates the strategies in order of *effectiveness*, from direct contact at the top to advertising at the bottom. We'll look at each of these strategies in more detail later in this chapter, but notice that there is a strong connection between effectiveness and the know-like-and-trust factor. Strategies 1 through 3 are much more likely to create a personal relationship between you and the buyer than strategies 4 through 6. The exact order of

Figure 1-2: Marketing Strategies for Professional Services

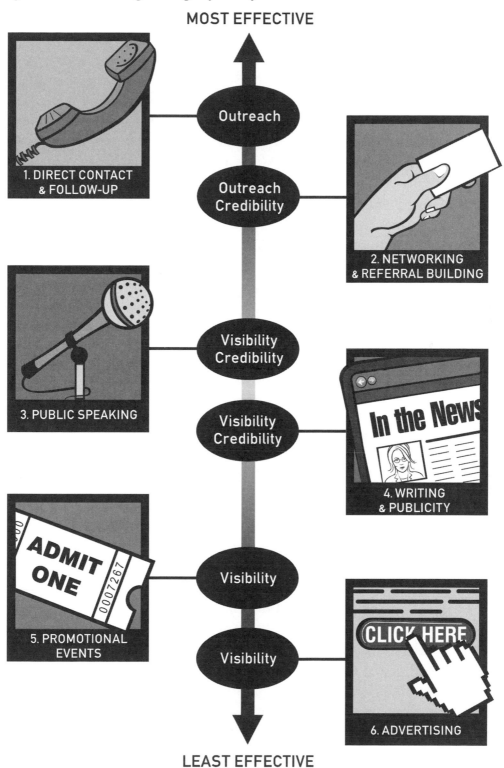

the individual strategies on the diagram is unimportant, but the overall effectiveness ranking is critical to making the right choices about marketing. Direct contact and follow-up is an effective strategy all by itself, but advertising, used alone, almost never works to find clients for a professional, consultant, or coach.

The effectiveness of any one strategy can vary with the situation and your own abilities and preferences. A psychotherapist, for example, would see that direct contact and follow-up with potential clients would be inappropriate, and therefore rely more on networking and referral building. A consultant who does poorly at public speaking would do well to avoid that strategy and concentrate on writing and publicity instead. But in any case where a particular strategy might not be best, you'll have the most success if you choose another with the highest effectiveness rank possible.

Keep in mind that the effectiveness rating shown in the diagram for these strategies refers specifically to their use in marketing your own services or the services of your firm. This is what the Get Clients Now! system is designed to address. If your business also includes product sales as part of a service package, or as an added option for existing clients, rest assured that this diagram is completely relevant to your business.

For example, a chiropractor who sells nutritional supplements to his clients or a corporate trainer who suggests that training clients purchase her companion workbook will both find this ranking of strategies to be quite accurate. However, defining appropriate marketing strategies to sell products *separately* from your services—whether in your place of business or online—is outside the scope of this book.

The third level of information shown in Figure 1-2 is the *impact* that each strategy creates: outreach, visibility, and/or credibility. Knowing the impact of a strategy will also help you determine how to use it. Direct contact and follow-up is an outreach strategy, and networking and referral building is both an outreach and a credibility strategy. Public speaking and writing and publicity have the impact of both visibility and credibility, and promotional events and advertising have only the visibility impact.

Notice also that the impacts themselves have an effectiveness ranking. Outreach strategies are clearly the most effective, and visibility-only strategies are the least. Strategies that combine visibility with credibility are ranked in the middle.

Looking at this diagram, you may wonder where the Internet and social media fit in. How effective is online marketing or social media marketing compared to the six strategies shown here? The answer depends on how you choose to use the Web to market your business. The relative effectiveness of your online marketing activities follows exactly the same pattern as any other type of marketing you could choose. So online networking will be more effective than online publicity, for example, and writing for the Web will be more powerful than advertising on the Web. The Internet and social media are not marketing strategies in and of themselves; they are simply additional channels for employing a wide variety of marketing choices. You'll learn more about these choices in the remainder of this chapter.

It's a Matter of Trust

Elinor Stutz, www.smoothsale.net

"Building business is all about establishing credibility and trust," asserts Elinor Stutz, CEO of Smooth Sale, LLC, and author of *Nice Girls DO Get the Sale: Relationship Building That Gets Results*. Stutz adds,

> With the development of social media, we no longer get word out about our business solely in local neighborhoods but instead we message worldwide. Posting online for all to see is quick and easy, but more than ever, to build relationships and trust, your words, actions and deeds all need to be in alignment with integrity.

> Whether you network in person or online, use video and blogs or tweets and posts, others will quickly notice whether you are attempting to serve the needs of your clientele or just serve yourself. Within seconds, people make a snap decision about whether to ignore your communication or take action on it. Contacts will help spread your marketing messages when they receive useful information and sense your integrity. Your intended audience will ask to connect for further conversation.

> Check your client list to see how you are scoring in this regard. What are your percentages for returning clients, referrals, and testimonials received? These results provide the measuring mechanism for how successful you have been in developing trust throughout your marketing efforts.

> You need to know just how far you are willing to go for business and when to put on the brakes. How do you wish to be remembered? What type of role model do you wish to be for your family and/or community? Are you willing to bend the truth to make a sale? Your words, actions, and deeds become part of your brand. What you stand for, provide to clients, and uniquely deliver, should be apparent in each and every communication.

WHAT GOES INTO A STRATEGY?

Think of marketing strategies as the highest-level organizing principle for your marketing and sales activities. When you are trying to decide if you should spend more effort on networking or publicity, for example, remember that networking is ranked as more effective. If you are wondering whether to plunk down a large sum of money for an ad special, ask first what that money would buy if you spent it on promoting yourself as a public speaker, since speaking has a higher rank than advertising.

Every strategy is made up of one or more tactics, or to put it another way, you use specific tactics to execute a chosen strategy. After the definition of each strategy in the sections below is a list of tactics you might use to employ it. And Part III of this book contains detailed marketing recipes that will tell you much more about how to use these tactics.

The following descriptions of marketing strategies will help you begin to consider what activities you will include in your Get Clients Now! program. Don't worry about selecting specific tactics at this point. Focus on the overall strategies and think about which ones might work best for you.

One important note before you begin to read about marketing tactics: you are not going to use all of these tactics in the next twenty-eight days! You are not even going to use all the tactics listed for each strategy that you choose to adopt. The first secret of successful professional services marketing is to choose a set of simple, effective things to do, and do them consistently. You will be using only a few of these tactics at any one time. So don't allow the list of possibilities to overwhelm you, just let it inform you.

STRATEGY:
DIRECT CONTACT AND FOLLOW-UP

Direct contact means making person-to-person contact with a prospective client, in person, or by phone, mail, fax, e-mail, text message, or online. To get results, your first contact must be truly personal, not a form letter, bulk e-mail, or generic social media post. If you make contact in writing, address your communication to a specific person and mention some issue you know he or she is facing, or a connection you both share. If you don't do this, you are merely generating advertising, whether you send a letter in the mail or post it on a social media platform.

After your initial contact, more impersonal direct communication, like postcards, e-zines, or broadcast e-mail can become effective follow-up techniques. But for interested prospects, use one-to-many approaches like these as a supplement to personal contact, not a substitute for it.

Note that the marketing strategy of direct contact and follow-up refers here to contact with a prospective client. It does not refer to the contact and follow-up activities you may do with colleagues and others while you are using the strategy of networking and referral building.

Tactics for Direct Contact and Follow-Up

▶ **Cold Calling**. Call a complete stranger on the phone. Works best if you have reason to believe the person currently needs your service and you can easily explain why that is.

▶ **Warm Calling.** Call prospects with whom you have some connection—people you have met before, who have been referred to you, or who belong to a professional or personal community where you are also a member.

▶ **Lunch or Coffee (with prospects).** An excellent follow-up tactic when your services are expensive or difficult to explain, or the sales cycle is long.

▶ **In-Person or Phone Appointments.** What many people do to hold a sales conversation to discuss their services in detail. May lead to a proposal or quote, or directly to a sale.

▶ **Personal Letters and E-mails.** Send a personal letter by postal mail or e-mail to a hot prospect. Most effective when it is truly personal, not just boilerplate, and is coupled with a follow-up phone call.

▶ **Text Messages, Instant Messages, and Social Media "Shouts."** Brief messages sent by text, instant message, online chat, or social media post aimed at an individual. Useful for quick hellos, reminders, or requests to prospects who are active on the platform you are using.

▶ **Announcement Card or Letter.** A great way to let everyone know what you're doing if you're just getting started or have made changes in your business. Best when followed up with phone calls.

▶ **Nice-to-Meet-You Notes.** When you meet someone and collect his business card, send a follow-up note by mail, enclosing your card. Or an e-mail with your contact information.

▶ **Sending Articles or Links.** Keep in touch with prospects in a nonpromotional way by mailing articles or forwarding links to websites or online posts they might find useful.

▶ **Extending Invitations.** Invite prospects to a meeting or seminar you are planning to go to anyway. It's a good reason to re-contact them without doing any selling.

▶ **Reminder Postcards or Mailers.** An occasional mailing reminds people what you have to offer. Postcards and self-mailers can be easier and cheaper than a print newsletter.

▶ **Newsletters and E-Zines.** A powerful follow-up technique when your services provide valuable information. Use print or e-mail newsletters to show off your expertise and remind people you're available.

▶ **Broadcast E-mail and Autoresponders.** Broadcast e-mails can provide prospects with additional reasons to hire you. You can set up an automated sequence of e-mails to follow up with prospects over time. Broadcast e-mail should only be used when a prospect has already expressed interest in your offerings, and opted in to receive your e-mail.

STRATEGY:
NETWORKING AND REFERRAL BUILDING

Don't limit your picture of networking to mean circulating through a room exchanging business cards. Nor should networking be defined by the time you spend making social media posts. A broader view of networking is creating a pool of contacts from which you can draw clients, referrals, resources, ideas, and information. You can network by phone, e-mail, and online as well as in person, but networking is by definition interactive.

Some of the people you meet through networking will be prospective clients, but you will also make other valuable contacts. Just as you would follow up with a prospect by placing a call or suggesting lunch, you can build your network of colleagues and referral sources in the same way.

You don't have to wait for word of mouth to build in order to start getting referrals. You can seek out potential referral sources by identifying people who are in contact with your target market and getting to know them. After an initial meeting or conversation, you can stay in touch using some of the same tactics as shown for direct contact and follow-up, plus the following tactics more specific to networking and referral building.

Tactics for Networking and Referral Building

- ► **Attending Meetings and Seminars**. One of the best ways to meet people, because many of them have come for the express purpose of making new contacts. Also a good follow-up technique if you keep returning to the same group.
- ► **Developing Referral Partners.** Get to know people who serve the same type of clients you do, no matter what their business is. Some professionals get most of their business from alliances with partners like these. *divorce attorneys*
- ► **Participating in Online Communities.** Interacting with the members of online discussion groups, message boards, chat rooms, and social networking platforms, or the readers of blogs, allows you to network without leaving your home or office.
- ► **Lunch or Coffee (with contacts).** A good way to become acquainted with referral partners, colleagues, and centers of influence. Your goal is to get them to know, like and trust you.
- ► **Staying in Touch with Former Clients.** Your best source of referrals can be people who have already worked with you. Keep in touch and don't be afraid to ask them to refer others.
- ► **Volunteering and Serving on Committees.** Volunteer your professional services for a high-profile nonprofit to get recognition. Serve your professional community as an officer or committee chair to gain more visibility.
- ► **Sharing Information and Resources.** Pass along articles, posts, or websites of interest, invitations to events, and other ideas and opportunities to the people in your network. They will come to think of you as a resource and refer others to you.
- ► **Collaborations and Strategic Alliances.** An excellent way for any small business to expand contacts and visibility. Your collaborator may know another whole circle of people.
- ► **Swapping Contacts.** Exchange leads or past clients with a referral partner in a noncompetitive business. You could even send letters introducing each other.

- ▶ **Leads Groups.** A group of people who meet regularly to exchange contacts, leads, and referrals. If you can't find one you like, start your own.

- ▶ **Giving Referrals.** One of the best ways to get people to refer you business is to refer business to them. Always be on the lookout for opportunities to refer.

People Do Business with People

Maria Elena Duron, www.mariaduron.com

"Anyone can look good in a short exchange, Twitter tweet, or Facebook status update," shares Maria Elena Duron, "but relationships and trust are built from ongoing interaction." Duron is a marketing coach who acts as a personal "buzz agent" for her clients. "Consistent interaction gives us a chance to sample someone's competence, motivation, and character." Duron goes on to explain,

> Regular networking produces the cornerstones for a growing business—good relationships and new connections. It also provides access to insights from others. Other people's experience is just as valuable as other people's money. From access to knowledge to referrals, your business connections can yield plenty as they become relationships through networking. It makes good business sense to have a regular networking schedule and a list of people you want to connect with in different ways.

> No matter whether you represent a company or you are a solopreneur, people do business with people. To take it one step further—people do business with people they know, like, and trust. And, in our fast paced, time deprived society, this is one activity that is worth our time. Even if we can accelerate it through social networks, time is still a key ingredient for developing relationships and trust.

STRATEGY: PUBLIC SPEAKING

Think of speaking in front of a group as an immensely powerful form of networking. People are much more likely to remember you if you are standing in the front of the room instead of seated in the back. If you are new to public speaking, try starting out small. Volunteer to introduce speakers at an event, or offer your services on a panel. Then gradually work your way up to solo presentations or full-length workshops.

A word of caution about public speaking: Look for an already organized group to present to rather than trying to invite your own guests. Hosting a program of your own is a promotional events tactic, and often less effective than speaking for someone else's group. You may be surprised to find how many civic, business, and professional groups are eagerly seeking free speakers for their meetings. Getting booked as a speaker can be easier than you may think.

Tactics for Public Speaking

- ▶ **Acting as Master of Ceremonies.** Any excuse for standing up in front of a group will make you more visible and memorable. If you serve a group as an officer or committee chair, you'll have opportunities to make announcements or introductions.

- ▶ **Serving on Panels.** An easy way to break into public speaking without having to prepare an entire talk. Let colleagues know you are available to speak on your area of expertise.

- ▶ **Making Presentations.** Every meeting or conference needs speakers. Most of them are people like you, speaking for free to promote their business. It brings you visibility and credibility both.

- ▶ **Virtual Speaking.** Many speaking opportunities exist on webinars, teleseminars, and online chats sponsored by associations, vendors, and professional schools. You can speak to an international audience without traveling.

- ▶ **Giving Classes or Workshops.** If you really enjoy speaking or teaching, this is an effective way to expose prospective clients to your expertise. If they like you, they will want more of you.

STRATEGY: WRITING AND PUBLICITY

Writing articles, a column, or a blog about your specialty is an excellent way to gain visibility and credibility you couldn't manage otherwise. If you have never been published before, you might begin by publishing yourself. You can provide articles to an online article directory, or write for your own newsletter or blog. The newsletters or blogs of colleagues can also be good places to get exposure for your writing. Once you have had a few items published, you can graduate to better-known venues. Don't rule out these tactics if you're not an expert writer. A ghost writer or professional editor can help turn your words into publishable prose.

Just as you can publish your own writing online, you can also generate your own publicity via social media. Posting on platforms like Facebook, Twitter, LinkedIn, Google+, and YouTube allows you to share news and expertise with those who follow you.

Getting interviewed by the mainstream media or trade press can be considerably harder, but you can start small or wherever you have connections. Local radio and newspapers like to profile local experts. Associations and online communities often feature their members. Vendors sometimes interview their customers. When approaching the media, always remember that you need to provide them with an engaging story. Tell the editor or producer exactly why their readers will be interested in what you have to say.

Be aware that unless your piece appears on the home page of the *New York Times*, you shouldn't expect a deluge of phone calls and Web traffic. You are more likely to receive congratulations from people you already know than to hear from a flock of new prospects. Writing and publicity techniques are better for steadily building your credibility and name recognition than for filling your marketing pipeline all at once.

Tactics for Writing and Publicity

> ► **Publishing Articles or Tips.** When you publish an article or brief tip online or in print, people not only read it and get in touch; you can also send it to your mailing list, link to it from your website or social media posts, and use it in your marketing kit.

> ► **Reprinting Previously Written Articles.** Get more mileage out of each article you write by finding multiple publications and websites to publish it.

> ► **Writing a Column.** When you appear regularly in the same publication or site, people who read your column will remember you and consider you an expert.

▶ **Publishing a Blog.** Making regular posts to a blog can prove your expertise, keep you in touch with prospects, and attract new people to your pipeline.

▶ **Being Quoted by the Media.** You can make this happen by writing to journalists, commentators, or bloggers when you see or hear your area of expertise being discussed. Next time, they may contact you for a quote or refer to your work.

▶ **Having Stories Published About You.** Send a press release about your work, opinions, or achievements to editors that cover your area, or publish a release online. You can also contact a freelance writer in your field, and let her know how interesting you are.

▶ **Being Interviewed on Broadcast Media.** Pitch yourself to producers as a fascinating subject for radio, TV, or webcast interviews. Once you have appeared in just one media outlet, others will often be eager to have you as a guest.

▶ **Getting Others to Link to Your Website.** Increase your Web presence by letting people know about the useful content on your website via your e-zine, blog, or social media posts.

▶ **Posting to Social Media.** Making posts on social networking platforms can expand your visibility and credibility, once you have built a network of followers. You can post helpful tips or resources, news about your business, updates on your professional activities, or photos and videos showing your work.

Your Parents Love You, But Who Else?

Susan Harrow, www.prsecrets.com

"Publicity markets your services more effectively than advertising . . . or your parents," points out Susan Harrow, media coach and author of *Sell Yourself Without Selling Your Soul*. Harrow says,

> Your parents love you. They think you are the best thing that ever walked this earth. And they're right. They're also biased. And everyone knows that. So when they say great things about you to anyone who will listen, those people's eyes tend to get that opaque and uninterested glaze. A similar thing happens when an audience reads or sees advertisements. Even when someone is looking for a specific product or service, they know that anyone who has the money can buy space to plug their products.

When a journalist writes a story about you or your business, you are already one step ahead of those people who choose advertising. Why? You have literally and symbolically passed through a gatekeeper—the editor or producer who has judged that you have something of value for his audience.

People perceive a journalist or producer as an unbiased source of information. The person who is included in an article or is on a radio or TV show has passed through a journalist's or producer's screen. We credit the media with knowing a good story when they see one. You can't buy the kind of prestige that puts you on the front page of a major newspaper.

STRATEGY: PROMOTIONAL EVENTS

Putting on a show, or being part of someone else's, is a time-honored way of attracting customer attention. Participating in a trade show, or co-sponsoring a fundraiser, can put you in direct contact with potential clients, and bring you an audience you couldn't afford to reach alone. But look out for the cost! Renting a booth, setting up a display, and distributing literature to hundreds of people can be extremely expensive. Before committing to a live event like this, evaluate the cost per head of each likely prospect you expect the event to generate, and see if you couldn't beat that price by using some other marketing method.

If you want to try producing your own live event, such as a seminar or reception, figure out how much it might cost you to put on the event and fill the room; then see if the expected business will be worth the expense. Publicizing events like this can require a substantial outlay for paid mailings and advertising. Look to see what the result might be if you spent the same amount of time and money on generating business through other strategies.

Hosting a virtual event, such as a webinar, teleseminar, or online contest, can be inexpensive to produce. But you still have to publicize it in order to get people to participate. If you don't already have a substantial prospect list or social network you can invite, you may find it no easier or cheaper to find prospects for your promotional event than it is to find paying clients.

Tactics for Promotional Events

- ▸ **Trade Shows.** Booths at big shows can be very expensive, but many associations put on more affordable tabletop expos. Trade shows are better for making contacts than for closing sales.

- ▸ **Live Seminars, Workshops, or Demonstrations.** Offer a free demonstration or low-cost workshop to your existing prospect list. If you can fill the room, this can be a useful credibility booster.

- ▸ **Virtual Seminars.** Offering a workshop via webinar, or giving a talk via teleseminar allows you to invite prospects from around the world.

- ▸ **Open House or Reception.** Find an excuse to throw a party, and invite prospects and referral partners. People who don't return your calls may surprise you by showing up.

- ▸ **Co-Sponsored Events.** Co-sponsoring a workshop, symposium, or fund raiser with a nonprofit will attract clients who support the cause. Collaborating with colleagues on an event will maximize your resources and extend your reach.

- ▸ **Networking Lunch, Breakfast, or Mixer.** Invite clients, prospects, and referral partners to meet each other for their own benefit. Tell everyone to bring a guest.

- ▸ **Giveaways, Contests, and Surveys.** Offer a free gift, or a drawing for one, in return for collecting a prospect's contact information. Or conduct a survey of potential clients and offer to share the results with all participants. Be sure to target your audience carefully to avoid cluttering up your prospect list with people who will never become clients.

STRATEGY: ADVERTISING

Many professionals, consultants, and coaches have found paid advertising to be quite ineffective at filling their marketing pipeline with paying clients. Remember the know-like-and-trust factor: Ads don't allow clients to get to know you personally, nor do they build trust. This doesn't mean that advertising should be completely eliminated as a possible strategy. Increasing website visibility, for example, is an advertising tactic that many businesses will want to pursue at some point.

For some professional service providers, print or Web advertising can be a reliable source of new prospects. A paid ad in an online or print directory, for example, can bring new inquiries to professionals who people often seek in an emergency, like attorneys; need only rarely, like a résumé writer; or prefer to locate privately, such as a psychotherapist. For professionals with date-dependent offerings like seminars and groups, advertising via direct mail, flyers, and online calendars is often necessary. But in most cases, advertising alone rarely generates business; it must be coupled with direct contact and follow-up tactics in order for it to pay off.

To determine what role advertising should play in your marketing, ask yourself this question: "How do clients usually find a service like mine?" If your immediate answer is "by referral," you will probably find most advertising to be a waste of money. But if your clients often do find businesses like yours from advertising, you may need to consider some forms of it.

Take a look at your competition and see where and how they are advertising. Ask questions of your colleagues about what type of advertising has and hasn't worked for them. Advertising can be an expensive proposition. Evaluate the potential return on any advertising investment. How many clients will it bring you before it pays for itself? And is there some other more effective way you could spend the same money?

On the Web, for example, you might choose to have a website for your business but not to invest additional funds in advertising it with pay-per-click ads or paid directories. You can instead use some of the other approaches discussed in this chapter to attract traffic to your site. Strategies like public speaking or writing and publicity are more likely to generate Web visitors that quickly turn into clients. You'll have a much harder time closing sales with people who get to your site by clicking on an ad.

Tactics for Advertising

▶ **Increasing Website Visibility.** A website by itself is a tool rather
    than a tactic. You may wish to use your site primarily as an online
    brochure: sending visitors to it with other tactics rather than expecting
    it to attract traffic on its own. Or you can increase website traffic
    without paid ads by getting your site ranked more highly in search
    engines and local search directories. Building a site that includes

relevant search terms in its text, and offers extra value with helpful articles, a blog, or other useful tools will improve your rank, and encourage others to link to your site.

▶ **Pay-per-Click Advertising.** You pay for these online ads each time someone clicks on one to visit your site. Costs can add up quickly, so evaluate your potential return carefully before choosing this option.

▶ **Online Directories.** Listing your business in directories used by your prospective clients can increase your visibility. Some directories charge a fee to list you; others are free.

▶ **Print Directories.** Use of general print directories like the Yellow Pages is waning, but consumers still turn to them in emergencies and for household services. Specialized directories for your industry or profession can be a better bet.

▶ **Online Classifieds.** Best used when your business serves consumers who may be regular users of classified services such as Craigslist. Ads can be free or paid. Your ad should be narrowly targeted and ask for an immediate response, perhaps with a special offer.

▶ **Newspaper or Magazine Classifieds.** May appear in the print edition, Web edition, or both. Track every response you get to see whether your ads are worth the investment.

▶ **Banner Ads.** For these display ads on websites, in e-zines, and via smartphone apps, you'll typically pay a flat fee for a length of time or per issue. Be sure you know the number of viewers who will see your ad before you buy.

▶ **Print Display Ads.** Ads like these in newspapers, magazines, and trade journals are typically more for visibility than direct response. You usually need a big budget, and repeat advertising, to make them work.

▶ **Event or Conference Programs.** Another visibility booster that may need a big budget. Works best if people who already know your business will notice the ad.

▶ **Unsolicited Bulk E-mail or Text Ads.** Sending unsolicited bulk e-mail or text message ads (otherwise known as spam) to market your professional services is probably the least effective advertising tactic you could choose, and the most likely to annoy your prospects. Just don't do it.

▶ **Direct Mail.** Postal mass mailings to people who don't yet know you have nowhere near the impact of personal letters, and are often a waste of money. Consider narrowing your target group and using direct contact and follow-up tactics instead.

▶ **Brochure or Flyer Distribution.** Brochures and flyers can be used to develop interest with a targeted group. They can be left at a place of business your target audience frequents or posted on a bulletin board in your community.

▶ **Radio or TV Ads.** You need a substantial budget to go this route. Ads must be repeated to have any effect. If you do this, get professional help in scripting and producing your ad.

▶ **Billboards.** For professional services? Well, people have done it. You can probably find better ways to spend the money—like one of the other tactics already mentioned.

MAKING YOUR FIRST SELECTION

After reading this overview of potential marketing strategies and tactics, you probably have some idea of which strategies you might like to use in your Get Clients Now! program. Consider which two, three, or four strategies you think you would most like to employ. More than four strategies are too many to attempt in a twenty-eight-day period, and fewer than two won't give you enough flexibility. Two or three is usually best.

If you're unsure which strategies might be best for you, keep reading. You'll find more guidance on selecting strategies in Chapter 2.

Get Personal About Your Marketing

Tony Alessandra, Ph.D.; www.alessandra.com

Tony Alessandra, the author of 27 books, including *Collaborative Selling* and *The Platinum Rule for Sales Mastery*, points to experienced salespeople as powerful role models for professionals selling their own services. He asserts,

> The successful sales rep seems to just sit back and respond to calls. The orders roll in, and she seems to be getting rich without effort. What we generally don't see are the years she spent building her network, and investing in her personal visibility.

This successful salesperson is using personal marketing. She's marketing herself just as a company would market a product. Just as it takes time to build brand loyalty, it takes time and hard work for personal marketing to pay off, but it's worth it in the long run. If your best potential clients have been made aware of you in advance of your contact with them, you'll find it much easier to set up an appointment, establish a relationship, and consummate the sale.

Keep in mind that it's better to work on getting multiple exposures to a smaller target group than to spread your effort and have fewer exposures to more people. Potential clients in your target market should be reading your articles, receiving mail from you, hearing you speak or give a seminar, bumping into you at a social function or trade show, and hearing about you and your expertise from their fellow association members and friends.

The reason it's so important to invest your time in these methods is that the quality of an incoming lead is almost always better than the lead you get in a cold call. The prospect who calls you has already identified his need for your service, and he's calling to get your help.

When you effectively use personal marketing, you'll find that little by little, people will start to recognize your name, your company, your product, and your face. Pretty soon the phone will start to ring for you, and your image as an established expert will start to take hold.

BUT WHAT ABOUT SELLING?

In thinking about what marketing strategies to use, it may have occurred to you to ask where selling enters the picture. This is another way in which marketing a service can differ from marketing a product. When you are selling professional services, marketing and sales are not two separate activities that occur at different times; instead, they must be seamlessly integrated. Think about it. If you are talking to someone about what you do, you may think you are networking. But if she expresses an interest in doing business with you, you are instantly in a selling situation.

The opposite is equally true: If you make contact with a prospect in order to sell your service, the person may tell you that he isn't interested but has a colleague who might be. Then you would switch from selling to networking.

The marketing strategy of direct contact and follow-up could also be thought of as personal selling. But it would be misleading to call it that, since in many cases when you make contact, you are not "selling" at all. You may be asking a potential client how her business is going or what she's working on these days. You could be inviting her to your upcoming open house or speaking engagement. When you are speaking with a prospect, selling may not always happen, but it can begin at any point in the conversation.

So think about everything you do to get clients as being both marketing and sales at the same time. Think about every marketing strategy as a selling strategy, and vice versa.

A WORD ABOUT TERMINOLOGY

Before moving on to the next chapter, it might be helpful to review some of the terminology used so far. Up to this point, you have encountered marketing strategies, tactics, and types of impact. Each overall strategy (e.g., direct contact and follow-up) is made up of tactics (e.g., cold calling, warm calling, or personal letters), and has a resulting impact (outreach, visibility, or credibility). In a few pages, you will also learn about stages of the marketing cycle. If you remember the distinctions among these terms and the elements they represent, you will be able to follow the process of building your Get Clients Now! program more easily.

CHAPTER 2

Where Do You Start?

The Marketing and Sales Cycle

THE UNIVERSAL MARKETING CYCLE

Marketing and sales for the professional services business operates on a predictable cycle, with four separate stages:

1. Filling the Pipeline
2. Following Up
3. Having Sales Conversations
4. Closing Sales

The activities that take place within each stage of the cycle will vary depending on your business, but the cycle is the same for everyone. Knowing more about how this cycle works will enable you to determine exactly where to focus more time and energy in your marketing.

Figure 2-1 depicts the Universal Marketing Cycle as if it were a water system. At the top are the collection buckets for the prospects, contacts, leads, and referrals with which you are filling the pipeline. On your desk, computer, or favorite handheld device, these will be represented by the names and phone numbers of people and organizations. *Prospects* are people you have reason to believe will be interested in your services. *Contacts* are people you meet through outreach strategies like networking, or just in the

Figure 2-1: The Universal Marketing Cycle

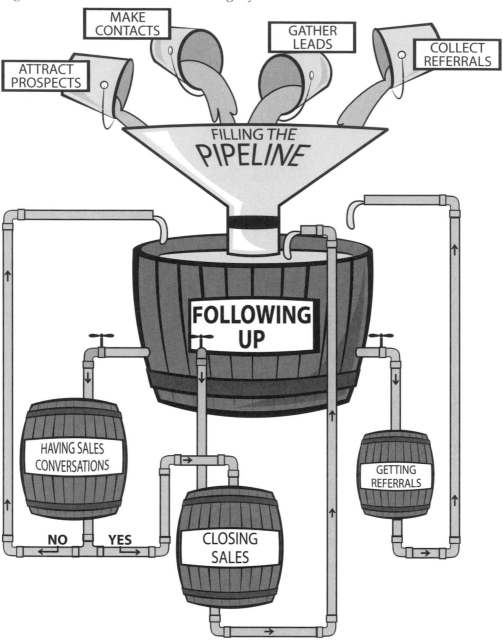

course of business or life. *Leads* are people you identify through research or hear about from your contacts. And *referrals* are people who are referred to you by contacts, clients, and others.

Don't worry too much about the distinctions among these categories. They are all people in your pipeline.

The marketing pipeline empties into the follow-up pool, which you dip into in order to move potential clients and referral sources further along in the system. They don't move along by themselves; you must make this happen. Your goal is to keep the follow-up pool constantly circulating, with new prospects entering the pipeline and existing ones flowing into the next stage of the cycle.

The arrows in the bottom half of the diagram indicate the direction of flow. With potential clients, you want to move quickly to having a sales conversation. This is where you find out about their needs, tell them more about what you do, and see if there is a match between the two of you. The actual conversation may happen in a formal presentation or scheduled appointment, or informally, in person, by telephone, or even by e-mail. Some professionals offer a complimentary consultation or sample session as a lead-in to a sales conversation. When the sales conversation concludes, you may be ready to ask for the business, or you may need to prepare a detailed proposal first. In some cases, the conversation stage may last 15 minutes, and in others, it can take many months.

Your desired result, though, is always the same: to move prospects forward to closing the sale. If they say yes at the end of the sales conversation, you have a new client. If they say no, they stay in the closing sales stage, where you continue to follow up with them as long as it seems worthwhile. Sometimes continued follow-up will lead directly to closing the sale after all, and at other times, you may need to have yet another sales conversation.

When the sale is closed, you begin to serve the client. As you are providing service, and after you complete your service, the client must also return to the follow-up pool. By continuing to follow up with this client, you may close another sale or get referrals.

Some of the people and organizations in your pipeline may never enter the prospect area of the cycle at all. They may be contacts who can become referral sources for you. You must follow up with these people also, regularly reminding them that you are around, thanking them for referrals, and putting them right back in the follow-up pool.

In any of these cases, what follow-up looks like and how often it happens depends on the nature of your business and the type of contact that seems natural for you. Refer to the tactics listed in the previous chapter under direct contact and follow-up. Every one of these is a potential follow-up technique.

Keep Your Prospects Cycling

Donna Feldman, www.donnafeldman.com

Donna Feldman is a business coach who helps clients with marketing and social media. She has facilitated dozens of Get Clients Now! programs. "One day when teaching Get Clients Now!," Feldman recalls, "I noticed that the Universal Marketing Cycle is a closed system. There's no way out of it! Even when someone tells you 'not now,' they're still in the system and you can always contact them next year." Feldman explains,

> There are really two kinds of follow-up: immediate and long-term. When you meet someone or they contact you, you should follow up right away, but then you also need to follow up with people over time. With a regular newsletter, for example, or invite them to become a LinkedIn connection or to like your Facebook page.

> When you keep contacts in the system, you're able to stay in touch. If you see them post something interesting on LinkedIn, it gives you a reason to contact them. Because they've heard from you again, they might end up hiring you, or signing up for your next class, or referring you to someone else.

> By keeping them in the system and continuing to follow up, you stay front and center. When they or someone else needs your services, they remember you.

HOW DOES THE CYCLE WORK?

Let's look at two examples, one for a professional in the business-to-business (B2B) marketplace and one for a professional marketing business-to-consumer (B2C) services.

Suppose you are a B2B computer software consultant who typically works with large corporate clients. At a breakfast meeting of the Association of Information Systems Professionals, you met the director of information technology (IT) in a major corporation. You spoke for a few moments about his company and exchanged business cards. The director is now a contact in your marketing pipeline.

When you returned to your office, you entered his name and other information into your computerized contact management system, and set up an automatic reminder to place a follow-up call the next day. He is now in your follow-up pool.

The next day, the IT director's name and phone number popped up on the reminder list displayed on your computer. You called him, got his voice mail, and left a message reminding him of your meeting, briefly describing the kind of work you do, and suggesting it might be to his benefit if the two of you were to talk. Then you set up another reminder to follow up again three days later.

The IT director did not return your call, so when he popped up on your reminder list again in three days, you placed another call. This time you reached him, but he didn't have time to talk. He did mention, however, that some changes were coming in his company that might indicate a need for your services. With this new information, the IT director is now a likely prospect rather than just a contact. He is still in the follow-up pool.

You now send the IT director an e-mail, telling him how you could be helpful to him during this upcoming project. You provide a link to your website, referring him to some biographical information about you, a summary of the type of services you provide, and a list of satisfied clients. A week after sending the e-mail, you haven't heard from him and call him again. After three phone calls over ten days, you once again reach him in person. This time you suggest a meeting, and he agrees to meet the following week. He has just moved from the follow-up pool to the sales conversation stage.

At the meeting, you spend about half the time asking questions and learning about his company and the upcoming project. Then you describe how you can help him, and why you are uniquely qualified to do so. You answer his questions about your background and expertise. At the end of an hour, you ask if he is interested in using you on this project. He asks you to prepare a proposal, outlining what you would do and how much it would cost. You agree, and before leaving you schedule a phone appointment with him a week later to go over the proposal. At this point, the IT director is still in the sales conversation stage.

One week later, you meet by phone to discuss the completed proposal you sent him the day before via e-mail. You explain what you have written, and the rationale for your process and pricing. After answering his questions about the proposal, you ask if he is ready to sign a contract with you. Your prospect has now moved from the sales conversation stage to the closing sales stage.

The IT director tells you he must discuss your proposal with his team before making a decision. You make sure he has all the information he needs for that discussion, and offer to be present at the meeting. He declines your offer but tells you he will decide within two weeks.

Two weeks pass without the IT director's contacting you, so you e-mail him. He replies that he has not yet had time to meet with his team and suggests you try back in another couple of weeks. You e-mail again after two more weeks go by, and wonder of wonders, the IT director says his team is in favor of hiring you. You ask him when you can get to work, and he suggests you come to a project planning meeting next Monday. You send him a completed contract by e-mail, and he signs and returns it. Congratulations! You have just closed the sale.

That the entire process took over two months from beginning to end is not unusual. Sales cycles even longer than this are common, whether your clients are big companies or single individuals. Following up appears in the center of the Universal Marketing Cycle diagram for a reason: Consistent and persistent follow-up is central to successfully moving a prospect forward to making a sale.

Now for our second example, let's say you are a B2C career coach whose clients are professionals in job transition. You gave a talk entitled "Planning Your Next Career Move" to the Professional Women's Network. At the end of your presentation, you asked for anyone who was interested in finding out more about career coaching to give you a business card. Three women in the audience—Elsa, Mindy, and Dolores—gave you cards. They are now prospects in your marketing pipeline.

The following morning, you stapled each card to a page in your prospects notebook and noted where and when you met these women. You mailed each of them a copy of your brochure with a personal note. In your daily planner, you entered an action item for one week later to place follow-up calls to all three. They are now in your follow-up pool.

Two days later, Elsa called you. She had read your brochure and wanted to find out how much you charge. The moment you picked up the phone, Elsa was in the sales conversation stage.

You asked Elsa to tell you about her situation and explained how you thought you could help. After making sure she understood what she would get for her money, you told her your rates, and asked if she wanted to make her first coaching appointment. She said yes. You have just closed the sale with Elsa. And of course, five days later, you will still call Mindy and Dolores, who remain in your follow-up pool.

Your sale with Elsa closed easily only three days after meeting her, but closing sales with Mindy and Dolores might take much longer, or they might never close at all. You will continue to follow up with them until you are able to have sales conversations with each of them, or until you decide it is no longer worth your while to follow up because you have other more likely prospects on which to spend your time.

Self-Promotion Serves Your Clients

Debbie Allen, www.debbieallen.com

"You can't be truly successful if you aren't willing to let people know that you, your product, and your services exist," advocates Debbie Allen, motivational speaker and author of *Confessions of Shameless Self-Promoters*. "If you aren't willing to promote your talents, expertise, and products, others will quickly pass you by. The world is not going to beat a path to your door unless you pave the way. Resenting self-promotion is one of the greatest obstacles to success." Allen adds,

> Those who don't feel comfortable with self-promotion hold a negative belief system around it. They own this negative belief because they don't understand the difference between aggressive promotion and assertive promotion; between ineffective promotion and effective promotion. Yet there is a huge difference!

> Ineffective self-promotion comes across as rude, pushy, boastful, and self-serving. Just as many people who are opposed to it believe to be true. Yet that is ineffective, and not what I'm suggesting to you.

> Effective self-promotion comes from a different place—a place of caring from your heart. When done effectively, it comes out from a place of passion: a place of help and support first and foremost.

> Effective self-promotion comes across as serving others first, versus ineffective self-promotion that serves the person promoting first.

> When you effectively promote yourself, more prospects will be readily open to doing business with you. They will then return the favor to you in the form of increased sales, profits, success and wealth.

CHOOSING WHERE TO FOCUS

The Universal Marketing Cycle is a clever diagnostic tool to help you choose where to focus your marketing efforts. The key to marketing success is narrowing your focus to work with just one stage of the cycle at a time, even when you are following up on many possibilities. Think about your own situation as you review the cycle. Where in the system are you stuck? What stage of your marketing needs the most work:

1. Filling the Pipeline—knowing enough people to contact?

2. Following Up—contacting the people you already know, or know about?

3. Having Sales Conversations—getting from follow-up to conversation?

4. Closing Sales—getting from conversation to sale?

In most businesses, contacting prospective clients directly is one of the primary methods of follow-up, so knowing enough people to contact is an easy test to see if your pipeline is sufficiently full. But if you are in a field where direct solicitation of clients is inappropriate, such as psychotherapy or, in some cases, law, ask yourself if enough people are calling you. Another good test is to imagine you were using a newsletter or e-zine for follow-up. How many people who already know you could you send it to?

Do you already know where you are stuck or need more work? If so, skip ahead to the next section, "What Strategies Should You Use?" If not, try asking yourself some questions.

If you answer yes to the following questions, you need to focus on *filling the pipeline*:

▶   Are you brand new in business?

▶   If you sat down to call every lead you currently have, would you be through before lunch?

▶   Have you personally followed up with every prospect on your list within the past thirty days?

▶   Are you not contacting the prospects you have because you already know they don't need you or can't afford you?

▶   Are you in a business where it's inappropriate to contact prospective clients, and you're not receiving enough inquiries?

If you answer yes to the following questions, you need to concentrate on *following up*:

▶   Do you have a drawer full of business cards (or database full of contact information) from people you have met but have not been in touch with since?

▶   Have colleagues handed you leads whom you haven't gotten around to calling?

▶ Are there prospects who said no or didn't return your initial call who you haven't contacted in the past three months?

▶ Do you have a wide network of personal contacts with whom you never talk business?

▶ Are there people you haven't been in touch with lately who inquired about your services in the past, but weren't quite ready or didn't have the funds?

If you answer yes to the following questions, you need to work on *having sales conversations*:

▶ Do you follow up with prospective clients consistently, but can't seem to get their attention to discuss their needs and your offerings?

▶ Do people refuse to take your call, or brush you off quickly when you do get through to them?

▶ Are all your prospects already working with a competitor—or at least that's what they say?

▶ Does everyone you contact seem to think what you do is too expensive, will take too much time, or is just not for them?

Finally, if you answer yes to the following questions, it's time to focus on *closing sales*:

▶ Are you regularly getting to the sales conversation stage, but don't seem to close enough sales?

▶ Do your prospects seem to be going through the motions of allowing you to have a sales conversation, but have no serious interest?

▶ Are you encountering objection after objection that prevents the sale from going through?

▶ Do you often conclude a sales conversation and still don't know where the prospect stands?

Pick What's in Front of You

Robert Middleton, www.actionplan.com

Robert Middleton has been helping independent professionals become better marketers since 1984. "When helping my clients with their marketing, we'll often be working on how to contact new prospects most effectively," Middleton explains. "We'll look at associations, directories, and mailing lists, and discuss the most appropriate ways to get prospects' attention and get in front of them. Then I ask whom they know in their current network of business associates and past clients to contact as well." Middleton continues,

> It's not unusual that they have a contact list of several dozen, if not several hundred, people whom they have some business connection with. When I hear this, I suggest they put any cold contacts on a back burner for now, and pay closer attention on how to pick all that "low hanging fruit."

> The truth is, you may not need to make as much effort as you thought to generate new clients. They may be closer than you think. Still, you need a plan to contact these people, and make the best of those contacts.

WHAT NEEDS THE MOST WORK?

Now that you know where in the Universal Marketing Cycle you are stuck, it's time to choose where you will focus your marketing efforts for the next twenty-eight days. If you think you need work in more than one stage of the cycle, start with the first one in the sequence. For example, if you feel stuck on both follow-up and having sales conversations, choose follow-up. If you aren't sure where to start, begin with filling the pipeline. If that's not really where the problem is, you will find out soon enough and move forward to the right stage anyway. Just be sure to pick only one stage.

WHAT STRATEGIES SHOULD YOU USE?

Once you have chosen which stage of the Universal Marketing Cycle to focus on, the next step toward designing your own personal Get Clients Now! program is to determine which of the marketing strategies discussed in Chapter 1 you are going to use for your action plan. The following chart illustrates which strategies are most appropriate to use during each stage.

If you chose . . .   *You should use the strategies . . .*

Filling the Pipeline   1. Direct contact and follow-up
                              2. Networking and referral building
                              No more than one or two of the following:
                              3. Public speaking

	4. Writing and publicity
	5. Promotional events
	6. Advertising

| Following Up | 1. Direct contact and follow-up |
| | 2. Networking and referral building |

Having Sales Conversations	1. Direct contact and follow-up
	2. Networking and referral building
	No more than one of the following:
	3. Public speaking
	4. Writing and publicity
	5. Promotional events

Closing Sales	1. Direct contact and follow-up
	2. Networking and referral building
	No more than one of the following:
	3. Public speaking
	4. Writing and publicity

The strategies recommended for each stage are listed from most to least effective. Direct contact and follow-up plus networking and referral building are considered to be the most effective approaches overall, regardless of which stage you are in. While any of the strategies listed for your stage will work, the ones listed first in each case are most likely to produce results with the least struggle. It's a good idea to employ the most effective strategies, unless there is some reason that a particular strategy won't work well for you. If you are nervous about speaking in public, for example, you might choose writing and publicity as an alternative to add more credibility to your approach.

What are the best strategies for your situation? Review the marketing strategies you tentatively picked in Chapter 1 against the appropriate strategies for the stage of the Universal Marketing Cycle you are working on. Defining specific marketing strategies to use consistently is one of the most important ways the program will help you to focus your efforts. Therefore, you will need to stick with the strategies you select now for the entire program. Choose at least two, but no more than four, marketing strategies for your 28-day plan now.

Keep the Pipeline Flowing

Frank Traditi, www.coachfrank.com

Frank Traditi is an executive coach, small business marketing expert, and co-author (with C. J. Hayden) of *Get Hired Now!* "'How do I turn more prospects into clients?'" asks Traditi. "That's the burning question asked by nearly every service professional or consultant. Is there a secret code that unlocks the door to success? Not at all. The answer lies in your follow-up." He explains:

Following up is the focal point for all of your sales opportunities. It's why the follow-up bucket is so prominent in the marketing and sales cycle. While you may feel that your services are good enough to sell themselves, it is consistent follow-up that truly moves your prospect from "maybe" or "later" to "yes."

To keep all of your potential client opportunities flowing smoothly in and out of the follow-up pool, make following up a priority. If the sales process has slowed down, it's probably due to lack of follow-up. Try to engage in some form of follow-up activity every day.

Let go of any fear, uncertainty, or doubt about following up with your prospects. They actually expect your call and want you to help move the relationship forward. Remember to offer value in all your follow-up activities. Every contact with your prospects is a chance to demonstrate your expertise.

And keep track of your progress. Always know where you are in the sales cycle with each prospect. This will help you move every prospect toward a sale much faster.

FILLING OUT THE ACTION WORKSHEET

With your two to four marketing strategies chosen, you are ready to begin filling out your Action Worksheet. A blank worksheet is provided in Figure 2-2. Because you may wish to make changes to your worksheet later or repeat the program after the initial twenty-eight days, make an enlarged copy of the blank worksheet, or download a copy at www.getclientsnow.com.

Make your first entries on the worksheet now. Check the boxes that correspond to the marketing strategies you will be using and the stage of the Universal Marketing Cycle where you need the most work. Now let's go on to the next step: setting your sales and marketing goal.

Figure 2-2: Blank Action Worksheet

GET CLIENTS NOW!™ Action Worksheet

What strategies will you use?

DIRECT CONTACT & FOLLOW-UP	NETWORKING & REFERRAL BUILDING	PUBLIC SPEAKING	WRITING & PUBLICITY	PROMOTIONAL EVENTS	ADVERTISING
☐	☐	☐	☐	☐	☐

Where are you stuck or what needs the most work?

☐ Filling the pipeline ☐ Following up ☐ Having sales conversations ☐ Closing sales

How much business do you have now? _____

How much business do you *really* want? _____

What would that get you? _____

_____

What is your program goal? _____

What will be your reward? _____

Success Ingredients   Target Date

1. _____   _____

2. _____   _____

3. _____   _____

Daily Actions

1. _____

2. _____

3. _____

4. _____

5. _____

6. _____

7. _____

8. _____

9. _____

10. _____

Special Permission _____

No Marketing? No Business!

Stephen Fairley, M.A.; www.businessbuildingcenter.com

Stephen Fairley, the author of *Getting Started in Personal and Executive Coaching* and *Practice Made Perfect*, claims, "Most people who start their own professional practices are technicians—the people who really just want to do the actual work of consulting, coaching, law, etc., which is great and necessary. However, technicians typically underestimate the difficulty of the other three essential roles; that is, starting, building, and maintaining a successful practice. They also typically overestimate their ability to market and sell their services." Fairley adds,

> Other than the actual decision to start the business, the sales and marketing aspects are the most important function of your business. If there is no sales and marketing, there are no clients to service. If there are no clients, there is no revenue. If there is no revenue, there is no business. It is all a big cycle, and that cycle starts and ends with sales and marketing. To be successful in your professional practice you must accept that you are the chief marketing officer as well as the vice president of sales. There is just no getting around it. If you don't market yourself and sell your ability to help people, you will never get clients.

"The greater danger for most of us is not that our aim is too high and we miss it. But that it is too low . . . and we reach it."

—Michelangelo

CHAPTER 3

Where Are You Headed?

Setting Your Sales and Marketing Goal

HOW HAVING A GOAL WILL HELP YOU

In this chapter, you are going to set your sales and marketing goal for the twenty-eight days of the Get Clients Now! program. We will be using goal-setting techniques many times throughout this program, so let's take a moment to examine the system's core philosophy about goals:

1. Set goals that will stretch you, but that you believe are realistic.
2. Try your best to meet them.
3. When it becomes clear that a goal is unrealistic, change it.
4. Reward yourself for effort, not just results. Punishment is not allowed.

Rewards are a key element of the process. Marketing is unpredictable. Sometimes you do everything exactly right and still don't get the results you want when you want them. If you reward yourself only when you get results, all the challenging work that led up to the result often gets discounted. And in the meantime, you feel as though you aren't getting anywhere.

Get into the habit of rewarding yourself for effort, regardless of your results. To do this consistently, you will always need a goal. If you decide, for example, that you will make ten follow-up calls on Monday, and you make them, you deserve acknowledgment even if none of those people agree to buy today. If you hadn't set a goal for the day, you would have nothing to reward yourself for, and no cushion for the disappointment you may feel.

This approach is particularly important where Success Ingredients are concerned. These are the missing ingredients you need to be successful in your marketing and that you plan to create during the program. A blog, for example, could be a missing Success Ingredient. Having a blog might be important for the success of your business, but the blog by itself will not bring you clients. You will need to let people know about it, build a subscriber list, make some posts to it, and so on, before your blog starts turning into sales. Therefore, you need to reward yourself up front, as soon as you launch the blog, for all the effort that went into creating it.

While rewards are essential, punishment is strictly forbidden. When you don't meet a goal you've set, acknowledge it, see what you might learn from it, then move on. Don't consider it a failure, beat yourself up for it, or allow it to discourage you from trying again. Expecting that you will reach every goal you set is unrealistic. Just try your best to do what you intend, reward yourself for all you accomplish, and learn from what you don't.

Setting marketing goals on a monthly, weekly, and even daily basis can provide you with a number of significant benefits. The first one is an improved *focus*. Looking at your goals each day will keep them in the forefront of your mind. Knowing that you have only twenty-eight days to achieve the results you want will tighten your focus on marketing and help you to ignore distractions.

Second, your goals will produce *evidence*. By regularly measuring your level of effort and comparing it to the results you create, you will get a constant reality check on your progress. You will discover right away if you are not working hard enough or are spending precious marketing time on activities like cleaning out your desk drawer. You will also be able to tell when you have done enough and can take a day off without feeling guilty.

Your goals will also provide you with *direction*. For the next twenty-eight days, you won't need to worry as much about what you should do next to get more clients. Your completed Action Worksheet will indicate exactly what to do. Whenever you feel uncertain about your next move, ask yourself, "Which choice (action, decision, and so forth) is more likely to lead me in the direction of my goals?" Often that reminder is all you will need to stay on the right track.

Finally, your goals can help you with *motivation*. Post your Action Worksheet on the wall where you will constantly see it. Run a contest with yourself to see how early in the day you can complete your Daily Actions, and then try to beat your own record. Set up a reward for finishing each Success Ingredient project, or reaching a certain percentage mark toward your program goal. Invent a marketing or sales game and make up your own rules. The more fun you can have, and the more rewards you can collect, the easier the next twenty-eight days will be.

You Gotta Have a Plan

Rich Fettke, MCC; www.fettke.com

"There are hundreds of ways to market yourself," maintains Rich Fettke, master coach and author of *Extreme Success*. "You can create a promo kit to send the media, speak at business groups and functions, send out monthly postcards, e-mails, and faxes. You can call people on the phone and personally deliver your unique marketing message." Fettke continues,

> You can do any of these things, but will you? You can't do all of them at the same time. The trick to great marketing is to get the same people to hear about you over and over. The only way to do this without being overwhelmed and frustrated is to create a sales and marketing plan and then stick with it. Your plan needs to be specific, measurable, and attainable (with some risk), and include goal dates and deadlines. Setting up daily success habits for yourself will also lead you toward accomplishing your goals, step by step.

> I use the Get Clients Now! system with my own clients to give them an easy-to-follow structure for attracting more business. It gets them into action, and action creates results.

WHAT IS A GOAL, ANYWAY?

When you are planning to cook a meal, it's necessary to know if your intended dish is soup or pasta before you begin. To choose the right Success Ingredients in Chapter 4 and make the best selections from the Action Plan Menu in Chapter 5, you must first determine what sort of feast you wish to create. That's where a goal comes in.

A goal is your statement of intention. It is your own personal declaration of what you want, what you plan to focus on, and what you intend to accomplish. Having a sales and marketing goal gives you a destination for your business-building journey. Only when you know where you are going can you choose the right path to get you there. And you have to be clear about your destination to know when you have arrived.

Many years ago, some unsung champion of goal-setting came up with the acronym SMART to describe the five important characteristics of a meaningful goal:

Specific. Your goal precisely spells out your desired result.

Measurable. The goal states your target in measurable terms so you will know when you have arrived, as well as where you are at any specific moment.

Achievable. A goal is physically possible to accomplish within any defined limitations.

Realistic. Your goal can be accomplished within the specified time and with available resources.

Time-based. There is a calendar date by which you plan to achieve your goal.

Here are some examples of SMART goals you might set for the twenty-eight days of the Get Clients Now! program:

Two new clients with signed agreements by the end of the program
Fifteen paying appointments scheduled weekly beginning in Week 3
Twenty-two billable hours worked per week for the full month
Six thousand dollars in business booked for the following month by Week 4
Eight new qualified prospects by the end of the program

Your program goal will help you get into action. If you have a specific target that must be accomplished by a particular date, you will perform tasks that would otherwise languish on a to-do list. It will also help you measure your effectiveness. If you are moving toward your goal, your actions are effective; if you are not moving toward it, they are ineffective, or not effective enough.

Now you're ready to set a goal. As you answer the questions in the next section, write your responses on your Action Worksheet. See the sample worksheet in Figure 3-1 for an example.

Figure 3-1: Beginning to Fill Out the Action Worksheet

GET CLIENTS NOW!™ Action Worksheet

What strategies will you use?

DIRECT CONTACT & FOLLOW-UP	NETWORKING & REFERRAL BUILDING	PUBLIC SPEAKING	WRITING & PUBLICITY	PROMOTIONAL EVENTS	ADVERTISING
☑	☑	☐	☐	☐	☐

Where are you stuck or what needs the most work?

☑ Filling the pipeline ☐ Following up ☐ Having sales conversations ☐ Closing sales

How much business do you have now? __11 clients__

How much business do you *really* want? __20 clients__

What would that get you? __pay off my credit cards, take a vacation, feel less stressed__

What is your program goal? __4 new clients by the end of the program__

What will be your reward? __go out to dinner and a movie__

Success Ingredients

From Dream to Idea to Goal

Marcia Wieder, www.dreamuniversity.com

"In the early phases of a dream, or with a big dream, there may be no evidence that your idea is a good one, or that this is the right time to execute it," counsels Marcia Wieder, author of *Making Your Dreams Come True* and *Doing Less and Having More*. She advises,

> At that moment, it is essential that you believe in yourself and in your dream. Your belief will be the foundation, a place that you can stand and say, "I'm going for it because it matters to me and I believe in my dreams." Then, prove you really do believe in yourself by taking action.

> Make the call, write the letter, map out an action plan, hire a coach, share your dream. Do something and do it now!

SETTING YOUR GOAL FOR THE PROGRAM

The place to start in setting your program goal is to look at where you are
starting from. *How much business do you have now?* Answer this question in
whatever numerical terms you typically use to measure the amount of business you currently have. For example, you could choose (1) the number of
clients you have, (2) the quantity of paying appointments scheduled weekly
or monthly, (3) the billable hours you have put in or expect, or (4) the dollar
amount of business you have booked or already billed.

If you do not already have a way to measure business that works for you,
consider what would inform your marketing efforts the most. What number
would best tell you whether your marketing is succeeding? Following are
some examples:

If you are a(n) . . .	*Your measurement might be . . .*
Account representative	Total number of accounts
Life coach	Total number of ongoing clients
Real estate agent	Total number of listings
Contract trainer	Monthly number of training days scheduled
Image consultant	Monthly number of appointments booked
Psychotherapist	Weekly number of sessions held
Attorney	Billable hours worked monthly
Graphic designer	Billable hours worked weekly
Management consultant	Billable days scheduled monthly
Freelance writer	Dollar amount of assignments booked monthly
Interior designer	Dollar amount invoiced monthly
Financial planner	Dollar amount of assets under management
Salesperson	Dollar volume of sales closed monthly

The important thing to notice about all these measurements is that they
are based on numbers you can easily keep updated and track. During the Get
Clients Now! program, you will be measuring progress toward your goal each
day, so you always must be able to know exactly where you are. If you are an
interior designer, for example, it will probably be easier for you to track the
dollar amount of your invoices than the net profit you are earning on each
one. Be sure to pick a measurement that you can know on a daily basis.

Now, using the measure you chose, ask yourself *how much business do
you really want?* This should be not just what you want by the end of the

month, but the pie-in-the-sky, wave-your-magic-wand answer. Don't worry too much about how possible it seems. Allow yourself to think big. Whatever answer you give here is the direction you are headed.

If you had what you really want—that level of business you just named—*what would that get you?* Would it give you something tangible you have always desired, like enough free time and money to take a month-long tropical cruise? Or is an intangible outcome more important to you, such as peace of mind, or a feeling of success? There's no one correct response here, so choose something that is personally exciting, inspiring, or fulfilling. This answer is your motivation.

Still using the same measure, *what is your program goal* for the month of the Get Clients Now! program? Three new clients? Eighteen paying appointments per week? Twenty billable hours booked weekly? A monthly gross of $5,000? Your goal is what will give you the evidence that your program is working (or not).

Remember the SMART goal-setting characteristics in designing your monthly goal. A program goal must be a measurable target. "More clients" is not a goal; it is a wish. In order for a goal to help you track your progress, it must be numeric because you will be measuring your progress numerically as you move through the program. Your goal should also be a bit of a stretch. Be realistic, but challenge yourself to choose something slightly ambitious.

Finally, if you achieve your goal for the month, *what will be your reward?* Will you buy yourself a present, take some extra time off, have a special dinner? Choose something that will really represent success to you and that you will look forward to having earned at the program's end.

Merely by answering the questions above, you will already be on the path to success. It's part of the magic of goal-setting. When you set a specific goal and begin checking your progress against it on a regular basis, your day-to-day activities start to shift in the direction that supports your goal. This shift begins to happen without any conscious effort on your part. And, of course, additional effort in an informed direction can dramatically enhance the process, as you will see in Chapter 4.

If You Want It, Declare It!
Steven Robbins, www.steverrobbins.com

"When scheduling a meeting with myself to work on a report that was due a week ago, *of course* I find reasons to schedule something else on top of it," confesses Steven Robbins. Robbins is an executive coach and host of the iTunes Top 10 business podcast *The Get-it-Done Guy.* "After all, more important stuff comes up! Like that cute cat picture on social media. Commitments to ourselves are easy to break." He adds,

> But that's *so* not true about commitments to others.
>
> Declaring your intention to another person is powerful. It becomes more real. You feel peer pressure to get started. And by getting your intent out there, people will spot opportunities and send them your way.
>
> When I set my intentions, I declare it publicly: I tell friends so they can offer help. I tell loved ones so they can encourage me when I get discouraged. I tell enemies, so they can gloat if I miss the mark.
>
> Don't just say it in a phone call. Put it in writing, so you can't weasel out of it later. It's easier to make six prospecting calls than have the dreaded Accountability Conversation:
>
> "Did I say six phone calls a day? Nonsense. I'm sure I only said three."
>
> "Really? Let me find your e-mail. You clearly said six."
>
> If you want to amp it up even further, schedule regular check-in calls with people in your support network. Even if you procrastinate a bit, that upcoming check-in will spur you into action. Our most powerful psychological forces kick into action when we know we'll be accountable to someone else to produce results. Use this to your advantage. Declare your intention and watch how powerfully intention will turn into results.

TIME FOR A REALITY CHECK

Setting a realistic goal is important to your success. Choosing a target that is too easy to hit won't stretch you. You need to make an extra effort to produce your best results. But, if you set a goal that is unreasonably high, you will become frustrated and discouraged. So, how do you know if your goal is realistic? Here are four different ways of checking the reality of your goal. Choose whichever one you like best, or use all four:

1. **Straight-Face Test.** One way to use this method is to state your goal out loud, to a friendly audience, in a strong confident voice. If you can keep a straight face, it's probably realistic. Another way is to ask yourself the question, "Can I really do this?" If the most honest answer you can give yourself is a self-assured "Yes!" it is most likely a realistic goal.

2. **Prior Experience.** If the straight-face method seems too simplistic, review your prior experience. Have you ever had a month where you reached

the level of success implied by your current goal? If you have, no matter how improbable the set of circumstances was the last time, your goal is still realistic. If you did it before, you can do it again. And remembering that your goal is supposed to be a bit of a stretch, if you even came close to your current goal in some prior month, consider it realistic.

3. **Numerical Analysis.** If you got an inconclusive answer using the first method or are lacking sufficient experience to use the second, try looking at the numbers. Let's say you want to get four new clients this month. How many people do you think you will have to have sales conversations with in order to get four clients? Eight? Twelve? How many people will you need to make contact with to arrange that many conversations? Forty? One hundred twenty? Don't worry if you don't know for sure; just take a guess.

However many you think it is, do you have that many people already in your pipeline, and the time or resources to contact them all? Sit down with your calculator, and crunch some numbers. Starting from where you are right now, with the resources you have available, can you deliver the level of effort needed to reach your stated goal in one month?

4. **Peer Comparison.** Have others you would consider peers accomplished a similar goal in their business in one month's time? Do your colleagues or competitors who have been in business about the same length of time routinely get that much business? If so, you have probably set a realistic goal, no matter how unattainable it may seem to you right now.

If any of these tests make you fear that the goal you have set is unrealistic, change it now. There's no fun, and even less value, in struggling to meet a goal that was never achievable in the first place.

One final hint: if you are just starting out in business, you might consider setting a goal based on a certain number of leads acquired, prospects contacted, or sales conversations had, rather than closed sales. Remember the length of the marketing cycle for our software consultant in the previous chapter. If you are starting from scratch to fill your pipeline, closing a sale in the next twenty-eight days might be out of reach for you.

Set a Goal, Get Focused, Get Results
Loretta Love Huff, www.moreclientsbiggersales.com

"One of the comments I frequently hear from my clients is how focused on productive activities they become in the Get Clients Now! program," recalls marketing consultant and coach, Loretta Love Huff, the Dream Leader for Business. She recalls,

> One participant set a goal for the course and by the second week of tracking, had already achieved it. It wasn't that she had "sandbagged" her marketing prowess by setting an easy goal to reach. It was that once it was set, she stopped wasting her time on things that didn't really matter!
>
> She stopped thinking about marketing her business and worrying what bad things might befall her, and started actually talking with people about her business. She resisted the temptation to open her e-mail program until she had worked on the item on her Daily Actions list that scared her the most.
>
> She made calls early in the day to prospects and experienced the exhilaration of conquering her fears and completing her action items, feeling successful and accomplished even if they said no to her offers.
>
> Fueled by her increased productivity, she had time to pursue her more creative ideas without the guilt of thinking, "I should be doing something else." This increase in productivity and confidence ultimately led to the creation of a business mentoring and mastermind group which established her as a leader in her community.
>
> And it all started with setting a goal and staying focused on it.

ARE YOU RESISTING THIS PROCESS?

Have you read this entire discussion of goal-setting without yet setting a goal? Or did you choose one, but tell yourself, "I don't have to set a real goal. This is just an exercise?" It's time to ask yourself why. Or better yet, what is in the way?

Are you afraid? Of what? Failing? Succeeding? Offending someone? Looking silly? Do you have some negative past experience with goal-setting that is causing you to avoid it? Whatever it is that is preventing you from choosing a real honest-to-goodness, no-kidding, I-can-do-this goal, get it out in the open now. This program will not work for you unless you set a realistic goal.

Write out your fears and concerns, draw or paint them, talk them out with your business buddy, action group, coach, or a friend. Do whatever it takes to discover what is stopping you, and then stop letting it stop you. Make a conscious choice to try goal-setting one more time, or for the first time. Trust the process. It works.

LOCKING IT IN

Great work! Now that you have a goal, find someone to tell it to. If you are working with a buddy, group, or coach, you already have a place to share your goal. If not, tell it to a friend or colleague. Stating goals out loud grants them more reality than just writing them down. And telling someone else what you plan to accomplish creates a sense of accountability on your part to give you an extra push toward that goal.

PART II

The System

CHAPTER 4

What's Stopping You?

Selecting Your Success Ingredients

WHAT ARE THE MISSING INGREDIENTS?

With a realistic goal in place, you are now ready to take the next step in designing the action plan you will follow for the next month. You will be selecting your Success Ingredients—the missing ingredients you need in order to cook up a successful sales and marketing plan.

Success Ingredients are the tools, information, or skills that will successfully address the area of your marketing you have determined is stuck, or needs more work. Each stage of the Universal Marketing Cycle requires a different list of key ingredients for effective marketing. If you are working on filling the pipeline, for example, you may need to find some new networking events to attend. But if your focus is on closing sales, this ingredient won't be helpful. You might instead need to work on your selling skills.

The place to begin in choosing Success Ingredients is to ask yourself why you are not making progress in your chosen stage of the Universal Marketing Cycle. "Why can't I fill the pipeline?" you might ask. Or, "Why aren't I following up?" Your answer may point you to a needed Success Ingredient right away. Stop and think about this: What tools, information, or skills are you missing to help you fill the pipeline, follow up, have sales conversations, or close sales?

SHOPPING FOR SUCCESS INGREDIENTS

In the design of your Get Clients Now! program, you should have at least one, and no more than three, Success Ingredients that you plan to work on over the next twenty-eight days. You may have already thought of some missing ingredients by asking yourself why you are stuck in a particular stage of your marketing. To help you select just the right ingredients for your plan, see the Success Ingredient Shopping List in Figure 4-1.

In reviewing the shopping list, it is important that you look at only the section that applies to your chosen marketing stage. Don't overwhelm yourself by checking out all the other options. You have already determined exactly where you need to focus right now, so stay with it. If it turns out you are ready to move into another stage later in the month—or the next time you use the program—that will be time enough to look at the other possibilities.

Some of the items on the shopping list may be unfamiliar to you. To help you decide which ingredients are the best for you, see the Success Ingredient Guide in Figure 4-2. There is much more information about these ingredients in the detailed marketing recipes in Part III of this book. However, don't rush to go there right now. You don't need to worry yet about the how-to's of acquiring and employing the ingredients. All you need to do now is choose those you would like to work on first.

Using the "Black-Box" Principle

When an engineer needs to design a new process from scratch, many unknowns can surface—so many, in fact, that if the engineer were to try to answer every necessary question while creating the design, it might become hopelessly bogged down in detail, becoming almost impossible to complete. A handy solution to this obstacle is to enclose each unknown in a black box and design the rest of the process without knowing the details of what goes inside the boxes.

Adopting this idea to design your marketing action plan can be a convenient solution to a common problem experienced by marketers. Let's say you are working on the stage of Filling the Pipeline, and you're pretty sure you will need some "networking venues" in order to start meeting more prospects. Yet you have no idea what those would be or where to find them. Your lack of information might cause you to say, "I can't choose that; I don't know how to go about it," and ignore this important ingredient completely. Or, you might go the other direction and try to fill in the gap in your knowledge by chasing after information about networking in your industry, delaying getting started on your action plan until you have some answers.

By using the black-box principle, you can avoid both of those wrong turns. You can simply choose "networking venues" as something you need, and put it on your Success Ingredient list, without knowing yet how you will acquire it. This is exactly what you should do.

So refer to Part III of this book only if you need additional information in order to choose one to three ingredients with which you will start. You'll have plenty of opportunities to learn how to accomplish each one once you begin your action plan.

Which Ingredients to Choose

You can choose any of the ingredients listed under your chosen stage of the Universal Marketing Cycle, but you should look most closely at those designated for the marketing strategies you selected in Chapter 2.

Each ingredient shown in the Success Ingredient Shopping List in Figure 4-1 displays an icon to the left that indicates for which of the six marketing strategies that ingredient is typically used. (The icons are reviewed for your convenience below.) Some ingredients, such as "business cards" or "website," have all of the icons because they are tools that can be used with any of the strategies. The others are marked with only those icons representing the strategies which each specific ingredient supports.

For example, under the filling the pipeline stage you'll see "prospect list" as a Success Ingredient that supports the strategies of (1) direct contact and follow-up, and (2) advertising. This is because you might require a prospect list either for the direct contact strategy of cold calling or the advertising strategy of direct mail.

The best way to use the shopping list is as a source of ideas rather than as a prescription. You may already know exactly what ingredients are missing in your marketing. As you read through the list, keep asking yourself why you can't be or aren't being successful in your stuck area. Place a check mark next to each ingredient you suspect might be missing for you.

The Strategy Icons

 Direct Contact & Follow-Up   Writing & Publicity

 Networking & Referral Building   Promotional Events

 Public Speaking   Advertising

Figure 4-1: Success Ingredient Shopping List

To fill the pipeline...

- Description of services
- Market niche definition
- 10-second introduction
- Business cards
- Self-confidence skills
- Website
- Social media profile/page
- Prospect list
- Lead sources
- Live networking venues
- Online networking venues
- Networking skills
- Referral partners
- Speaking venues
- Speaking topics/bio
- Writing/publishing venues
- Articles or writing queries
- Blog theme/topics
- Publicity venues
- Press release/media kit
- Photos/audio/video
- Promotion concept
- Promotion plan
- Advertising venues
- Flyer venues
- Ad copy, layout, or script

To follow up more effectively...

- Contact management system
- 30-second commercial
- Brochure
- Marketing kit
- Model marketing letter
- In-house mailing list
- Postcard or mailer
- Newsletter or e-zine
- Broadcast e-mail system
- Bonus for online subscribers
- Personal connections

To turn more contacts into conversations...

- Telemarketing script/skills
- Qualifying questions
- Higher quality leads and referrals
- Better website conversion
- Professional visibility
- Competitive research
- Target market research
- New market position
- Better service package
- Narrower focus of services

(continues)

Figure 4-1: Success Ingredient Shopping List (continued)

To turn more conversations into sales...

- Professional credibility
- Testimonials or references
- Better-qualified prospects
- Stronger relationships
- Presentation script/visuals
- Presentation skills
- Portfolio
- Leave-behind
- Selling script
- Selling skills

Figure 4-2: Success Ingredient Guide

FILLING THE PIPELINE
- **Description of services**. A clear, specific description of the features, benefits, structure, and cost of the primary services you will focus on in your marketing.
- **Market niche definition**. Description of the target market you most wish to do business with and the niche area in which you specialize.
- **10-second introduction.** Self-introduction that describes what you do and who you do it for in a clear and memorable way.
- **Business cards**. To include your contact information and a brief summary of what you offer, such as a position, title, specialties, tag line, or key benefit.
- **Self-confidence skills.** A higher level of confidence, and key self-confidence tools to help you overcome fear, resistance, and self-doubt when marketing yourself.
- **Website**. A basic site that tells visitors what you do and why they should hire you, or a more powerful site that offers free resources and captures visitors' contact information.
- **Social media profile/page.** A profile for yourself or a page for your business that allows you to become active in social media networks or just be found more easily online.

- ▶ **Prospect list**. List of people or companies in your target market that you purchase, compile, or acquire from a lead source.
- ▶ **Lead sources**. Groups, institutions, publications, websites, media sources, and networking contacts that can give you information about potential clients on a regular basis.
- ▶ **Live networking venues**. Places, groups, and events where you can go in person to meet prospective clients and referral partners.
- ▶ **Online networking venues.** Social media networks, message boards, discussion groups, Web chats, and blogs where you can meet and follow up with people online.
- ▶ **Networking skills**. Techniques or experience to help you feel more comfortable about meeting people and interacting with them to build relationships.
- ▶ **Referral partners**. People, groups, or institutions that have contact with your target market, and are willing to refer potential clients to you on a regular basis.
- ▶ **Speaking venues**. Places, groups, or events—live or online—where you might be able to speak to promote your business.
- ▶ **Speaking topics/bio**. Description of one to three topics you are available to speak on, plus a summary of your background and speaking experience.
- ▶ **Writing/publishing venues**. Publications, blogs, or websites for which you can write articles, tips, guest blog posts, or an ongoing column.
- ▶ **Articles or writing queries**. Articles, tips, or blog posts you want to have published, or queries about pieces you'd like to write.
- ▶ **Blog theme/topics.** A concept for your blog that will give it a sustainable theme, and a series of topics you might blog about.
- ▶ **Publicity venues**. Print, broadcast, e-mail, and Web media outlets you can approach to get quoted, interviewed, or profiled.
- ▶ **Press release/media kit**. A release is the bulletin you send media outlets to attract press coverage. A media kit—print or online—provides more in-depth details about you.
- ▶ **Photos/audio/video.** Visual or audio samples to supplement your publicity efforts and demonstrate your expertise.
- ▶ **Promotion concept**. Idea for a promotional event, such as a free demonstration or workshop, complimentary teleclass or webinar, or an exhibit at a trade show.
- ▶ **Promotion plan**. Your plan for producing a promotional event or trade show appearance.
- ▶ **Advertising venues**. Places you can advertise to reach your prospects: e.g. direct mail, print publications, directories, websites, search engines, e-zines, or broadcast e-mail.

(continues)

Figure 4-2: Success Ingredient Guide (continued)

> ► **Flyer venues**. Places where you can post, distribute, or circulate a flyer.
> ► **Ad copy, layout, or script**. What your proposed ad will say and how it will look.
>
> ## FOLLOWING UP
> ► **Contact management system**. Organized method to keep track of all your contacts. Could be a notebook, desktop software, a cloud application, or a smartphone/tablet app.
> ► **30-second commercial**. Brief verbal summary of what you do, who you do it for, and key benefits and results you deliver.
> ► **Brochure**. Printed summary of the services you offer, benefits of working with you, and your qualifications.
> ► **Marketing kit**. Expanded brochure with multiple pieces (e.g., professional bio, client list, testimonial letters, or articles).
> ► **Model marketing letter**. Boilerplate language you modify to create letters you send to contacts, rather than writing each one from scratch.
> ► **In-house mailing list.** List of clients, prospects, and referral partners whose names you have accumulated from networking, referrals, visits to your website, speaking, etc.
> ► **Postcard or mailer**. Marketing literature you send by postal mail to remind prospects that you are still around, or make a special offer.
> ► **Newsletter or e-zine**. Collection of articles, tips, and/or announcements you periodically send by postal mail or e-mail.
> ► **Broadcast e-mail system**. System that allows website visitors to subscribe to your e-mail list, and allows you to send them e-mail broadcasts or autoresponses.
> ► **Bonus for online subscribers**. Free gift you provide website visitors as an incentive to subscribe to your e-mail list, e.g., an e-book, white paper, or video tutorial.
> ► **Personal connections.** Connections between you and prospects that encourage them to speak with you, e.g., referrals, introductions, or memberships you share.
>
> ## HAVING SALES CONVERSATIONS
> ► **Telemarketing script/skills**. Better language and techniques to help you improve at selling yourself by phone.
> ► **Qualifying questions**. Questions to ask your prospects to determine whether they are likely candidates for your services.
> ► **Higher quality leads and referrals.** The type of prospects who are most likely to buy, based on their profile or the source of the original lead.
> ► **Better website conversion**. Revisions to your website that encourage visitors to stay longer, return again, or contact you to discuss your services.

- ▶ **Professional visibility**. Making yourself more visible in your market niche to increase the likelihood that prospects know your name before you contact them.
- ▶ **Competitive research**. Information about the competition that enables you to better compete by emulating what works and improving on what doesn't.
- ▶ **Target market research**. Information about your prospective clients that tells you more about what they want and need.
- ▶ **New market position**. Influencing how prospects think of you in comparison to your competition by changing your marketing messages.
- ▶ **Better service package**. A different way of packaging your services or fees to make them more attractive to prospective clients.
- ▶ **Narrower focus of services**. Limiting what you offer your prospects to the one or two lines of business that your prospects are most likely to buy.

CLOSING SALES

- ▶ **Professional credibility**. How prospects perceive your ability to perform, based on what they see of your background, experience, credentials, or expertise.
- ▶ **Testimonials or references**. Letters or quotes from satisfied clients, or a list of verifiable references with their contact information.
- ▶ **Better-qualified prospects**. Prospects who are predisposed to become clients, because of their needs, desires, or ability to pay.
- ▶ **Stronger relationships**. Building connection and trust over time through exposure to you, your abilities, or others who already trust you.
- ▶ **Presentation script/visuals.** An outline of what you plan to discuss in sales conversations and supporting visuals to make your services more tangible.
- ▶ **Presentation skills.** Techniques or experience you need to get more comfortable with questioning, listening, or presenting.
- ▶ **Portfolio**. Tangible examples of your work that you can show to a prospect, e.g. case studies, photographs, videos, or samples of designs, writing, or reports.
- ▶ **Leave-behind**. Something extra you leave with, or send to, a prospect to use or review after a sales conversation.
- ▶ **Selling script.** A list of talking points to remember when closing the sale, including asking-for-the-business questions, and answers to common objections.
- ▶ **Selling skills**. Techniques or experience to help you do a better job at closing the sale.

Bridging the Gap from Idea to Action

Leslie Lupinsky, MCC, CPCC; www.leslielupinsky.com
Joni Mar, MCC, CPCC; www.jonimar.com

"Often what happens is people get very excited about their dreams, passions and visions," describe Leslie Lupinsky and Joni Mar, authors of *The Inspired Business Approach*, "but when it comes to the implementation phase, they fall into despair or fear about the work involved to achieve the results they are after." They go on to say:

> Once this starts, it can be a downward cycle. The person procrastinates on the necessary actions, producing more fear and despair. It takes a great deal of courage and support as well as a strong commitment to turn the cycle around.
>
> If you are losing momentum in your business, try asking yourself these questions:
>
> 1. Where are you now?
> 2. Where do you want to be?
> 3. What feelings are you experiencing in this gap between the two?
> 4. What's the cost to you and your business of staying here?
> 5. Sit with the experience of the gap, your feelings, and all of their implications for several minutes.
> 6. Now, where are you willing to move forward into action? What would support you to take the next step?

EDITING YOUR SHOPPING LIST

If you chose three Success Ingredients or fewer, you can skip to the next section, "Setting Target Completion Dates." If you selected more than three, it's time to prioritize. To ensure you are choosing the most important ingredients, first look at the marketing strategies you have decided to use. Since you will be using only those strategies for the present, you can eliminate any ingredients that you don't actually need to implement your chosen strategies.

For example, if you are working on filling the pipeline, but did not choose writing and publicity as one of your strategies, you should not be selecting "publicity venues" or "blog theme/topics" as Success Ingredients, no matter how attractive they sound. You have spent quite a bit of effort already in diagnosing the area that needs more work and picking the right strategies to address it, so don't second-guess yourself now.

If you eliminate those distractions and still have more than three Success Ingredients, ask yourself which three you need first. During your Get Clients Now! program month, you will be acquiring or creating the one to three ingredients you choose. As you complete your first choices, you can cross them off the list and start work on others.

Let's say you are focusing on following up, and are considering the Success Ingredients "model marketing letter," "contact management system," "30-second commercial," and "e-zine." It would make more sense to begin with the first three, since the model marketing letter, contact management system, and 30-second commercial would all help you follow up with hot prospects you already know are interested, while the e-zine would be more helpful with contacts you know less about or with whom you need to build more trust first. If you complete any one of the three within the month, you could then start work on the e-zine.

The Success Ingredients you choose don't necessarily need to be completed within one month; you are just deciding to work on them during that time. A 30-second commercial is something you might knock off in a couple of hours, but building a website could take you six weeks from start to finish.

If you're still not sure which ingredients you should choose, skip to Part III, which has a chapter for each stage of the Universal Marketing Cycle. See what the chapter for your chosen stage has to say about the Success Ingredients you are considering, and then pick no more than three to start with.

Make Your Projects Bite-Size

Caterina Rando, MCC; www.caterinar.com

"Finding space in your busy life for a big project like developing a website can be a challenge," points out Caterina Rando, speaker, success coach, and author of the bestselling *Learn to Power Think* and seven other books for entrepreneurs. She advises,

> Sometimes we have so much to do that we feel paralyzed. When that happens, write down everything you think you need to do. Decide what is urgent, and what you can put off. Ask yourself if there is anything you can forget about doing, and if there's anything that someone else can do.

> Try working in increments. Tell yourself you will give yourself a break in an hour. Psychologically, you will feel more at ease with the situation. At the end of the hour, take a break, even if it is just a walk down the hall. This is also

good for the creative process; it gives your conscious mind an opportunity to wander and come up with some new ideas.

If you are really dreading doing something, find a way to make it fun. I always pay my bills while watching a *Star Trek* rerun; that makes it tolerable. I have a client who returns all possible phone calls from her Jacuzzi early in the morning. Play upbeat music when working in your office.

Break down your project into bite-size chunks. I used to tell myself that I would take a whole day and do nothing else but clean my office. I never did it because the idea was too dreadful. Instead, what I do now is work on it in 15-minute segments.

I often procrastinate when I need to do some writing. The mental block that is in my way is that I believe or feel that I don't know how to say what I want to say. But if I sit down and start tapping on the keyboard, it will work itself out. So don't sit around wondering how you might get it done, simply start to do it and see what happens.

SETTING TARGET COMPLETION DATES

It's time to record those Success Ingredients on your Action Worksheet. Look at the example in Figure 4-3. List the ingredients you have chosen on the Success Ingredients section of your own worksheet; notice that the example shows target dates for each one. You need to do this, too, so think about what would be a realistic amount of time to allow yourself to complete or acquire each item. It's okay to choose a target date that is more than a month away.

In setting a target date for your Success Ingredients, use the guidelines introduced in Chapter 3 for realistic goal-setting. Review the "Time for a Reality Check" section if you need a refresher. You should consider both the working time and the elapsed time needed for completion.

If you decided you were finally going to finish that brochure you've been working on, it might only take you two hours of working time to complete a final review of the last draft your graphic designer sent you. But then it will take the designer time to make your changes and get it to the printer, and the printer will need time to get it on the press. So estimate how much elapsed time will be required to get it all done.

If you aren't sure, don't leave the target date blank while you check with the designer and the printer to see what is reasonable. Allowing others to determine your schedule may be one of the habits that has gotten you into trouble in the past. Try this instead: Decide when you would like to have the

Figure 4-3: Adding Success Ingredients to the Action Worksheet

GET CLIENTS NOW!™ Action Worksheet

What strategies will you use?

DIRECT CONTACT & FOLLOW-UP	NETWORKING & REFERRAL BUILDING	PUBLIC SPEAKING	WRITING & PUBLICITY	PROMOTIONAL EVENTS	ADVERTISING
☑	☑	☐	☐	☐	☐

Where are you stuck or what needs the most work?

☑ Filling the pipeline ☐ Following up ☐ Having sales conversations ☐ Closing sales

How much business do you have now? **11 clients**

How much business do you *really* want? **20 clients**

What would that get you? **pay off my credit cards, take a vacation, feel less stressed**

What is your program goal? **4 new clients by the end of the program**

What will be your reward? **go out to dinner and a movie**

Success Ingredients	Target Date
1. **market niche definition**	**03/06/13**
2. **10-second introduction**	**03/08/13**
3. **3 live networking venues**	**03/15/13**

printed brochure in your hand; then call the designer and say, "I need to have my brochure complete by the 31st. If I get you my final changes by the 20th, can you meet that date?" If your request is unreasonable, the designer will tell you. Then you can negotiate for a new date, and change the target date on your worksheet.

The function of having a target date for each Success Ingredient, just like setting a marketing goal, is to get you into action immediately. Once your brochure has a due date, you will make a call about it and say, "This is when I need it," instead of, "When can you have it?" You will immediately be in more control of your marketing, and much more likely to produce results sooner.

Changing the target date after establishing it is not cheating; it is being realistic. What is the point of beating yourself up because you failed to meet a target date that you already knew was impossible? It's much better to keep your target dates realistic so you can reward yourself for reaching them. This goal-setting technique is particularly important regarding Success Ingredients. Having a great brochure may be important for your business-building approach, but the brochure alone will not get you any clients. You will need to call, mail, follow up, and so forth before that brochure helps you land a sales conversation, and ultimately, a client. Therefore, you need to reward yourself at the beginning, for all the effort that went into completing the brochure, before waiting to see the results it helps you produce.

Climbing the Marketing Ladder

Grace Durfee, www.balancewithgrace.com

Grace Durfee is a personal coach who uses the Get Clients Now! system as one of her tools to help clients succeed. According to Durfee, "Success Ingredients in marketing are like the ladders in the classic children's game *Chutes and Ladders*." She explains,

> Your good efforts catapult you from one level of play to another, putting you closer to your goal. But it's not a lucky spin of the wheel that lands you on a ladder space and helps you get ahead. In marketing, intention, planning, and consistent action are what propel you forward. Careful selection of Success Ingredients is an important part of your marketing plan. You want to choose projects that have lasting impact—that get you out of a stuck place in your marketing, once and for all.

> How do you determine what the best Success Ingredients are for you at this time? A key question to ask is, "What would make the biggest difference?" If you're not sure, your excuses provide clues that will point you in the right direction. Examine the excuses you make over and over again. For instance, if you say, "I'm not good at networking because I get tongue-tied when people ask what I do," then working on a 10-second introduction would be a wise choice for a Success Ingredient. "I couldn't follow up with that prospect because I lost his business card," could mean that it's time to transfer your fish bowl full of business cards into a contact management system. Perhaps you say, "I'm uncomfortable putting myself out there as a professional, because I don't have _____ yet." Fill in the blank here with your missing link, whether it's a business card, marketing materials, or a website. You've just found your Success Ingredient project.

Completing a Success Ingredient will give you a burst of energy, confidence, and ideas for the next project. No chutes for you; you're finding the next ladder!

QUANTIFYING YOUR SUCCESS INGREDIENTS

When setting target completion dates for your Success Ingredients, you may be puzzled about what to do if your Success Ingredient is a skill set instead of something tangible. Let's say that you want to improve your networking skills. Pick a target date by which you would like to have this ingredient completed and imagine that you are scoring yourself on a scale of zero to 100 percent. If zero percent means you can't network at all, and 100 percent means you are a star networker, what would be your score today? Perhaps 25 or 50 percent? Now what would you like your score to be by the target date you chose? That's the answer you would write on your worksheet. For example, you might write "networking skills at 75%—Oct 27."

You can use this same scoring technique to set targets for other intangible Success Ingredients, like "professional credibility" or "better service package." Just pick your desired completion date and decide the score you would like to achieve by then. If this seems arbitrary, it is. Yet you are the only one who can accurately measure your own progress. The goal and your progress toward it have to make sense and feel good to you. That's the only way a goal can work its motivation magic.

Even tangible Success Ingredients might require some quantification in order to be specific enough to serve as a goal. If you chose "writing venues," for example, how many are enough? Pick a number that would make you feel as if you had satisfied that need for at least a month's time, and write it on your worksheet—for example, "10 writing venues."

Once you have chosen one to three Success Ingredients, written them on your Action Worksheet, assigned target dates to them, and quantified them in terms of number needed or scores you wish to achieve, you have completed four of the six steps in designing your Get Clients Now! program. In Chapter 5 you will be choosing the precise action steps you will take to get clients over the next twenty-eight days.

Feel Better to Sell Better

Brian Tracy, www.briantracy.com

"In numerous conversations with top salespeople over the years, we've found that they all have one thing in common," notes Brian Tracy, author of 45 books on sales and motivation, including *Eat That Frog! 21 Great Ways to Stop Procrastinating and Get More Done in Less Time*. "They have taken the time to sit down and create a clear blueprint for themselves and their future lives." Tracy adds,

> Even if they started the process of goal-setting and personal strategic planning with a little skepticism, they eventually become true believers. Salespeople are amazed by the incredible power of goal setting and strategic planning. Believers often accomplish far more than they ever believed possible in selling and they ascribe their success to the deliberate process of thinking through every aspect of their work and their lives, developing a detailed, written road map, and continually working towards where they want to go.

> Happiness has been defined as "The progressive achievement of a worthy ideal or goal." When you work progressively, step-by-step toward something that is important, you generate a continuous feeling of success and achievement. You feel more positive and motivated. You feel more in control of your life; happier, and more fulfilled. Feeling like a winner, you will soon develop the psychological momentum that enables you to overcome obstacles and plough through adversity as you move toward achieving the goals that are most important to you.

"I am only one, but still I am one. I cannot do everything,
but I can do something. I will not refuse to do the something I can do."

—HELEN KELLER

CHAPTER 5

Here's What to Do

Choosing from the Action Plan Menu

WHERE DO THE CLIENTS COME FROM?

The final—and most important—piece of designing your own personal Get Clients Now! program is to select the specific marketing and sales action steps you plan to take on a regular basis over the next month. These are the actions that will generate business for you.

At the beginning of this book, you learned the most important secret of professional services marketing and sales: *The magic formula is choosing a set of simple, effective things to do, and doing them consistently.* That's where the clients come from.

You are about to do exactly this. You are going to choose ten specific actions to take, and perform them daily or weekly for the next twenty-eight days. Your choices will be based on the "stuck" place you uncovered with the Universal Marketing Cycle, as well as the marketing strategies you selected to address that area in need of more work. These action steps are designed to enable you to dramatically improve your marketing. But you need to actually do them in order to find clients.

There is an interesting phenomenon that occurs when you get serious about marketing in a focused, consistent way. You begin to get results in unexpected places. The telephone rings, and it's a prospect you spoke to three months ago saying he is suddenly interested in working with you. You go to a networking meeting that seems like a complete waste of time while you are there, and run into a hot new prospect in the elevator on your way out. You get an exciting referral from someone whose name you don't even recognize. It's almost as if the universe has noticed how hard you are working and decided to reward you.

Don't make the mistake of thinking that these out-of-the-blue opportunities are accidents. There is a direct connection between the level of effort you put into marketing and the results you get out of it, even when it seems as if the results are completely unrelated to your efforts. This phenomenon is so common with people who use the Get Clients Now! program that it has a name: the Persistence Effect. If you persist in making ten calls a day, every day, you will get business, but it won't all come from the calls you made. If you consistently attend one networking event per week, clients will appear, but not necessarily from the events you attended. Don't worry about why it works; just know that it works.

The existence of the Persistence Effect can help you enormously in choosing the Daily Actions for your program, because there is one more secret to successful marketing: *It doesn't matter so much what you choose as it does* that *you choose*.

Picking ten things you can do about marketing—and actually doing them—will break you out of analysis paralysis, give you a plan, and get you into action. Even if you picked the "wrong" ten actions, the Persistence Effect would make this focused activity pay off for you in some way. Would it pay off as well as picking the "right" ten things? Probably not. That's why you are about to choose only actions that represent the stage of the marketing cycle you are focusing on and the marketing strategies you already selected.

Build a Fire Under It
Napoleon Hill, 1883–1970

"Persistence is an essential factor in the procedure of transmuting desire into its monetary equivalent," wrote Napoleon Hill in his classic *Think and Grow Rich* (1938). Hill elaborates,

> The basis of persistence is the power of will. . . . The majority of people are ready to throw their aims and purposes overboard, and give up at the first sign of opposition or misfortune. A few carry on despite all opposition, until they attain their goal. . . .

> Lack of persistence is one of the major causes of failure. Moreover, experience with thousands of people has proved that lack of persistence is a weakness

common to the majority of men. It is a weakness which may be overcome by effort. The ease with which lack of persistence may be conquered will depend entirely on the intensity of one's desire.

The starting point of all achievement is desire. Keep this constantly in mind. Weak desires bring weak results, just as a small amount of fire makes a small amount of heat. If you find yourself lacking in persistence, this weakness may be remedied by building a stronger fire under your desires.

ORDERING FROM THE ACTION PLAN MENU

There are two ways of going about selecting what Daily Actions to include in your program. One way is to choose from the selections already prepared for you that appear on the Action Plan Menu (Figure 5-1). The other is to design your own unique actions. Let's look first at how to design your own, which will help you understand how to make the best choices.

Suppose you are focusing on the closing sales stage, and you have chosen direct contact and follow-up as one of your marketing strategies. How could you use this strategy to close more sales? Perhaps you could follow up better by re-contacting people who you have already presented to, but didn't buy from you at the time.

To turn this into a specific, consistent action, give it a time frame and quantify it—for example, "Follow up with five prospects each week who previously said no." This action directly addresses the stage where you need more work, using a marketing strategy you have chosen.

How do you know how often to do something and how much of it to do? You guess. How much activity do you think will be necessary to achieve the result you want? How much do you have time for? The right answer is probably somewhere between those two. But really, there is no one right answer. It doesn't matter so much what you choose as it does *that* you choose.

Remember the Get Clients Now! goal-setting philosophy:

1. Set goals that will stretch you, but that you believe are realistic.
2. Try your best to meet them.
3. When it becomes clear that a goal is unrealistic, change it.
4. Reward yourself for effort, not just results. Punishment is not allowed.

You're going to use these same principles again in designing your Daily Actions. Pick a time frame and quantity that seem reasonable. Try it out. If

(text continues on page 84)

Figure 5-1: Action Plan Menu

Appetizers: *Choose 1 or 2*

To create Success Ingredients . . .

Spend 1 hour each day on my Success Ingredient projects
Complete 1 item each day from my Success Ingredient project list
Practice my skills or script once per day
Spend 1 hour each week doing research
Read or write every day for 1 hour
Interview 1 person per week
Collect 3 new facts per day
Observe how it's done once per week

Main Course: *Choose 7 or 8*

To fill the pipeline with direct contact and follow-up . . .

Spend 1 hour each day cold-calling

Send letters or e-mails to 10 new contacts each week

Place warm calls to 3 prospects per day

Spend 1 hour each week researching leads

Meet 3 new people in person each week

To fill the pipeline with networking and referral building . . .

Go to 1 live networking event each week

Contact 2 new potential referral partners each week

Have lunch or coffee with a colleague once per week

Add 20 new social media connections each week

Make 1 new online community contact weekly

Spend 15 minutes interacting with my online network daily

Post a comment to someone else's blog each week

Re-contact 3 former clients each week

Send an item of interest to 2 contacts each week

Volunteer in a visible position once per week

Ask for a referral once per day

Give a referral once per week

Follow up weekly with all new contacts met that week

To fill the pipeline with public speaking...

 Contact 3 groups each week about speaking

 Speak to a group once per week

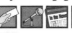 Spend 1 hour each week promoting my speaking events

To fill the pipeline with writing and publicity...

 Do 1 thing to get my name in print each week

 Post to my blog twice per week

 Write one article or tip weekly

 Find 1 new venue to post my articles each week

 Pitch 1 media outlet about interviewing me weekly

 Post updates to my social media network 3 times per week

 Spend 1 hour each week promoting my writing

To fill the pipeline with promotional events...

 Do 3 things each week to make my next event successful

 Spend 2 hours per week promoting my next event

To fill the pipeline with advertising...

 Distribute or post 30 flyers weekly

 Send 10 direct mail letters per week

 Update 1 page on my website each week

Evaluate 1 new place to advertise each week

Spend 1 hour per week refining my online advertising

(continues)

Figure 5-1: Action Plan Menu (continued)

To follow up more effectively . . .

Call 3 prospects or referral sources every day

Send an item of interest to 1 contact per day

Add 10 new names to my in-house mailing list each day

Enter contact activity in my contact management system daily

Send a letter or e-mail to 3 prospects each day

Send broadcast e-mail to some part of my mailing list weekly

Show up at a live event my prospects attend once per week

Invite a prospect or referral source to an event once per week

Have lunch or coffee with a prospect once per week

Interact with my online network for 30 minutes per day

Make my follow-up calls first thing every day

Follow up by e-mail or online with 5 prospects per day

To have more sales conversations . . .

Ask for an appointment with 1 prospect per day

Practice my telemarketing script daily

Make 3 follow-up calls each day

Send 2 follow-up letters per day

Ask my networking contacts for 3 introductions each week

Solicit one testimonial each week

Spend 2 hours per week researching my market

Meet with 1 new referral partner each week

Follow up with 3 potential referral partners weekly

Volunteer for a high-profile organization once per week

Make 2 queries about speaking or writing each week

Improve one area of my website weekly

To close more sales . . .

Follow up with all prospects within 7 days

Work to build relationships with 5 prospects weekly

Get 10 "no"s each week

Make 1 challenging phone call every day

Reconnect with 3 former prospects or clients every week

Practice selling with a coach, colleague, or mirror every day

Find a personal connection with 1 prospect each week

Attend 1 high-profile event weekly

Have lunch or coffee with a center of influence once per week

Volunteer for an influential group once per week

Make 1 contact about writing, speaking or media interviews weekly

Dessert: *Choose 1*

Plan my day each morning

Do all my "A-list" tasks first each day

Write in my success journal each evening

Exercise 3 times per week

Get 8 hours of sleep every night

Meditate for 1/2 hour per day

Schedule a day of fun each week

Add up my income and expenses each week

Spend 1/2 hour each day organizing my office

Visualize success daily

it's not working, change it. And reward yourself for what you did, not what you got.

You can choose to perform an action daily, weekly, or several times per week. "Daily" typically means five days per week, which is the recommended schedule for the Get Clients Now! program. The only rule is that all actions must be performed at least weekly, because you need to develop consistency in your marketing in order for the Persistence Effect to work. While it's okay to change the frequency of your actions once you start the program, it's generally not a good idea to change the actions themselves until you are ready to move forward to the next stage of the Universal Marketing Cycle.

Now that you know how the process of designing a Daily Action works, take a look at the Action Plan Menu in Figure 5-1. The menu is divided into three sections:

Appetizers—actions that will help you to create or acquire Success Ingredients

Main course—actions focused directly on getting business

Dessert—actions to help you be more effective and productive in general

You are going to choose ten Daily Actions, either from the menu or of your own design. As with a meal, you will need to balance your selections. The best combination for a satisfying marketing banquet is one or two actions from the Appetizer menu, seven or eight entrees from the Main Course section, and one Dessert item. This design will create an effective balance between project work (e.g., building a website), actual business development (e.g., making cold calls), and self-management (e.g., getting enough sleep) in your action plan.

It's Okay to Be Yourself
Joan Friedlander, www.joanfriedlander.com

"Many times, the first draft of a marketing action plan reflects all the false conceptions of what a person thinks they need to do in order to succeed at marketing," relates Joan Friedlander, a business life management coach who has facilitated more than 50 Get Clients Now! programs. "I love that moment when people figure this out and start coming up with plans that reflect who they are, and what they really like to do. They're much more successful, and happier, too." She explains,

There are probably 100 different marketing tactics that you could choose from. You are not going to be excellent at executing all of them. Do yourself a huge favor and choose only those action items that you can actually see yourself doing.

Are you most comfortable connecting with prospects one-on-one? Go to meetings and events where you are likely to meet prospects or referral partners. Then, rather than trying to land a client in that noisy environment, invite people you want to get to know better to have coffee with you instead.

Do you hate cold calling? Don't put it on your plan. Instead, build your Daily Actions around warm calling and referral building. A client I worked with made this one simple change and completely altered his results—as well as his feelings—about marketing.

The only thing you're required to become good at is talking to people so they can understand what you offer and that you can help them. This takes just two things from you: time and practice. It's okay to start right where you are.

START WITH THE FUN STUFF

In a few pages, you will be choosing your Main Course selections, those actions that will directly bring you business. It's a good bet that the process of making those choices may bring up some fear and resistance for you, so let's start with the fun stuff: Appetizers and Dessert.

Appetizers are action items to move you forward in the process of creating or acquiring your chosen Success Ingredients. By putting one or two Appetizers on your list of Daily Actions, you are making a commitment to do what it takes to get those missing ingredients in place. If you chose only one Success Ingredient, you probably only need one Appetizer, but with two or three ingredients to create, you may want two Appetizers to help you along.

The Appetizers on the Action Plan Menu are suggested actions for you to choose from, but you can also design your own. Remember that the time frame and quantity are up to you in either case. Here are some ways you can use the Appetizers on the menu:

> ► **Spend 1 hour each day on my Success Ingredient projects.**
> Good for projects like "lead sources" or "publicity venues" that may take a while to ferret out.

- ▶ **Complete 1 item each day from my Success Ingredient project list.** Use this for projects such as "website" or "contact management system" where you may have a list of many steps to complete.

- ▶ **Practice my skills or script once per day.** An excellent choice for ingredients like "telemarketing script/skills," where you need to practice to make progress.

- ▶ **Spend 1 hour each week doing research.** Appropriate for ingredients such as "speaking venues" or "competitive research."

- ▶ **Read or write every day for 1 hour.** Use this for information-gathering projects like finding "advertising venues," or creative work such as writing an "article or query letter."

- ▶ **Interview 1 person per week.** Good for projects such as researching your "market niche definition" or discovering how to find "better-qualified prospects."

- ▶ **Collect 3 new facts per day.** Another useful method of quantifying your progress in research or information-gathering.

- ▶ **Observe how it's done once per week.** A great way to improve your skills in areas like networking or selling.

When you have chosen one or two Appetizers, write them down as the first two Daily Actions on your Action Worksheet. See Figure 5-2 for an example.

Next, look at the *Dessert* selections. The Daily Actions on the Dessert menu are suggested ways in which you can be more effective and productive in everything you do. Choose just one. To make the right choice, ask yourself what is likely to get in the way of your success this month. Have you identified any habits or behaviors that tend to sabotage you? Is there something you need to do for yourself to perform at your best?

Use these descriptions of the Dessert selections on the Action Plan Menu to help you choose one or design your own:

- ▶ **Plan my day each morning.** If you often come to the end of the day and wonder where it went, this Dessert may be a good choice for you. Planning your day in advance will take only five or ten minutes. You could also make your plan the night before.

- ▶ **Do all my "A-list" tasks first each day.** Not everything on your personal to-do list is of equal value. Try giving every item on the list a

Figure 5-2: Adding Daily Actions to the Action Worksheet

GET CLIENTS NOW!™ Action Worksheet

What strategies will you use?

DIRECT CONTACT & FOLLOW-UP	NETWORKING & REFERRAL BUILDING	PUBLIC SPEAKING	WRITING & PUBLICITY	PROMOTIONAL EVENTS	ADVERTISING
☑	☑	☐	☐	☐	☐

Where are you stuck or what needs the most work?

☑ Filling the pipeline ☐ Following up ☐ Having sales conversations ☐ Closing sales

How much business do you have now? __11 clients__

How much business do you *really* want? __20 clients__

What would that get you? __pay off my credit cards, take a vacation, feel less stressed__

What is your program goal? __4 new clients by the end of the program__

What will be your reward? __go out to dinner and a movie__

Success Ingredients	Target Date
1. market niche definition	03/06/13
2. 10-second introduction	03/08/13
3. 3 live networking venues	03/15/13

Daily Actions

1. Spend 1/2 hour each day on my Success Ingredient projects
2. Send letters or e-mails to 5 new people each week
3. Place warm calls to 2 prospects per day
4. Go to 1 live networking event each week
5. Contact 3 new potential referral partners each week
6. Have lunch or coffee with a colleague once per week
7. Spend 15 minutes interacting with my online network daily
8. Send an item of interest to 3 colleagues per week
9. Ask for a referral once per day
10. Visualize success daily

Special Permission __I give myself permission to have enough time for everything__ priority of A, B, or C, then take care of all the A-list items first each day.

▶ **Write in my success journal each evening.** It's easy to get caught up in failures and shortcomings, but every day has successes in it. Start a success journal, where you write each day only those things you enjoyed, felt good about accomplishing, or for which you received recognition.

▶ **Exercise 3 times per week.** If you find that regular exercise gives you more energy, it may be just as important to effective marketing as a good telephone script.

▶ **Get 8 hours of sleep every night.** Depriving yourself of sleep is not good time management, and will backfire quickly. Not everyone needs eight hours, so substitute the best number for your needs.

▶ **Meditate for 1/2 hour per day.** Meditation, drawing or painting, listening to music, gardening, and needlework are just a few of the many activities that allow for relaxation and quiet reflection. Just plain wool gathering is fine, too. The idea is to give your overworked brain a rest.

▶ **Schedule a day of fun each week.** Relaxation takes many forms and you may need some pleasurable activity more than a rest. Scheduling fun time in advance will ensure it happens.

▶ **Add up my income and expenses each week.** Think of this as a motivational technique. If you know you need to make another $500 this week, you may want to pick up the phone on Friday afternoon. If you see your hard work paying off, you may be inspired to do a little more.

▶ **Spend 1/2 hour each day organizing my office.** Keeping track of where each prospect is in the marketing cycle can be crucial to closing sales. Time spent looking for important information that has gone missing is time you don't have available for marketing.

▶ **Visualize success daily.** This is a proven technique for improved achievement. Spend a few minutes each day visualizing yourself succeeding at marketing, selling, and earning the rewards that are important to you. You may even want to do this three times a day.

After reading these descriptions, you may be tempted to choose more than one Dessert. Yet you do need to leave enough room for the Main

Course, so limit yourself to just one. If one of the Desserts on the menu caused you to say, "That would really help me," that's the one to pick. If you have a self-sabotaging habit that none of these Desserts addresses, make up your own to help you start changing that habit.

Record your Dessert as the last Daily Action on your Action Worksheet (see Figure 5-2).

Strength of Purpose Defeats Avoidance
Dr. Stephen R. Covey, 1932–2012

The late Stephen Covey, educator, businessman, and motivational speaker, was the author of *7 Habits of Highly Successful People*, named the most influential business book of the twentieth century. In his blog at www.stephencovey.com, Dr. Covey wrote:

> As I think of the struggles many people go through, I am reminded of a powerful quote by Albert E. N. Gray: "The successful person has the habit of doing things failures don't like to do. They don't like doing them either necessarily. But their disliking is subordinated to the strength of their purpose."

> If you are someone who has to make important changes in your life, you may want to ponder on this idea. What are the things you know you have to do but are avoiding? If you were to discipline yourself and create a plan for doing those things, would you find positive, even breakthrough rewards?

> In my case, I know when I'm trying to avoid doing something, I eventually see that I've paid an even higher price by avoidance. For example, when I've neglected my health by not eating right, exercising, or getting enough sleep because I find it hard to stick to a disciplined regimen, I have found myself feeling sluggish and not doing my best work. When I finally subordinate my dislikes to the strength of my purpose, things turn around.

> Identify something you are avoiding and make a promise that you will do it. Make a promise and keep it. Subordinate the things you dislike doing to your greater purpose. The more you do this, the more strength you will build—and the more success you will find.

TIME FOR THE MAIN COURSE

The Daily Actions in the Main Course section of the menu are activities directly aimed at getting you clients. The Main Course items are grouped into categories that match the stages of the Universal Marketing Cycle: filling the pipeline, following up, having sales conversations, and closing sales. Because the possible activities for filling the pipeline are so varied, that area is subdivided into six sections, based on the marketing strategies each activity uses:

▶ Direct contact and follow-up

▶ Networking and referral building

▶ Public speaking

▶ Writing and publicity

▶ Promotional events

▶ Advertising

You will be selecting seven or eight Daily Actions from the Main Course menu (or of your own design), to reach a total of ten Daily Actions all together. The first rule to follow in making your choices is this: Don't read the whole list! Look solely at the category that pertains to the marketing cycle stage you are working on. And if your chosen stage is filling the pipeline, look only at the sections relevant to the marketing strategies you have chosen.

Icons that indicate which of the six Get Clients Now! marketing strategies each activity is related to appear on the left-hand side of the menu. For a key to the strategy icons, refer to Chapter 4. Some actions are applicable to only one strategy, while others could relate to several, depending on how they are used.

Here are two different approaches to making your selections:

1. **Just pick 'em.** As you have worked your way through the exercises in this book, you have already learned quite a bit about marketing. You know where in the Universal Marketing Cycle you are stuck or need more work, what marketing strategies you plan to use, and which missing ingredients you need to be successful. Maybe you already have enough information to make choices from the Daily Actions listed on the Menu for your marketing cycle stage. When you are ready to begin using your selected actions, you can read more about them in the marketing recipes in Part III of the book.

2. **First understand the theory.** Each Daily Action on the list represents an activity that has been proven effective in professional services marketing. Sometimes the purpose of an activity will be immediately apparent.

It's difficult to misunderstand what "spend 1 hour each day cold calling" is about. Other activities are more subtle. For example, "have lunch or coffee with a center of influence once per week" is listed for closing sales because this activity will simultaneously increase your visibility and credibility. When a prospective client hears about you from someone she respects, it can greatly increase your likelihood of closing the sale.

If you want to understand more about the purpose of the Main Course activities before making your choices, read now the specific chapter in Part III of this book that describes your chosen stage of the marketing cycle. You can skip any sections that relate to marketing strategies you will not be using.

Is one of these approaches to selecting Main Course actions more successful than the other? Actually, no—the difference is in you. If you are comfortable shooting from the hip, use the first approach. It's quicker and easier. If you don't like to commit to a course of action until you have thoroughly evaluated your choices, use the second approach. It will increase your level of commitment to the actions you choose.

How to Make the Best Selections

Here are the questions you should consider to make the best possible choices from the Main Course menu:

▶ **Where are you stuck or in need of more work?** You already know which stage of the Universal Marketing Cycle you need to focus on, so choose only Main Course items that pertain to that stage. If you don't see seven or eight actions that seem right to you on the list for your stage, it's fine to take one or two actions from the stage just before or after yours. However, don't pick actions from several different stages. This will dilute your marketing efforts and sabotage the Persistence Effect.

▶ **Which marketing strategies will you be using?** The icons shown in front of each action indicate what marketing strategy or strategies they relate to. Look for the actions that match up with the strategies you chose in Chapter 2. In each marketing cycle stage, you'll find that a majority of the Main Course actions support the strategies of direct contact and follow-up, and networking and referral building, because this is where the Persistence Effect has the most impact. For some of the other strategies, fewer choices are available.

▶ **How can you [stage] using [strategy]?** To include more actions to support your strategies, feel free to make up some of your own. Ask yourself how you could address your chosen stage (e.g., having sales conversations) using one of your strategies (e.g., writing and publicity). As an example, you could send a copy of your white paper to three hot prospects each week. Just be sure you are designing an action you can perform daily or weekly, rather than a one-time project. Projects to create missing tools or improve needed skills are Success Ingredients, not Daily Actions.

▶ **What will you actually do?** If you are paralyzed by cold calling or public speaking, there is no point in including these actions in your program, because you will simply avoid doing them. You might choose a Success Ingredient to help you improve your future skills in these areas, but your Daily Actions need to be activities you are willing to do this month. Instead of choosing actions you could find immobilizing, ask yourself . . .

▶ **What are you naturally drawn to?** If you are typically outgoing and enjoy talking to people, choose actions that will get you to networking events and give you plenty of time on the phone. But if talking to strangers makes you so uncomfortable that you will do anything to avoid it, select actions that will allow you to concentrate on building referrals with people you already know or writing articles for publication. If you choose activities you like, or are at least willing to try, you will do them.

▶ **How much available time do you have?** If you are full time in your business but have few or no clients, you may have quite a bit of time available for marketing. You may be able to spend as much time marketing as you would on working for your clients. But if you have another job or are busy with client work, you will have to fit your marketing activities into what may be an already full week. Time constraints may require you to conduct more of your marketing by phone or online than in person, or during evenings and weekends. Make sure your choices reflect the reality of your situation.

▶ **How soon do you need to produce results?** The sooner you need to find more clients, the more aggressive your marketing action plan should be. If your situation—financial or emotional—is becoming desperate, choose actions that are ambitious enough to accelerate your progress.

To make your selections, look at the section of the Main Course menu that corresponds to your stage of the marketing cycle. Place a check mark next to each Daily Action that seems to fit your situation. It's all right to pick some actions that are easy for you or that you are already doing consistently, but you should also choose some that will stretch and challenge you.

One note about filling the pipeline: If you are working on this stage, you may wonder why there are fewer actions listed under direct contact and follow-up than there are under networking and referral building. After all, isn't direct contact supposed to be the most effective strategy? While this is certainly true overall, keep in mind that your objective in filling the pipeline is to locate qualified prospects with whom you can quickly close sales. Making a completely cold approach by researching, calling, and mailing people you do not know is much less effective than being connected to them via introduction, referral, speaking, and so on. So when filling the pipeline, a better approach is to couple direct contact activities with networking and other strategies to warm up your approaches.

After checking off the Action Plan Menu items that seem to be the best fit, you end up with too many activities, ask yourself which ones would make the most efficient use of your time. What do you think will bring you the most return with the least effort? And remember: It doesn't matter so much what you choose as it does *that* you choose. Everything on the menu works.

When you have selected your seven or eight Main Course actions for a total of ten Daily Actions overall, adjust the quantity and frequency of each one to suit you. Then write them on your Action Worksheet as in Figure 5-2.

Nobody Wants a Drudger

Cat Williford, MCC, CPCC; www.themoderngoddess.com

"If you're not having any fun doing what you do, think back to a time when you were," suggests business and personal coach Cat Williford. "What 'drudge' do you currently have that wasn't there when you were having fun? How can you eliminate the drudge when you are marketing your business?" Williford says,

> When you're not having any fun in your marketing, you are wasting your time, which just adds to the drudge. Don't you want to do business with people who seem to enjoy life and what they do for a living? If you wouldn't want to do business with yourself, *you* may be the problem in your marketing!

> If you can eliminate the drudge by having fun when you market yourself, you will draw to you the type of clients you really want.

A WORD ABOUT CLOSING SALES

If you are working on filling the pipeline or following up, it may have occurred to you to wonder how you are actually going to make a sale. After all, the Daily Actions on your list are all focused on the earlier stages in the marketing cycle.

The key word to understanding the answer is *focus*. You have chosen to concentrate your effort on a particular stage of the marketing cycle because that is where you are feeling stuck or need more work. This doesn't mean, however, that you should ignore the routine functions of the other stages while you are doing this. If your pipeline-filling activities turn up a hot lead, follow up immediately. If your follow-up generates a possible sales conversation, schedule it. If your conversation leads to closing the sale, great! That's what you want.

Your Daily Actions in the program are in no way intended to be a list of everything you must do about marketing and sales for the next month. You need to continue pursuing solid leads with the same energy you always have (or perhaps a little more, because now you have a goal to meet). The intent of the Daily Actions is simply to focus more effort on the area of your marketing that needs it the most.

The Get Clients Now! program should hold the same place in your marketing and sales activities as an exercise program does in your life. You don't quit walking to the bus stop because you are now doing twenty-five sit-ups each morning, and you don't stop playing ball with the kids because you decide to run a mile three times a week. Routine life goes on while you are exercising; regular selling goes on while you are improving your performance in the areas of pipeline-filling and follow-up.

Marketing Alone Won't Do It
Howard L. Shenson, CMC; 1944–1991

Howard Shenson, the "consultant's consultant," published over sixty books, reports, and other tools for consultants during his lifetime. In his guide, *Shenson on Consulting* (Wiley, 1994), he points out:

> Consultants must engage in both marketing and selling to build viable practices. Success requires that the professional understand the difference between these two promotional activities. Marketing involves all activities that

are designed to establish the image and reputation of the consultant and to make the market aware of the availability of his or her services. The opportunity to sell results from successful marketing and involves all activities that cause an interested prospect to engage the services of the consultant. Some professionals feel that they need do only one or the other, or they cannot see the fine distinction between the two. Both are vital. . . .

Client awareness of and appreciation for the image and reputation of a particular consultant can be created through either indirect, public-relations-type marketing activities or direct marketing strategies or both. But even the best and most effective marketing does not eliminate the need for selling, for selling involves the art of demonstrating to an interested and informed client the wisdom of engaging the professional's services and allows the professional the opportunity to customize and particularize in relation to the prospect's specific needs.

WHAT IS GOING TO STOP YOU?

Look at what you have recorded on your Action Worksheet. You have an ambitious goal, Success Ingredients you are going to acquire or create, and a list of ten Daily Actions you are going to perform, all in the next twenty-eight days. If looking at this list makes you feel resistant, afraid, or overwhelmed, your reaction is completely normal.

If you have ever attempted a program before—dieting or regular exercise, for example—or taken a motivational seminar, or made some New Year's resolutions, you have probably experienced the following familiar scenario. You make new commitments when you are feeling enthusiastic, re-energized, or just plain fed up with the way things are. But then something stops you from following through.

What is that something? Lack of time—and its frequent companion, not enough money—are easy excuses, but the fact is that most of us make choices every day about where to spend our time and money. We choose whether to make a cold call or chat with a friend; pay the admission price to a networking event or buy a movie ticket. And it's not just choosing between work and play. Suddenly, deleting all the old e-mails in your inbox may seem more important than writing a marketing letter, or spending money on a new home entertainment system becomes more urgent than paying to have your website updated.

If you are really serious about making this time different, about following through on your commitments and getting the results you want, it's time to look at what may get in your way. Are you worried or afraid? If so, of what? Are you resisting something? What is it? Is there some special permission that you need in order to be successful with this program?

Many people, if not most people, are routinely blocked in marketing and sales by self-sabotaging thinking or behavior. If you thought you were the only one suffering from terminal procrastination or struggling with negative messages from your own inner critic, know you're in good company. Giving yourself permission to alter a longstanding habit can be a powerful step in the direction of lasting change. In the Get Clients Now! program, you will be consciously granting yourself a Special Permission every day. Here are some examples:

I have permission to ask for what I want.

I am able to do things I fear.

I deserve to be successful.

I can make a good living and still have time for family and fun.

The best way to design a Special Permission is to ask yourself what you routinely think or do that prevents you from being successful at marketing. For example, suppose you never seem to have time to make follow-up calls because you are busy working on client projects. You know this behavior backfires in the long run, because when you complete a project, there isn't another one waiting for you. The permission you might design for yourself is, "It's okay to put my marketing first."

Or, suppose that you are stalling in completing your portfolio, because then you will actually have to show it to someone. And if you did so, he or she might not like your work. Of course, you also know that if you don't show your portfolio to anyone, it's unlikely that anyone will hire you. In this case, you might choose this Special Permission: "I believe in my talents and abilities."

Are you wondering what is going to make you believe your Special Permission? After all, you just made it up. What will make it real for you? For one thing, there is the simple repetition of it. Repetition is one of the primary ways that we learn. You learned the alphabet by heart from saying or singing it over and over. If you look in the mirror each morning and say, "I believe in my talents and abilities," you will begin to internalize that information in the same way that you know *f* comes before *g* without reciting the alphabet from the beginning.

The other reason your Special Permission will work is that it's only for twenty-eight days. Whenever you find yourself questioning the validity of your permission, remind yourself it is only temporary. You can go back to your old way of operating at the end of the month (if you still want to). Just as Samuel T. Coleridge's expression "the willing suspension of disbelief" can be the key to enjoying a novel or play, you can temporarily allow yourself to believe fully in your Special Permission. If you are skeptical, try it.

If you already know your Special Permission, write it on the last line of your Action Worksheet. If you're still having trouble finding a permission that fits, just pick one of the examples above to start with. It's almost a guarantee that some block or obstacle will appear within the first few days of starting the program. Then you can design a new Special Permission to address it. And if at any point during the twenty-eight days, your permission stops working for you, change it.

Got Permission from a Rabbit

Shannon Seek, CPCC; www.seeksolutions.com

"I joined a Get Clients Now! group years ago when I needed to expand my business," remembers coach and professional organizer Shannon Seek. "In my false sense of courage I didn't even know I had fear at first, but I felt stuck. During the program, I recognized that I needed to give myself permission to be afraid. I came up with a metaphor that would help me visualize it: 'Be the bunny.' On the Native American medicine wheel, the rabbit represents fear, and working with Rabbit Medicine requires owning your fear when you have it. I imagined myself as a rabbit hopping through fear—timid-but-still-moving bunny—or a rabbit in a World War I fighter plane with goggles and ears flopping in the wind—fearless bunny. It made being fearful seem funny, safe, and okay enough that I could deal with the task at hand. It really got me unstuck."

"After seeing, there must be acting. Otherwise, what's the use of seeing?"

—THICH NHAT HANH

CHAPTER 6

You're Ready . . . Let's Go!

Putting the System into Action

THE TRACKING WORKSHEET

Your Action Worksheet is completed. You have chosen your Program Goal, one to three Success Ingredients, ten Daily Actions, and your Special Permission. It's time to put your own personal Get Clients Now! program into action.

Your next essential tool for the twenty-eight days of the program is the Tracking Worksheet, which you will use daily to measure your progress through the program. The Tracking Worksheet is quite a magical device. You will be amazed at how much difference this one simple tool can make in your marketing!

Remember the benefits of goal-setting discussed in Chapter 3? Using the Tracking Worksheet consistently will automatically provide you with focus, evidence, direction, and motivation for your marketing. If you arrange to work through the program with a buddy, group, or coach, you will also lock in place the accountability, perspective, and support to help you succeed.

Look at Lee Greenback's partially completed Tracking Worksheet in Figure 6-1. Each column represents a working day of the program, for which you will make daily entries like these:

▶ **Weather Report.** On a 1-to-10 scale, with 1 being the lowest and 10 the highest, how is your state of mind today? How does your body feel? This is an intuitive score; put down what you sense is correct. These numbers

Figure 6-1: Partially Completed Tracking Worksheet

GET CLIENTS NOW!™

Tracking Worksheet

Start Date: 03/04/13

Name: *Lee Greenback*

	3/4	3/5	3/6	3/7	3/8	3/11	3/12	3/13	3/14	3/15	3/18	3/19	3/20	3/21	3/22	3/25	3/26	3/27	3/28	3/29
Weather Report (1-10 scale)																				
Mind	8	7	8	9	8															
Body	7	7	8	8	7															
Success Ingredients (% done)																				
1 mkt niche definition - 3/6	50	75	100																	
2 10-second intro - 3/8	25	25	50	75	100															
3 3 live networking venues - 3/15	0	0	0	33	33															
Daily Actions (Y/N)																				
1 ½ hour/day on SI projects	N	N	Y	Y	Y															
2 ltrs/e-mails to 5 people/wk	Y	Y	N	Y	Y															
3 warm calls to 2 prospects/day	Y	Y	Y	Y	N															
4 1 live networking event/wk	Y	Y	Y	Y	Y															
5 3 new referral partners/wk	Y	Y	Y	Y	Y															
6 lunch/coffee w/colleague wkly	Y	Y	Y	Y	Y															
7 15 min online network/day	Y	Y	Y	Y	Y															
8 item to 3 colleagues/wk	Y	Y	Y	Y	Y															
9 ask for referral 1/day	N	N	N	Y	Y															
10 visualize success daily	Y	Y	N	Y	Y															
Total (# of 10)	8	8	7	10	9															
Program Goal (% of target)																				
4 new clients	0	0	0	0	25															
Special Permission (Y/N)																				
enough time for everything	Y	Y	N	Y	Y															

will go up and down from day to day, as your mood and physical condition fluctuate. This score tells you how much you should expect from yourself on any given day.

▶ **Success Ingredients.** For each of your one to three Success Ingredient projects, what percentage have you completed? If zero percent means you have done nothing thus far and 100 percent means the project is done, how far do you estimate that you have progressed along the range? This too may be an intuitive score, or for some projects you can compute it mathematically. These numbers will go up as projects move forward, but will not go down.

▶ **Daily Actions.** For each of your ten actions, did you do it today (Y) or not (N)? At the bottom of this section, record the total number of actions completed at the end of each day. This number will increase or decrease from day to day as your productivity varies and other activities require your attention.

When an action is designated as weekly (or several times per week) rather than daily, you should still score yourself for that action each day. This way you still have the possibility of scoring 10 out of 10 every day, instead of losing points just because some of your actions are weekly. You can accomplish this by giving yourself a "free Y" on any day that you carry out your plans for this action during the week.

Let's say you have chosen the action "Go to 1 live networking event each week." On Monday, if you planned to attend an event today and you went, give yourself a Y. If you planned to attend one today and didn't go, you get an N. If you didn't plan to go to an event today at all, you get a free Y, but look at your calendar now and determine which day this week you will attend one. Then score yourself each day based on how well you followed through on this intention. Going to a planned event gets you a Y, a day with no event planned gets you a free Y, and not going to a planned event gets you an N. If you don't make up the missed event by going to another, you will get an N for that action for the remainder of the week.

Whenever you reach the end of the week and still haven't taken a weekly action, you must give yourself an N for it on Friday. Be honest and remember—these scores are for you.

▶ **Program Goal.** What percentage of your goal have you achieved so far? Since all goals in the program must be numerical, you should be able to compute this exactly. This number will increase as your goals move forward, but will not decrease.

▶ **Special Permission.** Do you have your special permission today or not? Tell the truth. You will notice how difficult everything is on those days you don't have it.

On Day 1 of the program, you will start filling in your own Tracking Worksheet, based on the Action Worksheet you completed at the end of Chapter 5.

THE 28-DAY PROGRAM

For the next twenty-eight days, you will be working steadily on achieving your chosen marketing goal. But if you keep your foot on the accelerator the whole time, you will run out of gas!

You should plan ahead which days you will be working on your marketing and which days you will rest. There are rest days built into the program so you can have time to regroup and recharge. You may choose to spend some of a rest day working on a Success Ingredient project or the exercises in this chapter, but you will be responsible for completing your Daily Actions only on the days you have chosen as working days. In the program outline that follows, your working days are scheduled Monday through Friday, and your rest days are assumed to be back to back, on Saturday and Sunday. If your work week is different, you will need to adjust the program days to fit your actual schedule.

On your program working days, you should set aside—in advance—time to complete your Daily Actions, especially if you are already busy with client work or have another job. You may need to plan for some of your marketing activities to take place before or after the business day, or during lunch. Experiment to find the best time of day to fit these tasks into your schedule. Don't let the work you already have be your excuse for not finding the clients you really need or want. Make marketing your first priority instead of the last thing you do.

On working and rest days alike, read the entry for each day from the pages that follow. Try to do this as early in the day as possible so that you will keep your marketing in mind throughout the course of the day. On each working day, you should also spend a few moments on a Morning Review to plan how you will include your Success Ingredient projects, Daily Actions, and your Special Permission in the day's agenda. At the end of each working day, take another few moments to add up your daily scores on the Tracking

Worksheet. There are more details about these activities in the pages that follow.

On some of the rest days there are exercises provided to help you be more effective and productive in your marketing. To get the most benefit from the program, be sure to set aside some time to work with each of these, whether or not it is on the day suggested.

Day 1

Saturday is an excellent day to begin your Get Clients Now! program. Close the door, turn off the phone, and bring out your completed Action Worksheet from Chapter 5. Make an enlarged copy of the blank Tracking Worksheet in Figure 6-2, or download the worksheet from the book's companion website at www.getclientsnow.com. You can print the worksheet and fill it out by hand, or use one of the electronic versions and keep it on your computer, tablet, or smartphone.

Fill in the dates on the top line and the information in Column 1. See Lee Greenback's partially completed worksheet (Figure 6-1) for an example. On the top line, write the calendar dates of your working days for the next month. If the coming Monday were March 4, for example, you would label the first ten columns on your worksheet 3/4–3/8 and 3/11–3/15, skipping the Saturday and Sunday rest days in between. Next, write in Column 1 the Success Ingredients from your Action Worksheet with your chosen target dates for completing them. Then add your ten Daily Actions, Program Goal and Special Permission.

Award yourself a starting score on each of your Success Ingredients and your Program Goal. Are you starting from zero on your Success Ingredient projects and the goal you set for the month, or have you already made some progress? On Lee Greenback's worksheet, he gave himself a starting score of 50 percent on "market niche definition," believing he was already halfway there. On his "10-second introduction," he had done some work, but needed more, so he scored himself at 25 percent. For "live networking venues," Lee had yet to do anything, so he started at zero.

To give yourself an accurate score now and throughout the program, you may need to quantify your Success Ingredient projects. For Success Ingredients like "networking venues" or "referral partners," consider the question, "How many is enough?" If you're unsure, review the appropriate chapter in Part III for your chosen stage of the Universal Marketing Cycle. Write the number you choose on your worksheet, as Lee did for his networking venues.

Figure 6-2: Blank Tracking Worksheet

GET CLIENTS NOW!™ Tracking Worksheet		
Weather Report (1-10 scale)		
Mind		
Body		
Success Ingredients (% done)		
1		
2		
3		
Daily Actions (Y/N)		
1		
2		
3		
4		
5		
6		
7		
8		
9		
10		
Total (# of 10)		
Program Goal (% of target)		
Special Permission (Y/N)		

Start Date: _____

Name: _____

If you have chosen a more intangible Success Ingredient, such as "networking skills" or "telemarketing skills," score yourself intuitively. If zero equals "phone phobic" and 100 percent means "expert telemarketer," where would you rate yourself today? Would you like to be at 100 percent by the end of the program, or would 75 percent satisfy you? If it's the latter, write down "telemarketing skills at 75 percent," so you know what you're aiming for.

Now award yourself a starting score on your Program Goal. As described in Chapter 3, this is a numerical target for clients, contracts, appointments, billable hours, total revenue, or new prospects. You may be starting at zero, or you may have made some progress already. Either way, be honest with yourself, and be specific about what you are counting. Is a new client anyone who schedules his first appointment, or does this count only after the person shows up for it? Is your total revenue what you bill this month, or what you actually collect? Base your score on a way of measuring that you can track each week and will make this goal truly meaningful for you.

Keep the Tracking Worksheet where you will be sure to see it first thing Monday morning. Are you ready to make a commitment to the program you have designed for yourself?

> **Thought for the day:** Jay Conrad Levinson, author of the *Guerrilla Marketing* series, often says the following when asked about his work: "I hate to admit this, but mediocre marketing with commitment works better than brilliant marketing without commitment."

Day 2

Rest Day. Do something you really enjoy, perhaps an activity you haven't had time for in a while. You're going to be working hard for the next month, so take this opportunity to have some fun. Get plenty of sleep tonight so you'll be fresh and ready to go in the morning.

> **Thought for the day:** Even God rested one day a week.

Day 3

Are you ready to get clients now? It's time to let the Tracking Worksheet start doing its magic. First thing this morning, get your Tracking Worksheet in front of you. Each working day of the program, you will be using the worksheet at least twice: once at the beginning and once at the end of the day. To let even more of the worksheet's magic rub off on you, keep it where you'll see it all day long.

On this first Monday, begin by doing your first Morning Review. Look over your Success Ingredients and Daily Actions. Which of these tasks do you plan to work on today? Do you need to add them to your daily to-do list or schedule time for them? Check your Special Permission to remind yourself what you need to be successful. Okay, you're ready for the day—go for it!

At day's end, award yourself your first Daily Scores:

Weather Report: How your mind and body feel, on a scale of 1 to 10.

Success Ingredients: The status of each project from 0–100 percent complete.

Daily Actions: Y (for Yes) and N (for No) on each one. Be sure to score any weekly actions as well. Add up the total number of Ys at the bottom of the Daily Actions section.

Program Goal: Progress toward your goal from 0 100 percent accomplished.

Special Permission: Y if you granted yourself your Special Permission today; N if you didn't.

If you have any questions about how to score yourself, refer to the description of the Tracking Worksheet at the beginning of this chapter.

You made it through your first working day of the Get Clients Now! Program. Congratulations! Did you accomplish all that you wanted? If you did, great! If not, remember that punishment is not allowed. Notice what didn't get done, and we'll look at your list again tomorrow to see if you need to make changes.

Throughout the remainder of the program, the day-by-day guidelines here will focus on keeping you in action, on track, and motivated. Whenever you have questions about how to implement the Daily Actions or Success Ingredients you chose, refer to the appropriate chapter in Part III for your stage of the marketing cycle to find detailed logistical help.

> **Thought for the day:** A short poem about marketing:
>
> You have to sow a lot of seeds.
>
> Some are flowers; some are weeds;

Some will die while others grow,

But all depends on how many you sow.

Day 4

Begin the day with your Morning Review. Look at your Success Ingredients, Daily Actions, and Special Permission and plan how you will include each in the day's agenda. You will do this each working day of the program. In today's review, and for all of this first week, pay special attention to the Daily Actions you chose. How did it work for you to add these new activities into your day?

If you scored 8 or above on your Daily Actions yesterday, keep them as they are. If you scored lower, but yesterday was unusually busy or chaotic, give yourself another day to see how you do. However, if you're feeling overwhelmed and suspect that your choices may have been too ambitious, you have complete permission to scale back a bit. Rather than eliminating any of the actions you chose, try just reducing the level of effort. Is there something you committed to do daily that could happen three times per week instead? Or could you cut down on the number of calls, letters, or meetings you had planned? Now is the time to redesign a list of actions that will work for you within the reality of a normal working day.

At the end of the day, compile your Daily Scores. Did you do better today? Terrific! If you're still not satisfied with your scores, don't worry or feel guilty; we will continue to look at ways of making them improve.

> **Thought for the day:** You will never be completely ready. Start from wherever you are.

Day 5

Morning Review. Wednesday is the day to look at any once-per-week actions that have yet to be scheduled. Choose now the day you will do them. If a lunch or meeting is involved, lock it in place by calling to make the appointment or reservation.

Daily Scores. Have you reached a score of 8 or higher on your Daily Actions? If so, good work! Try setting up a reward for yourself if you reach a certain score tomorrow. Promise yourself a walk in the park, a bowl of ice cream, a movie, or whatever will motivate you to do your best. If today's score was 6, go for a score of 8; if 9 was your score today, make tomorrow's goal a 10.

Thought for the day: Everyone you meet is either a prospect or a potential source of referrals. Never pass up an opportunity to introduce yourself and your business.

Day 6

Morning Review. What will be your reward if you reach your Daily Actions target today? What do you need to do to make that score possible? Here are three suggested strategies to try:

1. **Do it first.** Avoid doing anything else until your Daily Actions are completed. Don't check your e-mail, tidy up the house, or answer the phone. Eliminate every possible distraction until you have reached your target score for today.

2. **Do it now.** You may have some Daily Actions that need to occur later in your day rather than first thing. Every time you think of one of them, do it immediately. Let's say you need to ask for one referral per day. When you are in conversation with someone, just ask for a referral as soon as you think of it—right then, no matter what you are talking about. If you find yourself forgetting, put a rubber band around your wrist, and let it remind you each time you notice it.

3. **Block out time.** If your schedule prevents doing all your Daily Actions first, block out time on your calendar. Make a specific appointment with yourself and honor it just as though someone else were expecting you. Use this appointment as an excuse if other people try to detain or distract you. If you're afraid you'll forget or get busy with something else, try setting an alarm.

Daily Scores. Did you earn your reward today? Congratulations! If you're still having trouble, review your Daily Actions list again. If you find it too ambitious, you can scale back your level of effort at any point during the program, as long as you stick to the guidelines for choosing Daily Actions given in Chapter 5. You may decide that you already have the right list, but the problem you need to solve is how to make it happen.

Try again tomorrow to use the three strategies listed above. Don't beat yourself up or feel as if you're failing. It may take you several attempts to successfully change your work habits so that marketing becomes a part of your day. Keep at it; the payoff will be worth the effort.

Thought for the day: Learning any new habit is like starting an exercise program. It can be painful at first, but as you exercise that particular muscle, it becomes stronger and supports you better. Over time, the pain gives way to tolerance, tolerance to satisfaction, and satisfaction to exhilaration as you see the results of your commitment and persistence.

Day 7

Morning Review. It's your last chance to complete any actions scheduled as weekly, so look now at how to fit them in. What Daily Actions score will you go for today?

Daily Scores. How did you do this week? If you got your Daily Actions score up to 8 or more, it's time to celebrate your achievement. You are on the path to success in reaching your Program Goal and getting more clients. If your scores are in the 5 to 7 range, you are getting close, but need to make some changes. Revisit the Morning Review for Days 4 and 6 to see what else you might do. If you are consistently scoring lower than 5 on Daily Actions, you are not failing at marketing; you are learning what it will take to market well. There is something in your way, and once you know what it is, you can begin to eliminate it. We'll look at some of these potential roadblocks tomorrow.

Complete your week by making a list of your wins over the last seven days. What worked? What went well? What great things did you do, say, receive, and achieve? Here's a sample "wins" list:

- ▶ Completed my 10-second introduction and tried it out at a networking event
- ▶ Met three potential referral partners at the Association of Accounting Professionals meeting
- ▶ Studied two chapters of a book about networking
- ▶ Had lunch with my former boss and got some inside info on local firms
- ▶ Read about two companies that might need my services in this month's issue of *Accounting Pro*
- ▶ Heard that the Helping Hand Foundation might need a volunteer accountant

Keep your wins list where you can see it, right next to your Tracking Worksheet. Then congratulate yourself—you stuck with the program through Week One.

> **Thought for the day:** There are benefits of doing business with you that you take for granted but that would thrill your prospects if they knew about them. Look for the hidden assets in your business, and be sure to reveal them in your marketing.

Day 8

Rest Day. In the first week of the Get Clients Now! program, you may have encountered two of the biggest obstacles to marketing success: fear and resistance. If looking at some of the items on your Daily Actions list made your stomach flutter or your throat get tight, that was fear. If you found yourself thinking, "Yuck," "Not me," or "Not now," and digging in your heels, that was resistance. Know that you are not alone in these feelings. You may not hear other folks talk about this at the Chamber of Commerce, but most people feel afraid, resistant, or both, about certain elements of marketing.

Identifying the source of these feelings and why you have them is beyond the scope of this book. What you need now is to get past them in order to be successful—and you can! The first step in removing these roadblocks is to recognize they exist; then, be specific about their nature. Answer these questions now:

1. **What are you afraid of?** Being rejected? Making a mistake? Failing? Succeeding (and not knowing how to deal with it)? Looking silly? Write down as many different fears as you can. If you feel stuck, ask yourself, "What do I think would happen if I . . ." and complete the sentence with whatever Daily Actions are giving you trouble—perhaps ". . . went to a live networking event?" or ". . . made a cold call?"

2. **What are you resisting?** Doing the perhaps-not-your-favorite work of marketing? Talking about your abilities and experience? (Maybe it feels like bragging.) Spending time on marketing when you have other urgent priorities? Finish this sentence in your best whining, annoyed, or stubborn voice, "I don't want to . . ."

Now that these barriers are out in the open, ask yourself if you are going to let them stop you. They don't have to, you know. You can feel afraid yet move forward; you can feel resistant yet still do what you are resisting. The next time you are having trouble, notice what you are feeling, and choose whether to let it keep you from taking action. Say to yourself, "Oh, there's the fear again," or "Wow, I'm really feeling resistant right now," and then keep going.

> **Thought for the day:** Courage is not the absence of fear. It is the ability to take action while feeling afraid.

Day 9

Rest Day. Reward yourself for a week well done. Spend an entire day not thinking about work. Do something relaxing and replenishing.

> **Thought for the day:** You are the biggest asset your business has. Taking care of yourself is taking care of business.

Day 10

Morning Review. Continue as you began last week with planning your day to include all your Daily Actions, and try for a daily score of 8 or higher. In this second week, we will shift the focus to your Success Ingredient projects. How has your progress been here? You are one-fourth of the way through the program, so you should be 25 percent ahead of where you started on your Success Ingredients. If you are working on three simultaneously, each should have progressed that far. If you are doing them in succession, the first should be near completion.

Daily Scores. Were you able to give your Success Ingredients enough attention today? Look now at the rest of your week, and see where you can fit them in. In order to stay on track, you should be halfway through by Friday.

> **Thought for the day:** Work expands to fill the time allotted to it. If you want to get more done, give each task only the amount of time it is worth to you. And if you want to work less, allow less time for work.

Day 11

Morning Review. Are you having trouble finding enough time for your Success Ingredients? If you are on track or ahead of schedule, good for you! If not, here are some strategies to help:

1. **Give something away.** What other tasks are currently on your to-do list? Is there anything you can hand off to someone else? If you can't unload an entire project, are there some pieces you could ask another person to do? If you are unaccustomed to delegating, you may need to expand your vision of what it looks like. You don't necessarily need an administrative assistant in order to delegate; you can delegate to a co-worker, a colleague, a friend, your spouse or partner, your children, your siblings, another committee member, or a hired professional. What are you doing that someone else could do instead? Can you ask someone else? Can you pay someone else? If it enabled you to spend an extra hour a day on marketing, could you afford to pay someone to handle some of your other responsibilities?

2. **Put something off.** What on your list can be done later? If you have a habit of planning more things than you can possibly do, you are already putting some things off by default. Why not choose up front what those things will be? Think in terms of your overall priorities. What is more important than marketing? There will certainly be a few things, such as serving your current clients or spending some time with your family, but it's unlikely that everything on your agenda is more important than marketing right now. Find some tasks that you can defer for the next seventeen days.

3. **Let something go.** If you have had a task on your list for several weeks and not gotten it done, does it truly require doing? If you haven't made time for it in this long, how important can it be? Try this: cross it off the list for one week, and see if it comes back to haunt you. If you can forget about it, that's one less thing to do. If you can't let it drop, revisit the first two options above.

Daily Scores. Did you make more headway on Success Ingredients today? What will be your target scores for tomorrow?

> **Thought for the day:** Studies estimate that the typical urban citizen is exposed to thousands of marketing messages per day. Remember that when you're wondering if it's too soon to follow up with someone who has heard from you before.

Day 12

Morning Review. You have three days left to hit the 50 percent mark on your Success Ingredients. What will it take? If you are having any logistical challenges or how-to questions, read the chapter in Part III that discusses the marketing cycle stage you are working on.

Daily Scores. Did you hit your target scores? Take a moment to celebrate! Are you still struggling? You may need some additional support. Call your business buddy or a friend and ask that person to help you in the following specific way:

1. **Set a fixed time to talk.** Whether you meet by phone or in person, set a start and end time for your conversation. This will tighten the focus on solving your problem. Half an hour is probably enough; an hour is plenty.

2. **Begin by clearing.** Ask your buddy to just listen while you recount what's going on. Your buddy can say things like, "Gee, that's tough," or "How awful!" but should avoid offering advice until you have told the whole story. Talk about not only what is happening but also how it makes you feel. If it sounds like complaining, that probably means you're doing it right. You might be saying something like: "I've been trying for two weeks to finish the new copy for my website but there's just been one emergency after another, and now my mother wants me to help with getting her computer fixed, and I'm so frustrated! All the words I write down just come out wrong, and I don't think it'll ever come together, and I needed it yesterday, and I'm so worried that. . . ." You get the idea.

3. **Set a time limit of five to ten minutes for clearing.** Then ask your buddy to summarize for you: "I hear how frustrated and worried you are. You seem to have two problems that need to be solved: finding the time to work on the website copy, and getting the words to come out right. Are you ready to look at some solutions?"

4. **Brainstorm possible solutions.** Now that your problems are out in the open, you can get some assistance in solving them. Your buddy's job is not to hand you the right answer; it is to help you expand your thinking to come up with some new ideas. Take your problems one at time and together with your buddy make a list of possible solutions. Don't edit the list as you are brainstorming; you will do that later. Anything and everything that comes up should go on the list. A basic principle of brainstorming is that you are not allowed to say, "That won't work," or "I already tried that." Here are the potential results of a brainstorm aimed at getting the right words for your website:

- ➤ Hire a copywriter
- ➤ Plagiarize my competitors' sites
- ➤ Use a thesaurus
- ➤ Ask my cousin, the writer, to help
- ➤ Design a website with pictures instead of words
- ➤ Don't have a website at all
- ➤ Look at sites I like for inspiration
- ➤ Take a class in copywriting
- ➤ Leave the site like it is and stop worrying
- ➤ Have some colleagues review it

5. **Look for a next step.** You can ask your buddy to help you with this or do it later on your own. If none of the brainstormed ideas seems right, look at each one to see if there's something useful in it. Maybe you can't afford a copywriter, but you know one you could ask for some free advice. Perhaps a class in copywriting would take too long, but you could buy an e-book on the subject and read it tonight. Find just one thing you can do that will get you moving forward again, and then do it.

> **Thought for the day:** It really doesn't matter what you choose; the important thing is *that* you choose.

Day 13

Morning Review. Set a target for your Success Ingredient scores today that is a no-kidding-whatever-it-takes goal. Remember that you said you needed these things to be successful.

Daily Scores. Did you make it? Congratulations! Not quite there? You have one more day to catch up. Take a moment to remind yourself of your Special Permission. Did you have it today? If not, what do you need to do, say, or believe to grant yourself that permission? Now that you have been working with the program for a while, is there any other needed permission you have discovered? It's okay to switch, or even have two of them if that serves you in moving forward.

> **Thought for the day:** If none of your prospects say your price is too high, you're not charging enough.

Day 14

Morning Review. It's the halfway point in your Get Clients Now! program. Where do you want to be at the end of the day?

Daily Scores. You have worked diligently this week so pat yourself on the back. If you achieved your target scores on Daily Actions and Success Ingredients, you are on your way to a successful conclusion by month's end. If you are unhappy with your performance, consider how much more you have accomplished in these two weeks than before you started the program. Congratulate yourself for all the effort you have put in, even if you haven't yet produced the results you want.

If you have yet to reach the 50 percent mark with your Success Ingredients, revisit Day 11's Morning Review or schedule another call with your buddy to see what else you might do.

Complete your week by making and posting your wins list. Hooray! You made it through Week Two!

Thought for the day: There is no failure, only feedback.

Day 15

Rest Day. During Week Two, it's a good bet that you found yourself having at least one conversation with your inner critic. Also known as "the committee," or negative self-talk, this is the self-defeating voice you hear in your head that says: "You're not good enough," "You don't know how," and "They won't like you." The inner critic often has much to say about sales and marketing. This is a place in your life where you are putting yourself on the line, often bringing up all your concerns with being inadequate. Negative self-talk is one of the biggest obstacles you must overcome to achieve success.

Everyone has an inner critic (yes, everyone!), but some people manage it better than others. It is possible to manage it so well that you hardly notice it. To begin managing your inner critic, here are some steps to follow:

1. **Raise your awareness.** Every time you find yourself fearful, nervous, hesitant, or second-guessing, stop and notice what is happening. You may have a particular behavior pattern that manifests itself when the inner critic is active, such as procrastinating, avoiding people or projects, or being distracted by trivial interruptions. Or there may be a body sensation you can recognize as a warning sign, like a tight throat, sweaty palms, or a sinking

feeling in your stomach. When you notice any of these possible signs of negative self-talk, pause to listen to the conversation. Write down what you hear your inner critic saying and keep a list.

2. **Take responsibility.** Once you have a catalog of your inner critic's greatest hits, be aware that you can choose to change the music. Just like with fear and resistance, you don't have to let these negative messages stop you. Begin by constructing a fair and accurate response to each of the messages you typically hear and use your response whenever you notice it. If your negative self-talk threatens, "They are going to say no to you," you might respond, "Yes, that's possible, but they also might say yes. I'll never know until I ask." If your inner critic tells you, "Don't do that—you might make a mistake," a good response is, "Yes, I might, but I'll learn from it and move on." Learning to manage negative self-talk is an attainable skill; the only requirement is that you be willing to try.

3. **Practice self-management.** Learning any new skill takes practice, and managing your inner critic is no exception. At first it may be difficult to catch your inner critic in the act; you may realize only later where the reluctance you were feeling was coming from. This is a normal part of learning self-management. Just use your positive response as soon as you think of it. Over time, you will become more skilled at hearing negative messages in "real time," and be better able to respond immediately. If you use this process consistently, the messages will begin to lose their power over you because you will stop believing them.

> **Thought for the day:** The main difference between a skill and a talent is a lot of practice.

Day 16

Rest Day. Have fun today! Enjoy an activity you haven't done for a while to make the day feel special. You deserve it!

> **Thought for the day:** Rule One in the Game of Life: You must be present to win.

Day 17

Morning Review. It's the first working day of Week Three, and you're past the halfway mark in the program. Good work! Your target scores for each day this week should continue to be 8 or higher on your Daily Actions, and 50 to 75 percent on your Success Ingredients. The focus this week will be on your Program Goal. At this point in the program you should have reached at least 50 percent of your goal. By the week's end, you will need to be at 75 percent. Ask yourself this morning, "What will it take to make this happen?"

Daily Scores. Did you see some movement toward your Program Goal today? If you are already at 75 percent or above, consider raising the stakes. How much more business could you generate by the end of next week? If you're below 50 percent, revisit your Daily Actions. Could you boost your level of effort in order to get more clients? Consider increasing the quantity or frequency of some Daily Actions to make up the gap between you and your goal. Make your weekly actions twice a week; spend more time on networking or referral-building; increase your target number for calls or meetings. If you are already scoring 8 or above on your Daily Actions, you can probably do this without too much more effort. You've only got two weeks left, so make the most of them.

> **Thought for the day:**
>
> If he who has a thing to sell
>
> Goes and whispers in a well,
>
> He won't be so apt to make the dollars
>
> As he who climbs a tree and hollers!
>   —Anonymous

Day 18

Morning Review. What can you do to ensure you're pulled toward your Program Goal rather than having to push to get there? Take a moment to reread the first section of your Action Worksheet from Chapter 3. How did you answer "What would that get you?" when you thought about the level of business you really want? Visualize now some of those results. Pick one to be your touchstone for the day and post a word, phrase, or picture somewhere to remind you of it: on your phone, computer, or dashboard.

Daily Scores. Did you feel some pull from your goal today? Try creating an even stronger touchstone for yourself this evening with one of these quick activities:

1. **Write about it.** Write down what it would be like to achieve your goal. What would you have? How would you feel? What could you then do?

2. **Draw it.** Draw a picture of what goal achievement would look like. You don't have to be an artist; even stick figures drawn with markers will do the trick.

3. **Visualize it.** Close your eyes, put on some favorite music, and imagine in detail your personal vision of success.

4. **Sing it.** If there's a song that represents achievement or good fortune to you, play it and sing along. Or change the words to any song you hear to be about you and your success.

Thought for the day: When doing business with the universe, remember that you must place an order if you want to get a delivery.

Day 19

Morning Review. Use the touchstone you created yesterday to help motivate you today. Post your essay or picture on the wall, recapture your visualization by briefly closing your eyes, or hum your success song.

Daily Scores. Are you past the 50 percent mark toward your Program Goal? Yes? Keep going with the plan you have; it's working! No? If you're still not there, revisit "Choosing Where to Focus" in Chapter 2, where you selected the stage of the Universal Marketing Cycle you would work on this month. Do you think you chose correctly? Has anything changed or shifted since you made your choice? If you're not sure, look at the Daily Actions listed in Chapter 5 for the other stage or stages you are considering. Do any of those actions seem more appropriate for where you are now?

If you've been working at a high level of activity for the last two and a half weeks, it is entirely possible that you have moved forward a stage in the marketing cycle. It's also possible that by becoming more active about marketing, you have discovered that your challenges are not what you originally thought they were. If either of these situations exists for you, consider redoing your Daily Actions list to better match where you are now.

Identify the Marketing Cycle stage that you think is the best fit for where you find yourself today, and choose some new Daily Actions that suit that stage. Try working with this revised list starting tomorrow, and see if it begins to produce more movement toward your goal.

> **Thought for the day:** When you are selling professional services, the client's resistance is often about taking the action that your service represents, and not at all about hiring you. If you can get the client to commit to taking action on what needs to be done, hiring you will be his natural next step.

Day 20

Morning Review. You have two days left to reach a 75 percent score on your Program Goal. What sort of game could you design for yourself to play that would make these two days exciting and fun? Could you see how many phone calls you could make in an hour or how many business cards you could collect at a single meeting? Is there a buddy with whom you could play this game and have the winner buy lunch?

Daily Scores. What was it like to be more playful with marketing today? Could you play the same game tomorrow or invent a different one? What could you reward yourself with this weekend if you get to 75 percent on your Program Goal by the end of Friday?

> **Thought for the day:** Struggle and adventure are two sides of the same coin. When you find yourself struggling, flip it over.

Day 21

Morning Review. Set yourself up for an exciting, adventurous day. Take some risks, put yourself out there, really go for it!

Daily Scores. It's the end of Week Three and you have been steadily in action about marketing for twenty-one days. You definitely deserve some applause. If you are at 75 percent or higher on your Program Goal, you are right on target. If you aren't quite there, congratulate yourself anyway on how much effort you have put in and how much you have learned. We'll look tomorrow at whether your goal needs any revision.

> **Thought for the day:** Marketing is like a box of chocolates because: (1) You never know what you're going to get; (2)

nobody likes all of it; and (3) there are plenty of treats, but you have to hunt to find them.

Day 22

Rest Day. So how did Week Three go? Does it look like you'll be able to reach 100 percent of your goal by the end of next week? It's time to revisit your goal one more time and see if it is serving you the way it should. Goals work differently for different people. Some folks like ambitious goals that they can't quite reach because it makes them try harder. Others find that this approach backfires because they always feel as if they're not doing enough; setting a goal that they know they can achieve is much more satisfying. What type of goal-achiever are you?

If ambitious goals excite you and make you want to get up in the morning, and your Program Goal is at 75 percent or more right now, raise it. Give yourself a reason to go all out in the final week. If, on the other hand, it's important to you that you reach every goal you set for yourself, and you're below 75 percent right now, lower your target. This is not cheating! If you can't win the game, there will be a piece of you that doesn't want to play anymore. By setting a more achievable goal, you will continue to be motivated by it.

> **Thought for the day:** Goal setting works the same way as target practice. Without a target, you don't know what you're shooting at, and until you start shooting, you don't know how far off your aim is.

Day 23

Rest Day. Did you promise yourself a reward for reaching your Program Goal target for this week? Today is a good day to keep your promise. If you didn't make your target, what reward do you get for the effort you put in?

> **Thought for the day:** Rest restores, repose repositions, recreation re-creates.

Day 24

Morning Review. You're on the home stretch with only five more days to go. Your target scores for each day this week should be 8 or higher on your

Daily Actions, and 75 to 100 percent on your Success Ingredients and your Program Goal. Picture the reward that you chose in Chapter 3 for achieving your Program Goal. If you reach your goal by Friday, that prize will be yours!

The focus of Week Four is on learning. As you have been working your way through the Get Clients Now! program, you have discovered some significant information about how you handle sales and marketing. If you can capture that learning and use it to become a better marketer, you will have accomplished an important result this month. Finding out that you never leave enough time for follow-up is just as valuable to your ultimate success as getting two new clients.

As you plan your day this morning and complete your Daily Actions throughout the day, notice:

- ▶ What have you learned about time management?
- ▶ Are you managing projects, priorities, and your schedule any differently than you did at the beginning of the program?
- ▶ What is working for you about the way you manage time?
- ▶ What still isn't working well?

Daily Scores. Were you able to balance all the program elements today: Success Ingredients, Daily Actions, Program Goal, and Special Permission? Take a few moments to write down what you have learned about time management over the last twenty-four days.

> **Thought for the day:**
>
> There once was a person named Lou
>
> Who found he had too much to do.
>
> So his very first task
>
> Was learning to ask
>
> Who to give Lou's to-do's to?

Day 25

Morning Review. Have you designed a getting-clients game to play this week? Or is there some other way you can keep marketing light and fun? Humor and a sense of playfulness are effective antidotes to fear and resistance. Notice throughout today what you are learning about these two tough adversaries.

Daily Scores. Write down your thoughts about these questions:

►   What have you learned about fear and resistance?

►   When do they surface for you?

►   What does their appearance signal?

►   What strategies have worked for you in handling these saboteurs?

►   Where do you still have trouble?

> **Thought for the day:** When you are faced with an obstacle, imagine you are an inquisitive child at a locked gate. Depending on your skills and talents, you might climb over it, tunnel under it, go for help, pick the lock, or break down the fence. The one thing you wouldn't do is stand there wondering how it got locked in the first place.

Day 26

Morning Review. Keep that reward visible; you're almost there! If you have you been working with a business buddy, action group, or coach, is there any extra assistance you'd like to ask for in these last three days to help you meet your goal? Consider today what have you learned about support this month.

Daily Scores. As of today, your Program Goal should be at 90 percent or more. Ask yourself what you should do in the next two days to reach 100 percent. Then take a moment to focus on your learning about support:

►   Is there any support you need to ask for now from your family, friends, or colleagues?

►   What kind of support has been most helpful to you in the past month?

►   Have you found yourself willing to ask for support, or do you wait until you are in a crisis?

►   What support structures would be beneficial to maintain after you complete the program?

> **Thought for the day:** Asking for help is not cheating. It's how anything important ever gets done.

Day 27

Morning Review. Is there anything that will get in the way of your being successful today? Are you willing to set aside whatever comes up? Notice what you are learning about self-management.

Daily Scores. Only one more day to go. Take a deep breath, and remember how far you have come since the program began. Notice what you have learned about your inner critic during the program:

- ▶ What are the "greatest hits" playing on your negative self-talk jukebox?
- ▶ Are there some counter-messages you designed that work particularly well?
- ▶ How does your inner critic interfere with your ability to market?
- ▶ What changes have you noticed in your ability to manage this interference?

> **Thought for the day:** If you don't like the music,
> don't dance to it.

Day 28

Morning Review. Are you ready to win? Are you planning your victory celebration? Can you taste your reward? You have earned it! Think about the element of motivation today:

- ▶ What really motivates you?
- ▶ How did having a specific goal for the month change your behavior?
- ▶ Does a far-off goal draw you toward it or do you need to be getting more enjoyment in the moment?
- ▶ Do you reward yourself for progress and learning or only if you achieve certain results?
- ▶ Are you satisfied with rewarding yourself or do you want acknowledgment from others?
- ▶ What motivational techniques backfire on you? Which are your favorites?

Daily Scores. You did it! Way to go! If you reached 100 percent or more on your Program Goal, you have achieved complete success in the *Get Clients*

Now! program. If your score is lower, you still deserve a huge commendation for sticking with the program, and for all the effort you put into it. Remember that punishment is not allowed. Completing the program is in itself a measure of success, regardless of the goal you achieve. And, you may have learned even more than those who did reach 100 percent.

What have you learned about goal-setting, about marketing, about selling? What did you learn if you didn't meet your goal? The fact is that sales and marketing are just like any other skills that you learn by practicing over time, and you have had a lot of practice this month. If you have always tended to reward yourself only for results, try acknowledging your progress regardless of the outcome. You may find this shift in thinking beneficial in more areas than marketing!

> **Thought for the day:** Success in marketing depends on success in management. The way you manage time, money, projects, people, and your own worst doubts and fears has as much to do with getting clients as networking , advertising, or cold calling do. Always remember that what you are really selling is you, so developing yourself is the best marketing investment you can make.

WHAT'S NEXT FOR YOU?

Whew! You've just completed an intensive 28-day program to get more clients. After you celebrate and catch your breath, you will probably be wondering what's next. The Get Clients Now! program is designed to be used over and over. Next month, or whenever you feel the need for a marketing boost, you can design a new program for yourself and start again.

Whether you are repeating the program immediately or not, review now your notes about what you learned over the past month. Look again at each of the areas you examined in Week Four—time management, fear and resistance, support, self-management, and motivation. How can you develop your skills in these areas to become better at marketing? What will you do differently in the future based on what you learned throughout the program about goal-setting, marketing, and selling?

Look also at your chosen Success Ingredients. Are any of these projects still incomplete? What additional projects back in Chapter 4 did you consider choosing, and is now the time to move forward on any of these?

Save your notes about learning areas and Success Ingredients to help design your next Get Clients Now! program. When you are ready to start again, begin by re-diagnosing your marketing condition with the Universal Marketing Cycle in Chapter 2.

If you went through the program by yourself this time, consider repeating it with a buddy, group, or coach to see how much difference the extra accountability, perspective, and support can make to your success. Or perhaps you see another way to make this program more effective for the way you think and work. Be creative, find your own unique solution, and above all, reward yourself for all you do.

PART III

The Strategies

YOU MAY HAVE REACHED PART III because you are reading this book from beginning to end, before completing the exercises or starting the design of your own Get Clients Now! program. The information here about marketing strategies, "recipes," and missing ingredients can certainly be used in this way to generate ideas and inspiration at any time.

A better way to make use of this material, however, is to reference it while you are in the process of building or implementing your action plan; for example, while:

▶ Selecting Your Success Ingredients (Chapter 4)
▶ Choosing from the Action Plan Menu (Chapter 5)
▶ Putting the System into Action (Chapter 6)

This part of the book contains instructions for preparing your chosen Success Ingredients, as well as marketing recipes to help you apply the strategies specified in your action plan. A chapter for each stage of the Universal Marketing Cycle is provided so you can quickly locate the ingredients and recipes you need:

▶ Filling the Pipeline (Chapter 7)
▶ Following Up (Chapter 8)
▶ Having Sales Conversations (Chapter 9)
▶ Closing Sales (Chapter 10)

You need only look at the specific chapter that covers the stage you are working on. Each chapter begins with an overview of the stage and some of the basic Success Ingredients it requires, then gives recipes for how to apply each marketing strategy during that stage. Only those strategies suitable for the stage are included, usually in this order:

- ▶ Direct Contact and Follow-Up
- ▶ Networking and Referral-Building
- ▶ Public Speaking
- ▶ Writing and Publicity
- ▶ Promotional Events
- ▶ Advertising

You need only study those strategies you are actually planning to use. For each strategy, additional Success Ingredients specific to that strategy are described within the recipe that most closely relates to them. For example, the ingredient "prospect list" can be found under the recipe for "Calling and Mailing," and the ingredient "press release/media kit" is described in the recipe for "Getting Media Publicity." The Success Ingredients covered in each section are listed at the beginning so you can find them easily.

Happy cooking!

CHAPTER 7

Filling the Pipeline

When You Don't Know Enough People to Contact

MAKING YOUR STRATEGIES WORK

Filling your marketing pipeline with prospects, contacts, leads, and referrals will be an ongoing process for as long as you are in business. By choosing to focus on this stage of the marketing cycle now, you are acknowledging that this is the area of your marketing that currently needs the most effort. Later on, when you have overcome some of your pipeline-filling challenges, you may decide to focus more energy on one of the other stages. But it is important to recognize that you will always need to keep your pipeline full.

This means that whatever marketing strategies you decide on for filling the pipeline, you should be willing to keep them up over an extended period of time. In marketing, more of the same works much better than a little of everything. Ideally, your pipeline-filling activities should become automatic and habitual. Even when you are busy, you should always allow time for making new contacts, networking, speaking, or whatever your chosen strategies are.

It's natural to wonder whether the strategies you have selected are the best choices. You may find yourself wanting to switch around just to see if something else might work better. Be patient and don't change your pipeline-filling strategies during the twenty-eight days of the Get Clients Now! program. It simply isn't enough time for you to judge your results accurately. It's okay to change individual *tactics* if it seems appropriate; you might switch from cold calling to warm calling, for example. But don't alter your overall *strategies*, from say, networking and referral building to promotional events.

The best way to determine how well a particular strategy is working to fill your pipeline is to track your results over time. There are three statistics that will be helpful to you in evaluating the strategies you are using:

1. How many prospects did each strategy generate?
2. How many sales resulted from those prospects?
3. What was the dollar value of those sales?

If you carefully note the exact source of each prospect, you can easily track these statistics for the month of the program. If you keep tracking your results for three months, six months, or a year, you will have a much more accurate perspective on which marketing strategies work best. Then if you decide to make a change, choose just one new strategy at a time to try out. And remember to keep tracking.

WHO BELONGS IN YOUR PIPELINE

There are two broad categories of people and organizations you want in your marketing pipeline: those who may someday be clients, and those who can refer clients. To find people who are likely to become clients, you will want to reach out to a market niche that is a good match for your services. To find people who may never be clients but could refer you business, reach out to those who serve or interact with people in that niche.

A person or organization who doesn't fall into one of these two categories probably doesn't belong in your pipeline. It is true that people you encounter while marketing your business may become personal friends or helpful with other aspects of your life, but you don't want to use up your precious marketing time in following up with folks who are neither likely to be clients nor refer them.

Whenever you meet someone outside your market niche who also doesn't seem to have much contact with it, think twice before putting that person in your pipeline. Always concentrate your efforts on the most likely prospects and referral partners. The way to win the marketing game is not to collect the most names and phone numbers, but to make the most sales.

BASIC INGREDIENTS FOR FILLING THE PIPELINE

SUCCESS INGREDIENTS:

Description of services	**Self-confidence skills**
Market niche definition	**Website**
10-second introduction	**Social media profile/page**
Business cards	

Ingredient: Description of Services

Being able to describe clearly the services you offer is essential for all aspects of marketing. A solid **description of services** can be the basis of numerous other marketing tools, such as a website, marketing letter, or telephone script. A complete description contains the features, benefits, structure, and cost of your services. It should not include everything you could possibly do for your clients, but rather just those services you plan to focus on in your marketing. The example in Figure 7-1 is for a certified public accountant serving small business owners.

Ingredient: Market Niche Definition

Your **market niche definition** identifies the people, organizations, goals, and problems that your business is primarily designed to serve. These people and organizations are the prospects you plan to pursue actively as clients. Don't make the mistake of thinking that your niche definition must encompass everyone who could possibly be a client. Instead, decide which clients you truly want to work with.

Choosing and defining a specific niche allows you to maximize all of your marketing efforts. Without a niche, your marketing attempts will be diluted and haphazard, leading to wasted effort, muddy marketing messages, and an overwhelming number of choices about where to go, who to contact, and

Figure 7-1: Description of Services Example

I provide tax preparation services for income, payroll, sales, and other miscellaneous taxes. I advise my clients on tax compliance and how to minimize their taxes. I also prepare business and personal financial statements. Other services I offer are analyzing employee benefit and retirement packages, valuing the worth of a business, and advice on accounting and financial software packages.

Benefits of using my service include saving money on taxes, complying with government regulations to avoid penalties, having accurate information to manage your business at your fingertips, and letting someone else worry about keeping up with tax laws so you don't have to.

I charge for my services on an hourly basis, at $100 per hour.

---

what to say. Making a name for yourself as a professional will be almost impossible because prospects won't be able to distinguish your true expertise.

The most powerful niche definitions include both a target market and a specialty. Your target market is the audience your business serves, and your specialty is the scope of issues you address with your clients—the goals you help them achieve and the problems you assist them to solve. For example, a real estate agent's niche might be "South Houston buyers of income property." The target market is "South Houston real estate buyers" and the specialty is "income property." If this seems too narrow a definition to you, consider the alternative. A broad description like "Gulf Coast buyers of real estate" will attract no one. It's far too generic to be useful in crafting marketing messages or focusing your marketing action plan.

Here are some questions to help you identify your market niche:

➤ Who needs your service the most?

➤ Who is able to pay what you plan to charge?

➤ Who is likely to give you large orders or repeat business?

➤ Whose problems and goals do you care about?

➤ What type of client work provides you with the most enjoyment and satisfaction?

➤ What sort of people do you enjoy spending time with?

▶ Where do you already have many contacts or an established reputation?

▶ Who would be the easiest clients to get?

Remember that what you are doing by defining a niche is targeting a particular group, not excluding all others. You are not limiting your options by choosing a market niche; instead, you are organizing yourself to launch an effective marketing campaign aimed at the clients you most want. If someone outside that niche shows up in your pipeline, by all means do business with them if you like. But focus the efforts that you initiate on filling the pipeline with those clients you are most interested in getting.

For the target market portion of your niche definition, it's important to describe your market using recognizable categories, such as demographics or industry classifications, rather than the presumed need of a client for your service. A contract trainer specializing in conflict resolution skills, for example, would find little value in defining her target market as "organizations that experience conflict." This won't help her focus her marketing, as it could be anyone.

"Organizations in need of conflict resolution training" won't do the job as a definition either. Could you look them up in a directory? Would a referral partner know who would be a good lead for you? Could you figure out where these people would go to network? No. You can't do any of these things with a need-based definition.

But if the trainer defined her market as "human resource development or training managers in midsize to large companies located in the Boston area," now she can find them—and so can her referral partners.

If your target market is organizations, here are some ways you could define them:

Classification (e.g., retailer, manufacturer, government agency)

Industry (e.g., health care, software, travel)

Size (by number of employees or annual revenue)

Geographic location

Special characteristics (e.g., well-established, rapidly growing, family friendly)

Decision makers (by department, division, or position title)

And here are some ways to define individuals as your prospective clients:

Age

Gender

Family status (e.g., married, with children, with aging parents)

Occupation (e.g., student, executive, self-employed professional)

Income (by individual or household)

Education (e.g., high school, college, postgraduate)

Geographic location

Interests and hobbies (e.g., plays sports, active investor, travels often)

For the specialty segment of your niche definition, choose words or phrases that your target audience would typically use themselves when describing the problems or goals they need assistance with. People seeking interior design help might have goals such as "furnish a new home," "remodel the kitchen," or "stage the house for sale." You could echo these needs by labeling your specialty as "custom home furnishings," "kitchen and bath remodeling," or "home staging." Stay away from generic, abstract phrases like "innovative designs" and "outstanding interiors." These may be useful in writing marketing copy for a brochure or website, but are inadequate as definitions of who you serve and how.

Join your target market and specialty together in one concise phrase that identifies your most-wanted target group and the problems or goals you address for them. For example: "computer network installation for small to midsize companies in the Denver area" or "career transition for midlife women."

A final word of advice: If you can't seem to narrow your focus to just one target market and specialty, you are better off defining two or three distinct markets or specialty areas than using one broad label intended to include them all in your niche definition. A financial planner seeking high-income individuals, for example, might choose "executives, established professionals, and successful entrepreneurs" as targeted groups. A target like this is much more helpful in locating prospects than saying "people with income over $100K."

A Bigger Pond Isn't a Better Pond

Michael Port, www.bookyourselfsolid.com

"No matter how much you might like to be everything to everyone, it's just not possible," declares Michael Port. Michael is a small business marketing expert, and *New York Times* bestselling author of *Book Yourself Solid*. According to Port:

> Even if you could be, you would be doing a disservice to yourself and your clients in the attempt. You can serve your clients much better, offer them much more of your time, energy, and expertise, if you narrow your market so that you're serving only those who most need your services and who can derive the greatest benefits from what you have to offer.
>
> If you're just starting out in your business, or if you've been working in your business for a while but are not yet booked solid, you may be tempted to market to anyone and everyone with the assumption that the more people you market to, the more clients you'll get. While narrowing your market to gain more clients may seem counterintuitive, that's exactly what you need to do to successfully book yourself solid.
>
> Think of narrowing your market this way: Which would you rather be—a small fish in a big pond or a big fish in a small pond? It's much easier to carve out a very lucrative domain for yourself once you've identified a specific target market. And once you're a big fish in a small pond, you'll get more invitations than you can handle to swim in other ponds.

Ingredient: 10-Second Introduction

Your **10-second introduction** is a concise summary of your business that you can use when you shake someone's hand, stand up in front of a group, or call someone on the phone.

It describes what you do and who you do it for in a clear and memorable way. One effective format is the benefits-oriented introduction, where you state the key benefit of your service before giving your occupation or job title. Here are some examples:

- ▶ "My name is Joyce Ozier and I help Vancouver retailers get more window shoppers into their stores. My company is Wow! Windows, and we provide retail display and design."
- ▶ "My name is Peter Marconi and I provide Chicago financial services firms with persuasive tools for winning new clients. I'm a marketing communications consultant."

▶ "I'm Carmen Sanchez, and I help working mothers take practical steps toward living a more fulfilling and balanced life. I'm a life coach."

▶ "I'm Fred Patel, and I deliver talented, high-caliber professionals to fill essential positions at information technology companies nationwide. I'm an executive recruiter."

The advantage of this format is that it positions you in the mind of your listeners before they have a chance to form their own opinions about what you do. If you introduce yourself as an attorney, for example, your listener may think you are a business litigator, estate planner, or do criminal defense work, none of which helps you get clients if you do family law. An introduction that begins, "I work with people going through divorce to help them get what they're entitled to," is both more specific and more memorable.

Notice that all these introductions use plain language rather than industry jargon. Unless you know exactly who your listeners are and what vernacular they speak, use terms a 12-year-old would understand.

Ingredient: Business Cards

The main purpose of a **business card** is to facilitate communication, not to give a complete description of your services. Put just enough information on your card for people to remember what you do, but not so much that they have no reason to call you or visit your website. If you turn your business card into a brochure, people may not contact you to learn more, nor will you have anything additional to provide them with after you talk.

Include your name, company name if you have one, mailing address, phone, e-mail address, and website. You might also include a social media profile, such as your Twitter ID or Facebook page. If you are operating a home business and prefer to keep your address confidential, provide at least your city and state. If your company name makes it clear what you do, that may be all you need. Otherwise, choose from one of the following ways to indicate your profession:

1. **Title or function** (e.g., graphic designer, event planning, business broker).

2. **Specialties.** List no more than three (e.g., employment law—employee relations—dispute resolution; errands—organizing—filing; psychotherapy—consultation—training).

3. **Tag line** (e.g., "Strategic research in values and attitudes," "Helping nonprofits thrive," "Stress relief for overworked professionals").

If you want to add more value to your card, instead of cataloging the features and benefits of your service, include a sample of your expertise or an invitation to take the next step. For example, a chiropractor might include the line "Call for a free initial consultation on pain relief," or a career counselor could print a brief "career satisfaction quiz" on the back of her card.

The more expensive your service is, the more expensive your card should look. Adding a logo or your photograph, using embossing, or choosing high-quality paper are all ways of improving the look of your card. You may need the services of a professional graphic designer to boost the image your card projects. If you plan to frequently mail information to prospective clients, your card will need to match the design of your letterhead, brochure, or marketing kit.

Avoid using perforated card stock to print cards from your own computer. Cards like these give the impression that you aren't willing to invest in your business and won't inspire trust. You can instead order professionally printed cards online at a very reasonable price.

When you are marketing more than one business, you need more than one business card. Even if you find yourself giving both cards to the same person, they will represent what you offer much more clearly than if you try to put everything on the same card.

Ingredient: Self-Confidence Skills

One of the most significant barriers to marketing that many independent professionals face is feeling as if they don't have what it takes. You may at times feel fearful, reluctant, or inadequate about aspects of marketing, selling, or the business itself. You may also think you are alone in feeling this way, or that there must be something wrong with you because you find promoting yourself to be such a challenge.

The first step to building stronger **self-confidence skills** for marketing is often to recognize that a certain amount of fear, resistance, and self-doubt is completely normal. Every entrepreneur or salesperson fears being rejected at times. It's natural to experience reluctance about tasks that we find difficult or distasteful. Wondering whether you have the skills or experience needed to promote or even to run a business is an ordinary occurrence. So you are definitely not alone!

Businesspeople who seem to not be troubled by inner saboteurs like these typically fall into two categories. Either they entered the world of business with a high level of self-confidence already, or they have learned to act more self-confidently in the course of building their businesses. You too can learn to do this.

Psychologists maintain that confidence is a learnable skill. Building your self-confidence can be accomplished in a wide variety of ways. Here are some suggestions:

▶ **Practice in a safe environment.** Try out your 10-second introduction, phone script, or speaking topic with friends, colleagues, or a coach. Ask them to focus not on helping you improve your content, but on receiving what you have to say positively and telling you what they liked about it.

▶ **Learn from role models.** Observe or read about a confident person who you admire. This could be a public figure (e.g., Sophia Loren or Martin Luther King, Jr.), fictitious character (e.g., Sam Spade or Princess Leia), or someone you know. How could you emulate what you admire about that person when conducting your business?

▶ **Prepare and learn.** Tackle the areas that give you the most trouble as if they were a school project. Research cold calling, for example, or take notes about networking. Write a paper about public speaking, or read articles on interacting with referral sources. Script out what you might say and rehearse in front of a mirror or video camera. Learning and preparation can take the edge off anxiety.

▶ **Take a confidence course.** Sign up for a ropes course, or take a martial arts class. Learn how to drive a race car or dive from a highboard. Try hang gliding, bungee jumping, or fire walking. Go on a vision quest or learn to scuba dive. Physically challenging activities like these with an element of danger can increase your confidence quickly.

▶ **Use positive self-talk.** Counter negative messages you are sending yourself with positive responses. When you notice yourself thinking, "I don't know how," remind yourself that, "I'm learning a new skill, and I'll get better with practice." If you feel as if, "No one will want to hire me," tell yourself, "Not everyone will hire me, but if I keep asking, someone will."

▶ **Relax and stay grounded.** Reduce tension and your overall stress level with relaxation and grounding techniques like deep breathing, meditation, visual imagery, slow tempo music, yoga, Tai Chi, hot baths, herbal tea, or massage.

▶ **Shift your perspective about marketing.** Remind yourself that marketing is an avenue to being able to serve more people, make use of your talents, and have an impact on the world. It's also the path to gaining the independence, flexibility, and fulfillment a thriving business can provide.

▶ **View your prospective clients differently.** When you are struggling to get business, it's easy to slip into the mindset that your clients are adversaries whom you must overpower, outwit, or reel in. Instead, think of you and your prospects as allies working together for a common cause—solving the problems or achieving the goals that your business addresses.

▶ **Practice gratitude and abundance.** Break away from feeling that marketing is a burden and clients are scarce by being grateful for all the progress you make and remembering that opportunities are everywhere. Try keeping a gratitude journal, where you note all the rewards your business brings you each day.

▶ **Act as if you were confident.** It's actually possible to build confidence by behaving as if you already have it. Imagine how you would act if you were twice as confident as you are now, then do your best to behave that way. Acting "as if" gets confidence into your bones by allowing you to experience what it feels like.

Choose just one of the approaches above, or another confidence-builder that appeals to you, and dedicate time to work with it regularly.

Get Your Confidence Rolling

Larina Kase, PsyD, MBA; www.larinakase.com

"When we leave our comfort zones, shadows become monsters," observes Dr. Larina Kase. Dr. Kase is a behavioral psychologist, confidence coach, and author of *Clients, Clients and More Clients*. She adds:

> Because we're anxious, everything looks threatening, scary, and overwhelming. When confronted with a situation that we fear we can't handle well, many people decide to avoid the opportunity completely. They choose to settle for the status quo rather than pursuing a change, because they fear failure and humiliation.

Others go after the opportunity before they are ready. They plunge right in (smartly knowing that if they don't take action, they never will). The problem is that they haven't adequately prepared. They haven't lined up the resources and support that they need. They haven't created a plan.

Still others retreat at the first sign of failure. Unfortunately many people escape from uncomfortable situations too early—before they have a chance to get used to the anxiety and achieve their goals.

You see, avoidance is the number one killer of confidence and high achievement. All of the mistakes above entail some form of avoidance.

To take on your biggest challenges, you will need some level of confidence that you can handle them. The way to build this confidence is by building momentum. Start out by strategically taking on opportunities that push you out of your comfort zone by about 20%. Then go up to 40%. Then 60%. Then 80%. Then 100% (your most difficult and important goal).

As Newton discovered, a body at rest stays at rest and a body in motion stays in motion. Get the ball rolling by taking on smaller challenges, and soon you'll have momentum on your side to help you with the larger challenges.

Ingredient: Website

A **website** can be a powerful tool for filling the pipeline, following up, or both. Many professional services sites are primarily online brochures. Their content focuses on describing the features and benefits of the services being offered and provides supporting details such as biographies or client lists. If your website matches this description, you will probably find that your site is primarily a follow-up tool. Most of your site visitors will not find you on their own, but will instead be people you direct to your site by way of other pipeline-filling strategies such as direct contact, networking, public speaking, writing, or advertising. The elements of a basic website like this typically include:

- ▶ Description of the services you offer
- ▶ Details about your target market and/or professional specialty (e.g., "I work with artists and designers" or "We specialize in qualitative market research")
- ▶ Features and benefits of your services
- ▶ Tag line, positioning statement, or competitive advantage

▸   Biography of you, your company, or both

▸   Client list, testimonials, or endorsement quotes

▸   Photographs or illustrations of you or about your work

▸   Contact information: address, phone, e-mail, and social media profiles

There's nothing wrong with having a website that follows this online bro-chure model. For many professionals, this may be all the Web presence you need. However, if you wish to use your site not just to follow up with prospects by directing them there, but also to fill the pipeline by attracting new visitors—without paid advertising—you will need more. To accomplish this aim, you will need to build a site that offers more value beyond just marketing copy and employs additional tactics to draw traffic.

Adding fresh, informative content to your site increases its value as a resource, which will bring you a higher ranking in the search engines, build your professional credibility, encourage other sites to link to yours, and cause more people to refer others to your site via social media, e-mail, and the like. These added information pages will also provide multiple links to your site in the search engines, because each one will be indexed separately. Posting new content frequently will also improve your search engine ranking.

Adding value to your site can take the form of:

▸   Educational articles about your area of expertise

▸   A blog or back issues of your e-zine or print newsletter

▸   Quizzes or assessments your visitors can use to score themselves

▸   Frequently Asked Questions (FAQs) about your field

▸   Resource guides or links to other useful sites

▸   White papers, case studies, or surveys relevant to your industry

▸   Tutorials or how-to guides that showcase your expertise

▸   Videos or audio recordings that educate, entertain, or inspire visitors

You can also improve the ranking of your site in search engine results when prospects search for specific keywords or keyword phrases. The higher your site ranks in the results, the more likely it is that a searcher will visit. This type of search engine optimization (SEO) is based on identifying what search terms your best prospects are most likely to use, then featuring these terms prominently in your website's copy. The best terms to focus on are those directly relevant to what you offer, but not so highly competitive that getting a high rank will be difficult.

Here's an example: A massage therapist in Tampa, Florida, found that typing "Tampa massage" into Google returned 7,900,000 results. Instead of trying to get a high ranking under that keyword phrase, she chose "Tampa deep tissue massage" for which there were only 180,000 results. In designing her site, she used the keyword phrase "Tampa deep tissue massage" in the page title on her home page. In the text on her page, she used the heading "deep tissue massage" when describing her work, and made sure to include that phrase and the word "Tampa" again elsewhere on the page. As a result of this keyword optimization, combined with other tactics she used to increase traffic to her site, when her home page was indexed by Google, it was listed in the top ten under "Tampa deep tissue massage." If she had resisted naming a specialty and focused her site around the more competitive phrase "Tampa massage" instead, it's unlikely she could have achieved a rank high enough for prospects to find her through a Google search.

SEO techniques can be sophisticated and change frequently. You may not wish to spend time learning enough to use them on your own. SEO experts and some (but not all) Web designers can provide you with professional help.

Regarding design and construction of your site, hiring a Web designer will save you a great deal of frustration and produce a higher quality result than you are likely to produce on your own. Web technology changes frequently, and a good designer can help you take advantage of the newest possibilities, as well as make sure your site is accessible to visitors using smartphones or tablets to browse the Web. Be sure to ask about the range of the designer's knowledge. If you are working with someone whose skills are mainly artistic or primarily technical, you may want to also hire a marketing pro to help with copywriting or search engine optimization.

Before you start building a site, spend some time surfing. Search for keywords you think prospective clients would use to find you, and explore what content your competitors' sites contain. Make a list of features you like and dislike, as well as what you think the competitive advantages featured on your site should be.

There are many ways to attract traffic to your website beyond those discussed above, and you'll find additional suggestions in this chapter under the recipes given for individual marketing strategies. Whichever methods you choose, however, beware of spending more time and money on building a site and attracting traffic to it than those visitors will ultimately be worth to you. In most cases, you will still need to have personal contact with prospects who find you on the Web before they decide to hire you. A well-designed website can be a significant source of new leads as well as a credibility booster, but it's not a complete sales and marketing strategy all by itself.

Climbing to the Top of Mt. Search Engine

Jill Whalen, www.highrankings.com

Jill Whalen is a search-engine optimization expert and publishes the newsletter *High Rankings Advisor*. Whalen says, "Top level search engine listings are absolutely critical for the success of your business on the Web. Why? According to most studies, the average user never goes past the third page of search results." She advises:

> Be realistic about your keyword choices. Never expect a high ranking for a single word—there are simply too many sites on the Internet for a one word search to be effective. In addition, it's practically impossible to create a one word search that is targeted to your specific website.

> For example, suppose you sell real estate in Florida. You might assume that using "homes" as your keyword would produce a lot of targeted traffic. Wrong. Just because people search for the word "homes" doesn't mean they're looking to buy or sell a home in Florida. However, if you choose "moving to Florida" as your keywords, most of your site visitors will be people actually interested in moving to Florida, and therefore probably needing real estate. This is the beauty of choosing the proper keyword phrases: you get an extremely targeted audience!

> Once you do have relevant keyword phrases chosen for your site, you absolutely must write good, professional, keyword rich marketing copy (or hire someone to do so) on every page of your website. Simply being found in the engines isn't enough. Once found, your site still has to sell its products or services.

> I believe that a big reason why our optimized sites end up getting so much new business is because we increase their overall appeal. That is, we write great, professional marketing text, and suggest other changes that may give the site a more professional appearance. These things are just as important to the bottom line as getting a high ranking in the first place.

Ingredient: Social Media Profile/Page

Social media channels have become an increasingly significant element in marketing, and it's worth considering whether to have a social media presence for yourself and/or your business. Social media networks such as Facebook or Google+ are designed to create a web of personal connections between you and your contacts. These virtual communities allow you to post your profile and access information others post about themselves. As a basic ingredient for filling the pipeline, a **social media profile or page** can enable you to be found more readily by prospects searching online. It can also give you an interactive platform for direct contact and follow-up, networking and referral building, and other marketing strategies.

You'll find more about tactics for using social media throughout Part III of the book. But first you'll need to determine whether a social media presence makes sense for you right now, and if so, where you should begin to build it.

Creating profiles for yourself or pages for your business on one or more social media services will often help you to be more easily found online by your prospects. People searching for a business like yours may search from within their favorite social media application, or your social media profile may rank higher in the search engines than your own website does. Some professionals use a social media profile as their online base (on LinkedIn, for example) instead of having a website at all.

Creating your own profile or page is also a necessary first step if you plan to become more active on social media, regularly posting updates and interacting with your network. But on some social media sites, you can simply create a profile to become more visible online without making a commitment to engage on a regular basis.

As of this writing, the major social media networks and media-sharing sites used by small business owners in North America are Facebook, LinkedIn, Twitter, Google+, and for video, YouTube. There are many others used by specific regions, professions, or industries. To choose how active you want to be on social media and which services you might wish to use, consider these questions:

- ▶ Do your ideal clients and/or referral sources spend much time online?
- ▶ Do people typically look for a business like yours online, or does most of your business come by personal referral?

► On what social media platforms do your clients and referral sources appear to be most active?

► Can your business take advantage of the national or international reach of social media, or are all your clients located nearby?

► Do you have the time and inclination to put effort into building an online network and interacting with your contacts?

► Are you comfortable communicating through the written word or by video, or are you better at connecting with people by phone or in person?

For a nationwide business which attracts many of its clients online, and whose owner enjoys communicating in writing or by video and spending time online, social media marketing can be an excellent choice. For a local business which gets most of its clients through personal referrals, and whose owner prefers less time on the computer and likes to speak with people in person or by phone, social media marketing is probably not worth the time and effort.

If you would like to simply have a presence on a social media channel to increase your online visibility or access networking opportunities on an occasional basis, you can set up a profile for yourself on LinkedIn and/or Google + . Fill out your profile as completely as possible to increase the likelihood that prospective clients will find you, or that people who already know you will locate your profile and add you to their network.

To become active on social media regularly, in addition to a profile for yourself, you may also wish to have a page for your business or brand. It's wise, though, to try out social media marketing for a while and see what results it produces for you before setting up multiple profiles and pages. For the twenty-eight days of the Get Clients Now! program, it is recommended that you set up no more than one new profile or page beyond what you had before. That way you can devote most of your attention to making use of any Daily Actions you chose that employ social media approaches.

STRATEGY: DIRECT CONTACT AND FOLLOW-UP

SUCCESS INGREDIENTS:

Prospect list

Lead sources

Recipe: Calling and Mailing

Sending mail or e-mail and placing calls are activities more typical of the following up stage than when filling the pipeline. This makes sense when you think about the whole purpose of your pipeline-filling activities: to find people you can call or mail, or to get people to contact you. So if you are working on filling the pipeline, you may not have a list of people to contact.

But there are two situations where you may wish to call and mail to help get your pipeline full: contacting new people to see if they might become prospects (more common in business-to-business marketing than when marketing to consumers), and contacting people you already know to stimulate referrals. You'll find more information about both of these subjects in Chapter 8.

Whenever you contact someone new, the best approach is to call before you mail or e-mail them, and call again after you mail. Even if you don't reach the person on the first call, you can find out more information from his voice mail or the receptionist, and leave a message to expect an e-mail or letter from you. On your post-mailing call, if you again don't reach him, you can mention your letter or e-mail, and prompt him to read it if he hasn't yet.

The purpose of your calls is twofold: to find out if this lead is actually a good prospect for you, and if so, to try to have a sales conversation. Remember that a sales conversation is defined as the time when you find out what your prospects need and tell them what you can do for them. This may happen in a formal presentation or scheduled appointment, or informally, in person, by telephone, or sometimes even by e-mail.

To accomplish your objectives, you will need to ask questions, not just give information. When you reach your prospect on the phone, don't rattle off a long introduction. Instead, give your name and mention any connection between you; then move immediately into conversation by asking a question. "Do you have a moment to talk about how I can help your company get better results from its training programs?" is a sample opening.

Be considerate when prospects tell you they are too busy to talk, especially if you are calling their cell phone. Tell them you will call another time, and if possible, find out when it might be convenient.

If they have the time to speak with you, be ready with two or three questions that will tell you immediately whether the person you are speaking with has a need for your service. If the need is there, ask for a phone or in-person meeting, or if she has the time, hold the conversation right then. Don't back away from asking for a meeting by offering to send literature first or referring your prospect to your website. You may never get this person live on the phone again. Only if she declines to meet with you or to take time for a sales conversation by phone should you offer to send something or suggest she visit your site. This is also a polite way to end the conversation if the answers to your qualifying questions indicate this is not a prospect for you.

The people you might be calling if you are trying to fill the pipeline are likely to be those you looked up on a **prospect list** you purchased or compiled from the Web, a directory, or your social media network, or obtained from a **lead source**, such as the media or a networking pal. (See "Finding Prospects" below for more information.) The best kind of mail to send folks like this is a personal letter or e-mail. "Personal" means addressed to them by name and mentioning some situation that you have reason to believe exists and that you can help with. If you are using postal mail, you can enclose a brochure or fact sheet, but don't send a lot of material. Wait for the follow-up stage to send anything more. And absolutely do follow up.

There's no hard-and-fast rule about whether postal mail or e-mail is a better choice for a cold contact like this. Sometimes an e-mail will get through to a prospect while a letter might be discarded by a gatekeeper or ignored. On the other hand, many people simply delete all e-mail from people they don't know. If you are using the call–mail–call sequence, your first call will alert your prospect to look for your e-mail, so he will be less likely to mistake it for an anonymous message sent to thousands of recipients. But with some prospects, only a postal letter will get their attention. You may wish to try both approaches.

When contacting people you already know in order to fill the pipeline, you are hoping to uncover needs they may have, or encourage referrals by reminding them who you are and what you do. Those you contact might be former clients, people you have had sales conversations with in the past who didn't buy, or networking contacts.

You might choose to get in touch with these people by phone, and place a "what's new" call. With centers of influence or likely referral partners, you might wish to schedule coffee or lunch. An easy way to contact a larger number of people, though, is by mail or e-mail. Again, personal mailings can have more impact than mass mailings of postcards or newsletters. An article, event announcement, or link to a useful website with a simple "thought you would be interested" note is a friendly and effective variety of reminder.

Recipe: Meeting People in Person

Getting out of your office to meet people in person can be a welcome break from calling and mailing. (There's lots more information about this under the "Networking and Referral Building" strategy below.) Keep in mind, though, that you don't have to go to an official networking event to meet people. You meet new people all the time—at the grocery store, dentist's office, or your child's soccer game. Do all these people know what you do for a living?

Get in the habit of carrying your business cards everywhere. Whenever you meet new people, use your 10-second introduction, and ask them a bit about themselves. Once you've had some conversation, offer a business card, and ask for theirs if they have one. You may feel awkward about this at first, but if you keep it up, it will soon become natural. If your service is primarily marketed to consumers rather than businesses—wedding planning, chiropractic, or home organizing, for example, this informal way of meeting new prospects can be quite fruitful.

And don't rule out this tactic if you market to businesses and organizations. All organizations are run by human beings, after all. That guy on the jogging path may turn out to be the marketing director of your city's fastest-growing firm, and the woman ahead of you in the espresso line might be the chief financial officer of a Fortune 500 corporation.

Recipe: Finding Prospects

The best ways to find prospects are by using the pipeline-filling strategies of networking and referral building, public speaking, and writing and publicity, described later in this chapter. This is because these approaches provide you with increased credibility, perceived endorsements, and personal connections, all of which build the know-like-and-trust factor that makes people buy. But you can also locate prospective clients through research techniques if you have done a good job of defining your market niche.

If you need a large number of prospects, you can license a targeted prospect list from a professional list broker or an online vendor of business lists or consumer lists (search the Web for "prospect lists" or "sales leads"). A compiled list like this can be useful if you are trying to market to many people at once. For example, sending out direct mail to invite people to a seminar, or hiring a telemarketer to pitch free initial consultations (as you might do when marketing a professional services business with several principals). But for a solo professional doing a call–mail–call campaign, licensing a compiled list may give you more names than you can possibly use during the term of your license.

Know that the day you obtain a list, it's already out of date. Ask the provider when the list you are getting was last updated, and what the undeliverable rate is expected to be, so you're not disappointed.

For smaller numbers, especially when marketing to businesses, it may make more sense to compile your own list. Here are some possible sources for compiling prospect lists:

▶ Internet searches for your target industry and geographical area (e.g., "Portland hospitals," "Atlanta restaurants")

▶ Online directories of companies or business contacts (e.g., Jigsaw, Manta)

▶ Your social media network and the networks of others you are connected to

▶ Yellow Pages (online or print) and other advertising directories

▶ Trade directories (e.g., Chamber of Commerce, Better Business Bureau)

▶ Association membership rosters (groups you belong to and others you can find online)

▶ Leading company lists (e.g., those published by *Forbes* or *Fortune*)

▶ *Book of Lists* published by your local *Business Times* or *Business Journal*

► Tenant directory posted in the lobby of an office building or industrial park

When compiling your own list of consumers you plan to call at their home phone numbers, be aware that for U.S. residents, the Federal Trade Commission's telemarketing regulations prohibit making sales calls to people with whom you have no prior relationship if their numbers are listed in the National Do Not Call Registry. While the FTC doesn't typically enforce these rules against small businesses that make a low volume of sales calls, you may wish to check the numbers on your list against the Registry, which you can do at the FTC's Do Not Call website. Registration for up to five area codes is free. Business-to-business marketing is exempt from these regulations.

You can also develop your own ongoing lead sources, which might be professional or trade associations; educational institutions; print, broadcast, or Web media; online communities; or personal networking buddies. Associations and schools produce publications and events that will keep you in touch with who's who in the industry or specialty they focus on. Print, broadcast, and Web media, and online communities like social media channels, message boards, and discussion groups can do the same. The more targeted the periodical, program, or community is to your market niche, the better.

The people who are speaking at these events, writing articles, being interviewed, and participating or being mentioned online are all potential leads for you. Make note of the names and affiliations you learn from these sources that might be prospects for you. Finding out how to contact the person mentioned is often the easy part.

Get a List and Get Going

Lisa Bowen, www.prospectstogo.com

"There's a lot of information available for free," points out list broker Lisa Bowen, "but you have to consider the time to find it, too. You can often get an already-compiled list for less than you think. For business-to-business (B2B) marketing, try InfoUSA or Dun and Bradstreet. For business-to-consumer marketing, InfoUSA is a good choice. Or work with a full-service list broker like me to license 5,000 names or more. You can get a list, and download the data into your contact management system. This can be absolutely worth it in terms of productivity. Instead of working on compiling the list, you can get on the phone." Bowen recommends:

To search out your own B2B prospects, try using a combination of LinkedIn and Data.com's Jigsaw. With Jigsaw, you can download lists of companies for free. On LinkedIn, you can search for companies and find out who the key players are. Then you can get phone numbers and e-mail addresses from Jigsaw. Either pay a membership fee to access contact information, or build up points by entering other contact information you've collected.

It's easy to find a list of companies that fit, but it's harder to get the names of all the marketing directors or human resource directors. You have to search online or call and ask, "Who is the person responsible for. . .?" But if you can't find a list that's exactly what you need, buying the closest match can be easier than compiling one from scratch.

Keep in mind the difference between prospects and suspects. Prospects are people you have talked to, so you and they both know they need your services. Suspects are people you think should need you, but they don't know it yet. When you buy a list, you're getting suspects. To turn them into prospects, you have to contact them.

A WORD ABOUT FEAR

It is perfectly normal to feel apprehensive about calling strangers on the phone. You have no idea how your call is going to be received, and if the person on the other end refuses to speak with you or isn't interested, it's hard not to take it personally. You may not even realize that you are afraid of making calls, but somehow, mysteriously, a hot lead will sit on your desk day after day and you just won't get around to picking up the phone. Perhaps you'll resort to sending a letter or e-mail without a companion phone call, which is nowhere near as effective.

Try asking yourself, "What is the worst thing that could possibly happen if I made that call?" Would it be hearing, "Don't bother me," or "Not interested"? Or would it be worse if the person you called was interested and you got tongue-tied and lost the sale? You know, though, if you don't place the call, you've lost the sale anyway. So how bad could making the call really be?

The fact is that most people are polite in their refusals. They say, "No, thank you," and hang up. And when someone is interested in what you have to offer, the conversation gets easy pretty quickly; your prospect may actually help you along.

So what do you think: Can you pick up the phone? You'll never know what you are missing out on unless you make the call.

What You Miss When You Fear to Persist

Alan Weiss, Ph.D.; www.summitconsulting.com

"The most common fright of all, perhaps, is that of rejection," muses Alan Weiss, author of forty-four books, including the bestseller *Million Dollar Consulting*. In his newsletter *The Balancing Act*, Dr. Weiss says,

> We simply don't want to be unliked, unaccepted, or unappealing. I've seen people with superb credentials and qualifications surrender to the less well-informed and educated because they don't want to incur displeasure. In normal negotiations, whether over salary, assignments, or opportunities, many people refuse to support their own legitimate positions because they are frightened of being rejected or seen as resistant. The inevitable results of such acquiescence is that people become angry at themselves later for missing the moment, and engage in the debilitating rituals of "I should have said. . . ." and "Why didn't I. . . ." In other words, not only do they abandon the negotiation, but they beat themselves up later for doing so.

> We're frightened because our egos are involved. Our carefully sculpted self-identities might suffer if we are unattractive to others, not accepted by our peers, and not compliant with everyone's needs. Ironically, in being so afraid to alienate others, we end up alienating ourselves. We sacrifice our potential to help others by delimiting our own growth and goals. My son used to tell me that he wasn't frightened by the dark, he was frightened by what might be in the dark. Fair enough. Buy a flashlight and shine it on the worst rejection you can anticipate. You'll find there's little to worry about except your ego, and then you can stop being so frightened.

STRATEGY: NETWORKING AND REFERRAL BUILDING

SUCCESS INGREDIENTS:

Live networking venues	**Networking skills**
Online networking venues	**Referral partners**

Recipe: Attending Live Events

Meeting people at live events is one of the easiest and most effective ways to fill your marketing pipeline—easy, that is, if you're not afraid of talking to strangers. All you have to do is match your market niche definition with the member profile of an existing association, organization, institution, or social group, and go shake hands.

The places where you go to meet people are your **live networking venues**. Here are some popular choices for networking in person:

▶ Chamber of Commerce mixers, workshops, and award ceremonies

▶ Service clubs such as Rotary, Lions, and Kiwanis

▶ Trade and professional association meetings where your *clients* are likely to gather

▶ Trade and professional association meetings where your *referral partners* are likely to gather

▶ Lectures, classes, workshops, and conferences hosted by educational institutions, vendors, community organizations, churches, and affinity groups

▶ Social, cultural, and sporting events or fund raisers that include receptions or other mix-and-mingle time

▶ Volunteer opportunities for a nonprofit that serves your niche or a community project

▶ Groups and clubs for people with shared interests, such as book clubs, running clubs, or single parents' groups

▶ Private gatherings organized for the purpose of meeting new people and schmoozing

▶ Lead exchange groups, where people in noncompetitive businesses gather weekly or monthly to swap leads and referrals

The best venues for networking are those intended to be a place for people to meet. If you attend a function like this, you can be assured that saying hello to someone you don't know will be accepted and welcome. Just walk up to anyone who looks interesting, stick out your hand, and say, "Hi, I haven't met you yet." Give people your 10-second introduction and ask about them.

If you are not naturally outgoing, you may find that groups with a more structured format work better for you than informal mixers and receptions. Many networking events offer "introductions," which means that members get a chance to stand up and tell the whole group what they do. Attendees may also be able to display or distribute flyers, brochures, or business cards. Even more structured than this is a lead exchange group.

Where do you find groups and events like this? Start by asking around. Anyone who is a likely referral partner for you can probably suggest some. Here are some other places you can look:

▶ **Websites that list events.** Do a keyword search for your city—e.g., "Boston events," or search Meetup.com or Eventbrite.com.

▶ **Associations or professional organizations.** Search online for groups that serve your niche and your area—e.g., "Austin psychology association" or "Nashville writers' organization".

▶ **Social media channels.** Look for the type of event you might like on your favorite social media site—e.g., search for "Seattle conference" in LinkedIn's Events area, or search for "Chicago networking" on Twitter.

▶ **Regional and local newspapers.** Look for a "Business Calendar" or "Community Calendar" section in print or online.

- ▸ **Chamber of Commerce.** Ask for a list of local business and community organizations.

- ▸ **Business Times** or *Business Journal* for your metropolitan area.

- ▸ **Specialized publications** aimed at your market niche's profession or area of special interest.

In looking for events to attend, keep in mind that the way to get the most value from a group is to be a member of it. You will have more success in your networking if you go back to the same groups over and over than if you keep going to new groups all the time. Find two or three that seem to have the right mix of prospects and/or referral sources, and keep going back.

So what if you are uncomfortable talking to strangers? Acquiring good **networking skills** will benefit you in all areas of your marketing. It's important to learn to introduce yourself smoothly, start a conversation with someone you don't know, and be comfortable when talking about your business in social settings. You might try practicing with friends, look for a workshop you could take, or read one of the many books on networking or mingling.

Recipe: Meeting People Online

The Internet has created an abundance of new ways to network without leaving your home or office. In addition to the major social media sites, for any given market niche, you will find hundreds of online communities, blogs, and Web-based events dedicated to serving it. If it makes sense for your market niche and your preferred working style to network online, you will need to identify some **online networking venues.** As with live networking, you will get the most value from regular participation in one or two networks, rather than choosing a large number of networks and dropping in only occasionally.

Here are some of the many channels you might take advantage of to get more prospects or referral sources in your pipeline:

- ▸ **Social media networks.** The best way to meet new people through social media is to begin by connecting with people you know. You can search for people by name or affiliation, or connect your address book to locate everyone you have an e-mail address for. Then expand your network by requesting to connect with second-degree contacts or friends of friends, as you might on LinkedIn or Facebook. Or follow others to encourage them to follow you back, as you might on Twitter or Google +.

▶ **Message boards and discussion groups.** Membership organizations, media outlets, vendors, services like Google Groups and Yahoo! Groups, and social media networks like Facebook and LinkedIn all offer online discussion forums where participation is often free. You can read and post questions and comments on any topic related to the forum's theme. Answering a posted question is an excellent way to attract prospects by demonstrating your expertise to a large number of people at once. Don't promote your services directly (unless the forum encourages this). Instead, include a brief signature box with your reply that lets members know what you do and how to reach you; for example:

Breeze Carlile, Move Coordinator

It's a Breeze ~ Moving Gracefully

San Francisco Bay Area ~ (415) 309-1860

www.itsabreezemoving.com

Relocation & reorganization for households and estates

▶ **Web chats and webinars.** These online discussions and presentations on specific themes are typically offered by membership organizations, educational institutions, vendors, and subject matter experts. Unlike discussion forums, these conversations take place in real time. Some are moderated or have a guest speaker who teaches a class or leads a discussion. Others consist of open conversation among all the participants. In live Web chats or Twitter chats, you interact by typing messages on your keyboard that others can see on their screen. In a webinar or Web conference, online visuals are combined with an audio presentation or discussion.

In either case, you can often connect privately with other participants during the conversation using an instant messaging or direct message option. This allows you to identify people in the chat environment that you would like to meet, then contact them directly to introduce yourself. Again, avoid being overly self-promotional. One appropriate approach is to offer another participant additional resources at no charge in answer to a question he or she asked.

▶ **Blogs.** While publishing your own blog is primarily a writing and publicity tactic, reading and commenting on others' blogs can be a powerful networking approach. When you comment on a blog post, you are making a connection with the author and all of her readers as well. The readers of many blogs become a strong virtual community, following each others' comments as well as the opinions of the blog's author. People reading your thoughts about the blog's topic will become acquainted with your work, and may contact you directly to find out more. Many blog readers are also blog writers. So if your comments are valuable, you may find yourself being quoted or linked to by other blogs.

Adding More Links to Your Marketing Chain

David Teten and Scott Allen, www.thevirtualhandshake.com

"If becoming an expert in your field is part of your marketing strategy, online networks give you a much more accessible outlet than the media," suggest David Teten and Scott Allen, authors of *The Virtual Handshake: Opening Doors and Closing Deals Online*. "You can speak up in a mailing list, discussion forum, or blog, and reach hundreds or thousands of people. Say something useful, original, and profound, and your online comments will get quoted and linked to, reaching even more people." According to Teten and Allen,

> Every signature on a post and every online profile is an opportunity to reinforce your brand. Link to your website in your e-mail signature. Link to the communities you belong to from your website. Link to your personal profile page from your community page. Link, link, link. Focus on awareness, not persuasion. Your participation, your signatures, and your profiles will create awareness. Those who are interested will be attracted to you and will come to you for information and assistance.

> A common mistake many marketers make when dealing with online communication is in thinking that it can be turned on and off like an advertising campaign. Online networks are generally not very receptive to marketing messages from brand new members. You must earn the right to talk about your product through participation in and contribution to the community. Long gaps in your participation will be noticed, and if your participation conveniently peaks for the two weeks before your marketing campaign, people will see it as manipulative.

Recipe: Following Up with New Contacts

If you don't follow up with the new people you meet, you are wasting your time in meeting them. It is simply untrue that someone will "contact you when they need you." The truth is that if they have met you only once, they probably don't even remember you, and it's even less likely that they will remember where to find you.

In networking, remembering the know-like-and-trust factor is critical. If you give people a chance to know you better, they will be much more likely to do business with you or refer others. But building relationships like this takes repeated contacts over time. There is much more about follow-up in Chapter 8, but the focus here is on how to follow up with new people you meet at live events or online.

When you return from attending a live event, sort all the new contacts you've collected into three categories: prospective clients, useful networking contacts, and other. Now sort the prospect category into hot, warm, and cool leads. A hot lead would be someone who already expressed an interest in doing business with you. A warm lead would be someone who mentioned a problem or goal you know you can help with.

Stop right there and follow up with all the hot and warm leads. Call each one on the phone, reintroduce yourself, and try to have a sales conversation or make an appointment for one. If directly soliciting business is inappropriate due to your profession (psychotherapy, for example) or the nature of the relationship (maybe it's your child's teacher), you can still make contact, perhaps by sending a "nice-to-meet-you" note. When you get voice mail or someone requests more information, send a letter or e-mail with a fact sheet or link to your website. For all your new contacts, capture them in your contact management system to keep track of their contact information and prompt you when to follow up again. If you use a broadcast e-mail system for follow-up, you might also capture them there, with their permission. You may also wish to add them to your social media network by requesting to connect or following them.

Next, go to the useful networking contacts and sort them into two categories: people whom you believe can lead you directly to prospective clients and people who can lead you to other marketing opportunities, such as a new networking group or a speaking engagement. Stop and follow up with the people who might ultimately have leads for you. Call them to suggest coffee or lunch, or offer to stop by the office. Remember your intention to build an ongoing relationship. Listen for clues about their interests, concerns, and goals. Consider what you might be able to offer them to create some reciprocity in your relationship. Then capture them in your contact management system for later follow-up.

You should now have three groups left: cool client leads, people who can lead you to marketing opportunities, and other. If you are short on time or have other hot leads in the pipeline, send those cool leads a nice-to-meet-you note, and tuck them away in your contact management system in case you need them later. If the new marketing opportunities fit into your current plans, go ahead and contact those people. Otherwise treat them just like the cool leads.

And those people in the "other" group? Unless they belong to people you would like to have a personal friendship with, toss them out. If they aren't worth following up with now, they don't belong in your contact management system.

With new contacts you meet online, it's also important to categorize and track them so you can follow up appropriately. Once online acquaintances have asked about working with you or otherwise shown interest in what you offer, it's appropriate to capture their information from the online venue where you met them and enter them into your contact management system for future follow-up. Until they express this interest, however, many online community members consider it a breach of protocol to directly approach fellow members as prospects. Some online communities expressly forbid any unsolicited selling to other members, so make sure you stay within community guidelines.

The best way to convert your network members from online acquaintances to true prospects or referral sources is to be an active participant in the network. On social media networks, post updates regularly, and make sure to provide helpful or entertaining content, not just promotional messages. Comment on the updates posted by other members as well. On message boards and discussion groups, reply to queries from other members with relevant, useful information. On blogs, comment on the original post, or in response to comments posted by others.

Before participating in any online forum, spend some time observing how the existing members tend to communicate. When you have a good sense of the accepted protocol, start making your own contributions. Remember that your goal in online networking is the same as for any other networking environment: building relationships. Serving as a helpful resource and getting to know people better over time will further your marketing goals. Using the community as another advertising medium for your marketing messages will not get you clients, and may even get you banned from membership.

Recipe: Networking with Referral Partners

A **referral partner** is a person, group, or institution willing to refer potential clients to you. Building relationships with referral partners can be an almost effortless way to fill your marketing pipeline. If enough people begin referring business to you, you will eventually achieve the enviable position of being able to respond to client inquiries instead of having to initiate each contact yourself.

A prospective client who is referred to you is much more likely to buy what you have to sell than someone who hasn't been referred. The endorsement of the person making the referral carries a lot of weight, increasing the know-like-and-trust factor immediately. Referred prospects are less likely to shop for the lowest price, ask fewer questions about your background and expertise, and typically come to a decision much more quickly. If soliciting business is inappropriate in your profession, referrals may be your primary source of clients.

For all these reasons, concentrating effort on building referrals can be a very worthwhile use of your time. While some of the best referrals come from past clients, there are many other possible referral partners for any business. Here are some examples:

▶ **Other prospects.** People you have spoken or met with but aren't ready to buy from you now will still refer you to others, if you remember to keep in touch with them.

▶ **Colleagues.** Others in your field can be excellent referral sources. If you offer noncompetitive services, you may even decide to collaborate on projects, form a strategic alliance, or approach prospective clients together.

▶ **Competitors.** Don't rule out your competitors as referral partners. You may have an area of specialty that they don't. They may also have times when they can't handle all the business that comes to them or can't take on a particular client because of a conflict of interest.

▶ **Others who serve your market.** Anyone who is in regular contact with your market niche is a potential referral partner, regardless of the field he or she is in. A computer network installer might easily collect referrals from the owner of a moving company, a commercial property manager, or a security systems salesperson—all people who might know about an upcoming office relocation. A strategic alliance with a partner like this could also allow you to bundle your services or products together.

▶ **Salespeople.** Regardless of what they sell, salespeople are used to the process of giving and receiving referrals. If you make friends with someone who sells for a living, he or she will naturally be on the lookout for possible leads for you. Start with the salespeople who sell to *you*.

▶ **Centers of influence.** These are the people in your field or geographic area everyone seems to know. You see them at networking events, read their names online, and hear them mentioned everywhere. People like this get asked for referrals all the time, so you want your name to be in their contact management system.

▶ **Organizations.** When a prestigious nonprofit or educational institution refers you, it is an implied endorsement, and makes you very attractive to prospective clients. Building relationships with organizations like this typically requires volunteering your professional services or teaching for them.

To begin identifying potential referral partners, develop a list of categories that represents the type of people or groups you think would be good candidates. For example, if you were an executive recruiter specializing in high-tech start-ups and rapidly growing companies, your referral partner categories might be:

▶ Accountants who serve this market
▶ Attorneys specializing in stock offerings, contracts, patents, trademarks, and other relevant areas
▶ Business development consultants
▶ Business and investment bankers
▶ Entrepreneurship centers
▶ Human resource management consultants
▶ Marketing consultants
▶ Venture capitalists

When you have identified some promising categories, look through your existing contacts to see whom you already know who fits. Call those people up, and say, "You know, I think we may be able to help each other get more clients. Can we get together and talk about it?" When you meet, ask them if there is anyone else they might suggest you talk to. After you have contacted the people you already know, and the people whom *they* know, you can add to your circle of referral partners further by employing the same strategies you are using to discover and attract clients.

The best referral partnerships are reciprocal. If the two of you are operating in the same market niche, the possibility of referrals flowing both ways is quite high. You might simply refer each other prospects when an occasion arises, or help each other more strategically by swapping contact lists or introducing each other to your contacts. But even if you can't imagine how you would be able to refer business to the person you are contacting, don't let that stop you. Savvy businesspeople are always looking for qualified professionals to add to their referral bank, because it helps them take good care of their own clients.

When you speak with a potential referral partner, find out as much about the partner's business as you tell her about yours. Exchange marketing literature and several business cards, or familiarize yourself with your partner's website. Ask who would be a good referral for your partner, and explain what type of client you are looking for. End your conversation by asking, "Is there anything else you need to feel confident in referring prospective clients to me?"

Be sure to thank your partners for each and every referral, whether it turns into business for you or not. A prompt "thank you" will generate more referrals. Keep in touch with your partners over time, just as you do with prospective and former clients. And remember to be on the lookout for referrals you can give to your partners. That's the best way possible to stay in touch with them.

Reframing Can Lead to Referring

Bob Burg, www.burg.com

"Referrals are the direct result of doing the correct things in the referral-gathering process," declares Bob Burg, author of *Endless Referrals* and co-author of *The Go-Giver*. "Most people ask, 'Do you know anyone who would be a good prospect for my widgets?' This approach usually elicits a couple of seconds of deep thought followed by, 'Well, I can't think of anyone right now, but when I do, I'll call you.' Ah, but how often do they ever actually call?" Burg explains:

> The problem is you're asking them to pick individuals out of a crowd in their mind of about 250 people. That's the average person's sphere of influence. It's like being asked if you've heard any good jokes lately. Personally, although I'm exposed to jokes every day over the Internet, I can never think of one at the time I'm asked.

Tom Hopkins, in his book *How to Master the Art of Selling,* advises helping your referrer isolate specific people they can identify and remember by narrowing their frame of reference. How? Here's a brief example:

"You: Dave, you're an avid golfer, aren't you?"
"Dave: Yes, I am. I play every weekend."
"You: Hmm. Is there a specific foursome you play with?"
"Dave: Absolutely, Tom Smith, Rita Jones, and Harry Browne."
"You: Dave, would any of them seem to be good candidates for . . . ?"

One more example. We know Dave is a Rotarian. Instead of asking if "anyone" in Rotary would be a good prospect (that's still too large a frame), try:
"You: Are there one or two people in your club that you tend to sit with every meeting?"
"Dave: Just one—Mike O'Brien. Been friends for years."
"You: Do you feel Mike would be a good candidate for . . . ?"

Have three or four specific frames of reference that you know in advance you are going to ask about. All it takes is one name to trigger off an avalanche of referrals.

STRATEGY: PUBLIC SPEAKING

SUCCESS INGREDIENTS:

Speaking venues
Speaking topics/bio

Recipe: Learning to Speak in Public

Speaking in public creates positive visibility, boosts your credibility, and establishes you as an expert in your field. It puts you in direct contact with potential clients in such a powerful way that you may find yourself closing a sale as soon as your talk is over. With all the benefits public speaking offers, it's unfortunate that surveys show most people are more afraid of speaking in public than of dying!

If this is true for you, don't include public speaking on your list of strategies just yet. You want to make a good impression on your prospective clients, and you're not going to do that if you're quaking in your boots. Work on getting some practice first. The best way to reduce the fear of public speaking is to get experience speaking in public.

Try taking a class at a nearby community college or from a local teacher. Join a local Toastmasters International group, where people meet regularly to practice their speaking and get feedback on their delivery. Or look for a Speaking Circle in your area. These are groups led by trained facilitators that assist you in developing a natural and authentic speaking style.

You can also work gradually on becoming a better public speaker by gaining more experience. Start by participating in a networking or lead exchange group that requires members to introduce themselves at every meeting. Your next step might be volunteering to host part of a program or make announcements for a group you are part of. After that, you might be ready to serve on a panel, where it is common to speak while staying seated and referring to notes.

Over time, you will get more comfortable at being in front of a group and be able to carry off a solo talk without experiencing panic. You may even grow to like public speaking, and graduate to conducting a breakout session at a conference or even a full-length workshop.

Recipe: Finding Places to Speak

When you are ready to get started with speaking to promote your business, you will first need to locate some **speaking venues**. These are the places, groups, or events where you can give free presentations to prospective clients or referral partners. "Free" doesn't mean there is no admission charge. It means you, the speaker, are not being paid, although in some cases you may receive an honorarium. Here are some suggested venues:

- ▸ Chamber of Commerce meetings and workshops
- ▸ Service clubs such as Rotary, Lions, and Kiwanis
- ▸ Trade and professional association meetings and conferences
- ▸ Lectures, classes, workshops, and conferences hosted by educational

institutions, vendors, community organizations, churches, and affinity groups

▶ Classes offered by community colleges, resource centers, and adult learning centers

▶ Groups and clubs for people with shared interests, such as job clubs, investing clubs, or writers' groups

▶ Teleseminars, webinars, Web chats, podcasts, and videocasts hosted by membership organizations, educational institutions, and vendors

If some of the entries on this list look suspiciously like those on the list of suggested places to network, you have noticed something very important! Public speaking is superpowered networking. You can speak to the same groups you might otherwise just visit, and you can find them using some of the same resources mentioned for networking and referral building earlier in this chapter. But as the speaker, you will be the center of attention instead of being just another member of the audience.

As with networking, you don't necessarily have to leave your home or office to be a speaker. In addition to the Web chat and webinar environments described in the earlier section on online networking, teleseminars, videocasts, and podcasts are an increasingly popular format for virtual speaking. Teleseminars, also known as teleclasses or teleforums, are seminars by telephone held on teleconference bridge lines. Dozens or even hundreds of participants listen live and can usually ask questions of the speaker during or after the session. Videocasts and podcasts are one-way presentations delivered over the Internet. Videocasts consist of live or recorded video, often combined with other visuals, viewed online. Podcasts are audio recordings which can be listened to online or downloaded to a portable MP3 player. Many of these virtual presentations take the form of an interview, where you as the guest expert are asked questions by the regular host.

Keep in mind that the strategy of public speaking has such a high effectiveness rating due to the perceived endorsement of the group hosting the event and the fact that the host organization invites and enrolls all the participants. Hosting your own speaking event is not a public speaking tactic; it's a promotional event, and is much less effective. So to use the public speaking tactics described in this section, you'll need to find groups to host you as a speaker.

Recipe: Getting Booked as a Speaker

To approach any of these groups about being a speaker, you will need to develop one to three **speaking topics** you would like to present. Your topics should be interesting, distinctive, and showcase your specialized expertise without being excessively self-promotional. They should also allow you to tell stories about your work and include examples of what you have done for clients. In this way, you can deliver valuable content to your audience and promote yourself effectively at the same time.

Most networking groups, service clubs, and professional associations give their guest speakers between 20 and 60 minutes for their talk. Conference breakout sessions and virtual speaking opportunities typically last from 60 to 90 minutes. Workshops and classes can run from 90 minutes to three hours. When you are speaking on an unpaid basis to fill your marketing pipeline, you will typically not want to present programs longer than three hours. Presenting longer seminars or multi-session classes should normally be reserved for paying engagements.

Give your presentation topics enticing titles that will attract plenty of prospects when publicized in a group's newsletter and announcement mailings. Write brief descriptions of each topic that will give group organizers enough information to decide if they like it, and can also be used to promote your talk once it is scheduled. (A sample topic description appears in Figure 7-2.)

The second essential tool for getting yourself booked as a speaker is a **speaker's bio** to accompany your topic descriptions. This can be the same professional biography you might display on your website or include in a marketing kit, with one important addition: include any prior speaking experience you have.

If you have given only one or two presentations, you might just add a line to your bio like, "Carlos Maldonado's presentations have been well received by organizations such as the Miami Independent Computer Consultants' Association and the South Florida Technology Consortium." If your speaking experience is more extensive, you can list the places you have spoken separately.

It's a good idea to include your website's URL in the bio you provide. If the group decides to invite you to speak, they will typically print your bio exactly as you wrote it. Then when the group's members see your program advertised, they will know how to find you, and may visit your site before or after your talk.

If you have never spoken in public and have no credits to list on your bio,

Figure 7-2: Speaking Topic and Bio Example

Speak Like a Pro: Tips and Techniques to Become a Polished Presenter

Wouldn't it be great to be able to stand in front of an audience of hundreds of people and hold them in complete captivation? Would you like to go into a presentation confident that they're going to love you, and overhear comments afterwards such as "He was excellent," or "She made a real connection with her audience"? This program offers proven tips that will help you speak like a pro . . . in a short time!

You will learn how to:

- ▶ Develop comfort and confidence
- ▶ Write and deliver a winning presentation
- ▶ Connect with your audience
- ▶ Persuade people to act on what you say
- ▶ Enroll clients to purchase your services and products

Your Presenter:

Sandra Schrift has spent 20-plus years working with over 1,500 professional speakers. She founded the first national professional speakers bureau in San Diego in 1982. Today she is a speech coach to executives who want to improve their presentation skills, as well as a career coach to both the emerging and veteran professional speaker who wants to grow a profitable speaking business. Sandra is also the founder of the first virtual university for emerging public speakers, Speakers University, which conducts ongoing teleclasses for anyone, anywhere in the English-speaking world. Find out more about Sandra at www.schrift.com.

---

don't let that stop you. If you believe you can do a good job, go for it. You have to give your first talk sometime.

With your topic descriptions and bio prepared, you are ready to start approaching your chosen venues. For networking groups, Chambers of Commerce, service clubs, association meetings, and vendor-sponsored programs, you will typically need to contact the program chairperson or program director. This is sometimes a volunteer working out of his or her own home or office. It's a good idea to find out more about the group before you contact the chairperson. You want to make sure the audience is right for you and be able to tell the chair why your topic would be of interest.

Visit the group's website to find out what sort of topics and speakers they usually have. Or, contact the group and ask for information about their upcoming events. Most groups will send you an information packet or newsletter. This will tell you more about the group and probably also give you the program chair's name, if it isn't on their website. If you still think this group is an appropriate venue for you, contact the program chair directly by phone or e-mail. Don't waste your time sending information to the group's main postal or e-mail address; it will probably be discarded.

If the program chair expresses interest, find out how far ahead the group is scheduling speakers, and send the chairperson your topics and bio. Then follow up after an appropriate interval to see if you are able to get yourself on the program.

With conferences, educational institutions, resource centers, and adult learning centers, study last year's schedule or the current catalog before you contact them. If they already have a program on your topic, see if you can find a new and different angle that hasn't yet been covered. When you're sure you have something fresh to propose, call the department chair or program director to see if the organization is interested. You will probably be asked to submit a proposal, for which the group may or may not have written guidelines. If no guidelines are available, send a description of your proposed topic and speaker's bio, with a cover letter explaining why you think this topic will be popular with the organization's audience. And don't forget to follow up.

Turn a Pack of Wolves into Purring Kittens

Carolyn Campbell, www.carolyncampbell.biz

Coach and trainer Carolyn Campbell reports that when people call her for help with speaking, they often begin, "I know I should speak more, but I hate getting up in front of people." Here are some ways Campbell suggests to overcome the speaking jitters and start having more fun:

▶ **Choose an inspiring topic.** Make a list of issues you're passionate about, and choose the one that most excites you. You'll be surprised how it will pique interest in others. Find out more about your audience and integrate their needs into your program.

▶ **Come early.** Arrive at least an hour ahead to set up. Test everything, especially anything technical, and adjust what you can to suit your needs.

> ➤ **Connect before you speak.** As people settle in, introduce yourself. Ask people's names and their interest in the topic. During your presentation, address as many as you can by name. They feel special, and you feel connected.
>
> ➤ **Honor your nerves.** If you are nervous, say so. Then quickly segue into your topic. Audiences appreciate your forthrightness as long as you swiftly gain confidence and demonstrate your expertise.
>
> ➤ **Create interaction.** Audience members enjoy connecting with speakers. Ask them questions, or have them ask you questions. Include a call and response or visualization. Choose a few different ways to interact that suit you and your style.
>
> ➤ **End strong.** Finish your talk with a powerful close. It might be a quote, a probing question, or a challenge for them to take action.
>
> ➤ **Invite further connection.** People who like what you say will want to know how to stay in touch, work with you, or donate to your cause.
>
> And most importantly, remember people came because they were interested in what you have to share. Don't worry about being perfect, focus on being connected.

STRATEGY: WRITING AND PUBLICITY

SUCCESS INGREDIENTS:

Writing/publishing venues	**Publicity venues**
Articles or writing queries	**Press release/media kit**
Blog theme/topics	**Photos/audio/video**

Recipe: Writing Articles or Tips

Just like public speaking, writing **articles** for your market niche can help you become more credible as well as more visible. A well-written article or a series of useful tips on a subject of interest to your niche will get their attention, demonstrate your expertise, and increase your name recognition. You can publish and publicize your articles in a wide variety of ways:

- ▶ Submit your articles to magazines, trade journals, newspapers, websites, newsletters, e-zines, and online article directories
- ▶ Publish articles or tips in your own e-zine or blog, and on your website
- ▶ Write a regular column for a publication or website
- ▶ Guest blog for other bloggers writing for your niche
- ▶ Include copies of your articles in your marketing kit or media kit
- ▶ Send copies of (or links to) an article to people on your follow-up list with a "thought-you-would-be-interested" note
- ▶ Send copies or links to all your clients
- ▶ Notify your social media network and blog readers of new articles and link to where they are published
- ▶ Use articles or a collection of tips as a handout at trade shows and speaking engagements
- ▶ When you speak to a group, offer to send articles or tips to anyone who gives you their e-mail address
- ▶ Leave an article behind with prospects after you have a sales conversation or include one with a proposal
- ▶ Frame your published article and hang it on your office wall
- ▶ Compile your articles or tips into a free e-book that you give to prospects or subscribers to your mailing list

The first step in getting an article published beyond your own newsletter or website is to identify appropriate **writing or publishing venues**. What print and online publications do the people in your market niche read? What websites do they visit? Ask your clients and prospects what publications they subscribe to, browse regularly, or buy. Notice which periodicals are lying on their desks or poking out of their briefcases, what publications they link to on social media, and which e-zines they forward to you.

For print publications, you can look up possible venues in directories for writers, such as those published by Writer's Market. For websites, blogs, and e-zines, you can look them up online by doing keyword searches for your target market or professional specialty.

As with public speaking, the best topics for your articles will be those that allow you to share valuable information with your audience, but are not self-promotional in nature. An article that is little more than a sales pitch for your services won't get much attention.

If you are new to getting your writing published, start with publications and websites that don't require much writing experience. Association newsletters are an excellent first target, as are the blogs and e-zines of colleagues, referral partners, and vendors in your niche. Online article directories that collect articles for free use by editors and publishers (e.g., EzineArticles or Articlesbase) will accept articles from first-time authors.

Other possibilities are employee newsletters, community newspapers, or advertising periodicals, like those that list homes for sale or job openings. Once you have been published in a few venues like these, you will have a track record as a writer and be able to approach publications and websites with more readers and a higher profile.

In most cases, you won't be paid for your articles. What you will receive, however, is an extended byline or "bio slug" printed at the end of your article, where you can describe your professional services and give your contact information and/or website URL.

Many venues will be happy to accept a completed article or allow you to pitch your article idea with a phone call or brief e-mail. Other publications, particularly the more prestigious ones, will require a **writing query** first. If you're not sure what a particular venue requires, look for editorial guidelines on its website, or contact the appropriate editor or blog owner and ask. Most print publications list the name and department of each editor in a box near the table of contents, or for newspapers, in the editorial section.

If you contact the editor by phone, be prepared to pitch your article idea on the spot. Describe your proposed topic, explain why it is of interest to readers, and tell why you should be the one who writes it. A brief e-mail query should contain the same details. If you're convincing enough, many publications will give you the assignment right then. Others will ask you to send a formal query letter and include links to samples of your writing.

If a publication's guidelines request that you query first, don't try to skip this step by sending a completed article in the hope that the publication will print it. It's likely the editor won't even look at it, and you will have wasted your time.

A query letter should begin with a strong lead paragraph, written just as if it were the opening paragraph of the actual article. You want it to capture the editor's interest, introduce your topic, and show that you can write. Continue the letter by describing two or three key points you intend to have your article to make. Then propose the article itself: "I would like to write a 1,500-word article on the benefits to employers of integrated disability management programs. I plan to interview three employers who have experienced significant cost reductions. . . ."

Conclude the letter with a brief description of your background that indicates why you are qualified to write the article. If you have previously been published, include links to two or three samples of your writing in your letter. Query letters are typically sent via e-mail.

The elapsed time it takes editors to respond to a query varies widely. Follow up after 30 days if you haven't heard anything. If the publication you are querying requests "first rights" for the articles it publishes, don't send the same query to another editor until you are sure the first one doesn't want it.

Once you have had an article published in one venue, don't stop there. Many publications and websites are happy to accept previously published articles. When you have an article published, make sure you are agreeing to give the publication only first rights or one-time rights. Then you can get a great deal of mileage out of the same piece by submitting it over and over to different venues. Again, check the editorial guidelines. If first rights are not required, you can offer articles that have been previously published.

After you have successfully placed a number of articles, you might consider finding a venue for an ongoing column. Landing a regular column with a publication or website respected by your target market is a major milestone in establishing your expertise, and can significantly boost your name recognition.

Virtual Customers Have Real Expectations

Steven Van Yoder, www.getslightlyfamous.com

"This is the age of the virtual customer," declares Steven Van Yoder, author of *Get Slightly Famous*. "Although the Internet has made it perfectly reasonable to land a major client you've never met in person, it has also created new expectations." Yoder adds:

> Prospects now "Google" around to find someone with your skills. They expect you to make a good virtual case for yourself. If you appear lackluster compared to your competitors, you will lose the potential client. Think about it. You have

probably used the Internet to research a company or person you're considering doing business with. Certainly potential clients are checking you out online, too.

Publishing articles online draws upon and displays your expertise by providing useful information that website visitors are actively seeking out. Online articles position you as an expert in your field and convey a level of authority that establishes trust and sets the stage for sales.

When high-traffic, high-credibility websites and e-zines publish your articles, you ride on the coattails of their loyal relationships with readers. Your articles are seen by visitors as referrals from trusted friends.

Some of the most prime real estate in the world these days is at the top of the search engine listings. The most widely used search engines rank websites by the quantity of other websites that link to them. This means that every article you publish that links to your website can improve your search engine rankings.

The only way to be truly successful in business is by establishing a good reputation. And understanding the way business has shifted in the Internet age can help you bring the potential of marketing your business into the virtual world.

Recipe: Publish Your Own Writing with a Blog

Publishing a blog allows you to combine both writing and publicity techniques in one activity. As a blog author, you are publishing your own stories on the Web. So you are not only the writer, you are also the media outlet.

A blog allows you to post articles, tips, comments, essays, news, and resource links to a website easily and quickly. Many blogs also include photos, graphic images, and audio or video clips. Blogs can help you fill the pipeline by attracting new clients who find you through search engines, social media mentions, or links from other sites and blogs. They are also an excellent follow-up tool, and you'll read more about that in Chapter 8.

To start authoring your own blog, you will need a **blog theme** and a series of **blog topics**. The concept for your blog should be a sustainable theme of continuing interest to your market niche. Coin a clever or evocative title for your blog that expresses the theme. For example, a communication skills trainer could name her blog "Can We Talk?" and a hypnotherapist could name his "Getting Out of the Habit."

Visit several blogs aimed at your market niche to see what topics others are writing about. You'll discover that some blog posts are lengthy articles or essays, and others are brief comments or tips. Many blog posts contain links pointing readers to articles, books, news, resource sites, and items written by other bloggers. You'll also notice that authoring a blog takes commitment. Keeping your blog up to date will require posting to it regularly, once per week at minimum. You will need to develop a substantial number of topics to begin with, and keep coming up with new ones over time.

You create and update a blog using blogging platforms like WordPress or Typepad. Some platforms are free to use and some require a fee. A blog can be hosted on an existing website or you can set up a special site just for your blog. Many blogging platforms offer free hosting, although some require you to display their ads on your blog.

Like any other website, a blog must be promoted in order to receive a lot of traffic. But the good news about blogs is that they are naturally rich in keywords relevant to your market niche, so they often achieve good placement in search engines without as much additional effort on your part. Also, as you make new posts, your older posts will be archived, automatically creating multiple pages that the search engines will index. If the topics you write on are interesting, informative, and useful to people in your niche, other sites and bloggers will begin linking to your blog, sending more traffic your way.

When you first launch your blog, be sure to announce it to your clients, prospects, colleagues, and referral partners. Mention it in all your marketing materials, and link to it from your e-mail signature, any other websites you maintain, and all your social media profiles. You can also submit your blog to blog directories, such as Technorati or Blogs.com.

Each time you post, mention your new post in your social media updates. You may also wish to summarize your newest posts in your e-zine or broadcast e-mail updates.

Give your blog visitors a way to subscribe to your blog, so that they will know when you publish new posts. You can allow people to subscribe via their favorite RSS reader, such as Google Reader or Pulse. Or they can have your posts sent to them via e-mail. Some blogging platforms have this e-mailing feature built in, or you can add it with services like Feedburner or AWeber.

If setting up a blog for the first time seems too technically complex or you need design help, hire someone to help you with design and installation. After your blog has been created, you should have no trouble posting to it without assistance.

Blogging that Makes Sense

Patsi Krakoff, PsyD; www.contentforcoaches.com

"The most frequent complaint I hear about blogging is 'I don't know what to write about,'" declares Dr. Patsi Krakoff in her blog WritingOnTheWeb.com. Dr. Krakoff specializes in helping professionals market their businesses online with blogs and other Web content. "This is because many business bloggers don't have enough clarity about their blogging goals." Here's how she helps her clients solve this problem:

1. Define your business Ps & Q (3 Ps + 1 Q):

   ▶ What Problems do you solve?

   ▶ Who are the People you serve?

   ▶ What Products and services do you offer?

   ▶ What makes you uniQue?

2. Create an outline or table of contents of your expertise on these problems as if you were writing a book or teaching a class.

3. Make a list of key words, categories, and topics that should be addressed in order to solve these problems, and that you're qualified to write about.

4. Make an editorial calendar for your blog that covers all the topics and categories you listed. Make sure your search engine optimization keywords are repeated frequently in posts and titles.

5. Set up a weekly schedule for blogging that includes writing the content, sharing it on social media sites, and formatting, editing, linking, etc.

When I'm working with clients on their blogs, I often find their content is all over the map. Quite often, they blog about whatever crosses their radar that day. It might be an e-mail from a client, something they saw online, or what they're doing that week. It's no wonder readers get confused and stop reading.

Clarity has to appear not only in your mind, but for your readers as well. When you blog according to an outline, you'll have a sequence of posts that make sense for your readers. There will be an order. Brains love order.

Recipe: Getting Media Publicity

Attracting the attention of the print, broadcast, and Web media can get you quoted, interviewed, or profiled. When prospective clients see you featured in the news, your credibility and name recognition may greatly increase. The more visible you are in your profession, the more likely it is that the media will contact you, but don't just sit back and wait. Generating publicity can be relatively easy, particularly if you start with smaller outlets.

Begin by identifying the best **publicity venues**—places your market niche and referral partners will be likely to notice a quote from you, article about you, or interview with you. Here are some suggestions, beginning with some of the easier targets for your first publicity attempts:

- ▶ Blog, newsletter, or e-zine of a client or colleague
- ▶ Blog, newsletter, or e-zine of a professional association or networking group of which you are a member
- ▶ Blog, newsletter, or e-zine for alumni of your college or training school
- ▶ Blog, newsletter, or e-zine of an organization you volunteer for
- ▶ Local newspaper for your neighborhood or small town
- ▶ Local trade journal for your profession
- ▶ Local radio show that focuses on a topic in your area of expertise
- ▶ Local or regional magazine that covers topics you can speak to
- ▶ Freelance journalists who write about your field
- ▶ Blog or website that covers news, events, and personalities for your market niche
- ▶ Daily newspaper for your metropolitan area
- ▶ Local television news, magazine, or talk show
- ▶ National trade journal for your profession
- ▶ Nationally syndicated radio show
- ▶ National magazine that covers topics you can speak to
- ▶ Web media that cover news, events, and personalities nationally or internationally
- ▶ National or international print news media (e.g., *Time Magazine*, *Wall Street Journal*)
- ▶ National or international news agency (e.g., Associated Press, Reuters)
- ▶ National or international television news, magazine, or talk show

To approach the media directly, you will need the name of the appropriate editor or producer. You can also approach reporters and freelance journalists who cover the topic you are seeking publicity about. You can usually get these names by reading, watching, or listening to the media outlet you plan to approach (which is a good idea anyway). You can also look them up in resources like *Bacon's Media Directories* or search the outlet's website.

An essential tool for approaching the media directly is a well-written **press release** or pitch letter, which may be one component of a complete **media kit**. A press release is a bulletin, typically 500 words or less, that you send to the media to announce news or alert them to a story. Successful releases issued by service professionals generally fall into one of three categories:

1. **News.** You are announcing something the venues you are approaching will consider newsworthy. For an association newsletter or neighborhood newspaper, this might be the opening of your business or landing a new client. For larger media, you need bigger news, such as publication of a book or survey, an invention or discovery, or winning an award. If you don't have a major event like this to announce, don't despair. Consider what kind of problems your market niche is currently experiencing that you have a solution for. Is there a potential news story in your solution?

2. **Commentary.** This type of release is positioning you as an expert on a currently hot topic. Or, instead of a release, you might choose to write a pitch letter where you propose yourself as an interview subject or suggest a feature story about your business. "Sandwich Generation Feeling the Squeeze" could be the headline for a geriatric-care consultant's release or the opening hook in her pitch letter. Then describe the situation that makes your comments topical, give a brief summary of your expertise, and add a pithy quote from you on the topic.

3. **Tips article.** Many publications will print your press release verbatim if it is written in the form of a brief article of significant interest to their readers. Articles with a seasonal angle can be very successful. A personal shopper might write 300 words on "How to Buy Lingerie for Your Valentine," with herself as the expert quoted in the article.

Figure 7-3 illustrates a sample press release of the news variety to show you the format and style the media expects.

When you are angling for a feature article about you or a live interview on radio, TV, or the Web, you will want to supplement your press release with other material, turning it into a complete media kit which contains

Figure 7-3: Press Release Example

FOR IMMEDIATE RELEASE
Contact: Barbara McDonald
Phone: (510) 282-9817
E-mail: logolady@yahoo.com
Website: www.bmcdstudio.com

Self-Taught Designer Wins Bay Area Logo Design Contest

A logo created by Berkeley-based graphic designer Barbara McDonald was chosen over more than 250 entries received in a design contest sponsored by The San Francisco Foundation. The contest, open to Bay Area artists of all types, challenged entrants to design a new logo for The San Francisco Foundation, an organization beginning its fiftieth year of service to Bay Area communities.

The San Francisco Foundation, which awards grants to nonprofit organizations in economic development, education, environment, culture, immigration, and youth, awarded McDonald $6,000 for her winning entry and will use it on all of its printed materials, signage, and website. "I was thrilled to have just made it to the finals of the contest," said McDonald, "but then to have my logo chosen by a prestigious organization like The San Francisco Foundation was quite an honor for me."

A self-taught artist, McDonald started her career painting sets and props for the Disney Design Center, then moved into graphic design while working for a large sign company in Los Angeles. Her business, BmcDstudio, was founded in 1994, and her clients range from small business owners like herself to local restaurants such as Picante and Greens, and medium-sized companies like The California Academy of Family Physicians.

"It has always been important for me to work with people and organizations who make a positive contribution to the community, and The San Francisco Foundation is the epitome of that type of client," stated McDonald.

###

---

photos, audio, or video. This is sometimes sent to media contacts after they have expressed some interest in your story, but more commonly it is made available online. You might have a page on your website called "Press Room" or simply "Media." Here are some ideas for what your kit might include:

- ► Brief biography of yourself

- ► Profile of your company or fact sheet about your work (include benefits you offer and results you deliver)

- ► High-resolution photograph of you (or several, if your work lends itself to action photos)

- ► Other media mentions you have received (list them or give excerpts)

- ► Upcoming events where you can be seen or heard

- ► Links to articles you have published

- ► Testimonials from clients or endorsements from influential people

- ► Sample questions and answers for an interview

- ► Audio or video recording of a previous interview or of you at work

- ► Contact information and social media links

Press releases and pitch letters are typically sent by e-mail. Just as you should do when approaching prospective clients, call your media contacts after sending them a release. Pitch your story on the phone and try to get them interested. If they want your media kit, tell them where to find it.

Learning how to write an effective release, compiling a media list, sending out releases, and pitching your story to the media may be more work than you want to tackle by yourself. Hiring a full-service publicist can be expensive, but you might decide to use the services of a public relations consultant a la carte, just to write your release, for example. There are also services that will distribute your press release to their media subscribers for a fee, as well as free release distribution services that will display your release online.

Another approach to gaining visibility in the media is to write to editors, producers, or journalists who serve your market niche. Commenting on a published piece or broadcast story can sometimes get your letter printed or read on the air. But it can also get you into a media professional's contact database. Conclude your letter with your contact information and an invitation like this: "The next time you run a story on carpal tunnel syndrome or repetitive strain injuries, please feel free to contact me for background information. I am an ergonomics consultant who specializes in helping heavy keyboard users set up their offices to avoid strain and injury."

Making the News

Jill Lublin, www.jilllublin.com

"In public relations, your job is to define your expertise to the media," advises Jill Lublin, co-author of *Guerrilla Publicity* and author of *Get Noticed . . . Get Referrals*. "One of my clients is an industrial designer for corporations—interesting, but not exciting. It turns out he runs his successful company as a 'virtual corporation,' so he became an expert on that topic. That caught the media's attention, and he has been featured nationally in newspapers, radio and television." Here are Lublin's key points to remember in using public relations:

1. Be ready to define your business concisely. Prepare a 30-second introduction that includes your business, your name, and a benefit of doing business with you.

2. Know who your public is, and target your audience. Yes, the universe can be your audience, but it's very expensive to market to. Define your audience with demographics.

3. Tell your story. Why would someone want to do business with you? Find out what makes you the most interesting and relates to the largest number of people.

4. Write a press release that answers the who, what, where, when, and why of your story. A well-written, concise release with an exciting lead paragraph will increase your chances.

5. Send your release to a researched media list. Have as many names as possible that are relevant to your topic including business editors, features editors, columnists, and producers.

6. Follow up your release with phone calls. Have alternative pitches ready in case your media contact doesn't like the first one. Be precise and to the point when leaving a message.

The media is accessible. We, the public, create stories. What you see in the news is about people like you and me. Read the paper you will be talking to, watch the television show, or listen to the radio program to see where you can fit in to make some news of your own.

Recipe: Making Your Own News Online

Editors, producers, and journalists are no longer the gatekeepers they once were, allowing only certain people and stories to become "news." With blogging and social media, you can publish or broadcast your own news and make it visible around the world in an instant. For example:

- ▶ Post written stories, photos, audio, or video to your blog
- ▶ Launch a regular podcast or videocast series
- ▶ Record a collection of audios or videos to make available online
- ▶ Host an Internet radio show
- ▶ Post your written, visual, audio, or video news on your social media channels

But just because your news *can* be seen from anywhere with an Internet connection doesn't mean it *will* be seen.

There are two components to gaining more visibility for news you publish yourself: (1) publishing useful content that informs, inspires, or entertains; and (2) building a network of people who are interested in your news.

Here in the "Filling the Pipeline" chapter, it may seem contradictory to talk about building a network being a prerequisite for attracting more prospects. But that's exactly how the online world works. If you want more people to read your blog, you need some loyal readers who will comment on your posts and share them with others. If you want more prospects to view your videos, you need some fans who will point others to them. If you want your posts on Facebook and Twitter to get more attention, you need to build your base of followers.

This is one of the many reasons that direct contact and follow-up, and networking and referral building, continue to rank as the two most effective ways for an independent professional to market. Your first followers, fans, and readers will almost always be people you already know, personally meet, or are referred to you by those who trust you.

Once you have an initial base of contacts like this, attracting more prospects online becomes significantly easier.

STRATEGY: PROMOTIONAL EVENTS

SUCCESS INGREDIENTS:

· ·

Promotion concept

Promotion plan

Recipe: Putting on a Show

Organizing or participating in a promotional event can consume a significant amount of time and money. Before making a commitment to put on a show, check your budget. Add up all the costs of producing the event, promoting it, and making a good showing at it. Divide the total by the number of clients you can honestly expect to get as a result of the event, to see how much each client is going to cost you. Do you still think it's worth it? Can you think of an easier or cheaper way to get the same number of clients?

Only if your event passes this test should you go ahead with it. Many professionals have found exhibit booths at trade shows to be an expensive mistake. On the other hand, free demonstrations or workshops have been a solid source of clients for others. Ask your colleagues what has worked, and not worked, for them.

To create a promotional event or participate in someone else's, a **promotion concept** is the starting place. Here are some ideas for promotional events you might consider:

▶ Display table at your networking group's business fair or expo

▶ Exhibit booth or demonstration at a trade show, vendor fair, or community event

▶ Hosting a networking event, reception, or open house at your place of business or an event space

> ▶ Being a sponsor for a fundraising event or awards ceremony

> ▶ Demonstrating or exhibiting your work in your office or studio, or a public location

> ▶ Offering a free or low-cost workshop

> ▶ Producing a free teleclass or a series of teleseminars or webinars

> ▶ Sponsoring a giveaway, contest, or survey

When you have come up with a concept that you like and tested its financial viability, you're ready to make a **promotion plan**. The more elaborate your event is, the more extensive your planning needs. Here are some elements your plan might include:

> ▶ **Advance Publicity.** Even if the event is sponsored by someone else, you will get more mileage from it if you invite your own prospects to attend. Many trade shows and fund-raisers will provide you with postcards, flyers, an e-mail announcement, sample social media posts, a social media page to share, or a website badge you can use to spread the word. If you are the sponsor, evaluate all the marketing techniques at your disposal to determine what combination might work the best. You may want to mail or e-mail invitations, distribute or post flyers, create an event page on a social media channel, post updates about your event on your blog and social media networks, issue press releases, purchase ad space, or ask colleagues to send announcements to their mailing lists and share the event with their social media networks.

> ▶ **Exhibit or Display.** Your exhibit booth or display table should reflect your level of professionalism and visually display your expertise. A banner or sign board will make your exhibit more visible when other exhibits are present. Use photographs, video, testimonial letters, press clippings, or samples of your work to make what you do as tangible as possible. Try to find out what sort of displays any other exhibitors will have. You don't want to look cheap or unprepared by comparison.

> ▶ **Marketing Literature.** If you participate in a large event, be prepared to give away many copies of your literature. Some attendees make a habit of taking something from each booth, regardless of whether they are actually interested. It's a good idea to have a relatively inexpensive piece available for the taking, such as a fact sheet with your contact information. Keep your

more costly brochure or marketing kit behind the table to give to serious prospects.

▶ **Script, Outline, or Presentation System.** If you are presenting a talk or workshop, design a program that will give your audience valuable information whether or not they decide to do business with you. Practice using any needed technology, such as a webinar system or PowerPoint presentation. For an exhibit, prepare in advance what you will say to people who come by your booth. Think of one good qualifying question you can ask at the outset of a conversation to see if the person you are speaking with is a prospect. Create a cheat sheet for any helpers you will have so they can answer predictable questions. If you will be conducting a demonstration, script and rehearse it. You will be the star of this show, and you don't want to flop.

▶ **Capturing Leads.** The traditional way to capture the contact information of people who attend an event is to collect business cards for a drawing or names for your mailing list. Offering a drawing for a free gift can result in collecting a large number of names with no way of knowing who is a legitimate prospect. Consider inserting a qualifier into your drawing: Ask people to answer a qualifying question on the back of their entry before dropping it in. To save time at an exhibit booth, use two stickers of different colors to indicate yes or no.

▶ **Logistical Details.** Plan ahead for all the small things that can make your event more successful—for example, extra helpers, extension cords, refreshments, giveaways, pens and paper, small bills to make change, or name tags. Try to have backup arrangements in case anything goes wrong, like an extra battery for your laptop, a backup teleconference line, or your presentation saved to a flash drive. If all the details are handled, you can concentrate on making a good impression.

STRATEGY: ADVERTISING

SUCCESS INGREDIENTS:

Advertising venues   **Ad copy, layout, or script**

Flyer venues

Recipe: Making Advertising Work

There are a number of reasons why advertising is last on the list of marketing strategies for professional services. First, there's the know-like-and-trust factor. Advertising is not an effective way to gain a prospective client's trust.

Second, advertising generates leads, not sales. People calling, e-mailing, or visiting your website because they saw an ad will take much more convincing than prospects whom you already know, or are referred to you. They will be more likely to bargain for a lower price, ask for references, or require a written proposal and lengthy sales cycle than will people who know you better.

Third, like any other marketing strategy, advertising must be done repeatedly to have an effect. Ongoing advertising can be very expensive. H & R Block can afford to advertise their tax preparation services because they have an enormous staff in many locations waiting to serve clients. The cost of this advertising is reasonable when divided by that many people, all working to generate revenue. But a two-person accounting office just can't generate enough revenue to pay for an extensive advertising campaign. This is why a small firm shouldn't copy what large companies do, thinking that is the best way to replicate their success.

The reality is that the other five strategies outlined in Chapter 1 will attract more prospects who become clients—and at a lower price—than advertising does, for the vast majority of professionals. Sure, advertising might bring you some clients, but your objective is to get the best result with the least investment of time and money.

And advertising *is* an investment—a high-risk investment. In using it, you should follow the same steps as you would to invest in anything:

1. Analyze your options carefully.
2. Choose the vehicle with the highest return at the lowest cost.
3. Don't invest what you can't afford to lose.

Does it ever make sense for an independent professional to advertise? Yes, it can. As noted in Chapter 1, advertising, *used alone*, almost never works to find clients for a professional, consultant, or coach. In other words, you should never rely on advertising to bring you clients. But it is possible to judiciously combine advertising with other strategies and produce results at a reasonable cost. For example:

> ▶ A brochure-style website, used alone, is merely an advertising tool. But combined with follow-up techniques like an e-zine, writing techniques like a blog, or networking and publicity via social media, it can become quite powerful and cost-effective.

> ▶ When producing a promotional event like a free workshop or webinar, you might advertise it to attract more attendees.

> ▶ You might run a pay-per-click ad campaign to drive traffic to a page where you collect the e-mail addresses of prospects in return for a free bonus, then follow up with them to build a relationship.

> ▶ You could produce a video to advertise your services and make it available on your website and social media channels.

> ▶ You might take the time to create a basic listing for your business in some of the online directories that offer this for free.

> ▶ If you offer products or paid seminars in addition to your services, you might choose to advertise those other lines of business. (As noted in the Introduction, the Get Clients Now! system is designed for marketing professional services; it's not a complete solution for marketing products and packaged learning programs.)

To examine the potential return on any investment in advertising, ask yourself these questions:

> ▶ How many prospects do you expect your ads to generate?

- ► What will each prospect cost you, based on the expense in time and money to create and manage your ads?

- ► How many will become clients?

- ► What will be the dollar value of those closed sales?

- ► Is there a cheaper way you could generate the same amount of revenue?

- ► How much can you really afford to spend?

Once you have made the commitment to advertise, and know how much you can afford to invest, here are some suggestions for getting the most from your advertising dollar:

► **Target the right audience.** The narrower your target, the better. Specialized publications and websites aimed at your market niche are often cheaper to advertise with than the ones with wide appeal. Targeting also permits you to tailor your ad for the people most likely to buy.

► **Place your ad where they "shop."** When is it most likely that a client will realize she needs you? Where might she be looking at that time? If you are a résumé writer, you can advertise in your networking group's e-zine and hope that people about to start a job search happen to see your ad. But it's more likely that job seekers would find you from an ad on a job posting website.

► **Request an immediate response.** Institutional advertising is for the big guys. You really can't afford to advertise just for name recognition; you need a direct response. A financial planner might headline an online ad: "How much will your investments bring you at retirement? Click here to find out with our free online calculator."

► **Repeat; don't scatter.** People often don't respond the first, second, or tenth time they see your ad, so give them more chances. When your budget is limited, buy repeat ads in the same venue, not one ad in several different ones. Make sure people see your ad often. For the same money that a large banner ad on a niche website's home page would cost each month, you could probably run a smaller ad on the same site's blog that would be seen along with multiple posts.

► **Appraise your website.** Before you start directing ad viewers to your website, make sure your site does a good job of capturing visitors and selling your services. There's no point in paying to get more traffic if prospects don't choose to interact with you when they visit.

▶ **Track and adjust.** Keep track of the response to every ad—not just the volume of calls or site visitors, but the value of the sales they generate. To do this, you will need to keep accurate records of where every prospect comes from, and how much each one spends with you. If an ad isn't bringing you paying clients after you have run it several times, dump it, even if you're getting plenty of inquiries. Revisit the points above, and see if you can come closer to your target, where they shop, and what will prompt a response. And if an ad is working for you, don't change it. You will get tired of your ads long before your clients do.

The variety of **advertising venues** available is truly enormous. Online, you can run pay-per-click ads in search engines or on websites, content-specific ads on social media channels, banner ads on websites and blogs and in e-zines, classified ads, calendar listing ads, and directory ads. In print, you can place display, classified, or calendar listing ads in newspapers, magazines, newsletters, trade journals, directories, or event programs. Out in the world, you can put ads on flyers, posters, signs, and billboards. And then there are other approaches both old and new, like ads on your T-shirt or car, or ads on smartphone apps. How do you even begin to choose?

This is where targeting is extremely important. There's no point in placing an ad somewhere that has minimal exposure to your target niche. There's also no point in running ads that cost more than the business they bring in. Pay careful attention to all the tips above on how to determine whether advertising is for you and how to make it work. And before placing any ad, ask yourself, "Is this the most likely place for prospects to be looking for a business like mine?"

Recipe: Distributing Flyers

Printed flyers can be one of the most inexpensive forms of advertising, and an appropriate medium for many professionals marketing to local consumers and small businesses. If you are already doing a fair amount of networking and referral building, you may often find yourself in places where you can hand out, post, or display flyers to increase your visibility and generate new inquiries. Likely **flyer venues** include the following places:

▶ **Networking events.** You may be able to hand out flyers when you introduce yourself, leave them on a table for people to pick up, or place one on each chair. If you don't know what the group's rules are, be sure to ask first so you don't offend anyone.

▶ **Trade shows.** If you have a booth, your flyers will be there, of course. If you don't, you could ask a referral partner to display flyers for you. Many shows prohibit the distribution of flyers by nonexhibitors, but creative marketers have been known to pass out flyers outside the show.

▶ **Educational institutions, association headquarters, health practitioners' offices, and resource centers.** Many organizations and businesses have bulletin boards, resource binders, waiting room counters, or literature racks where your flyers could be seen or picked up.

▶ **Community gathering places such as coffee shops, bookstores, libraries, or copy/shipping centers.** Bulletin boards and literature racks are common in places like these.

The **ad copy and layout** of your flyer will be important to its effectiveness. Special offers such as "free book or CD of your choice if you schedule before Oct. 31" or "free consultation with this flyer" can encourage people to call. Flyers that advertise only one service at a time typically get more response than those that contain a laundry list of everything you have available.

The most common flyer design is to use a full page and print on one side of colored paper stock. But you could also print your flyer on two sides and fold it into thirds to create the look of a brochure. (A true brochure is typically too costly to use for this sort of distribution.) Or, you could print on card stock and cut your page in half or thirds to create smaller-sized coupons or fact sheets.

The design and printing of your flyer should reflect your level of professionalism. If your flyer looks homemade, that's how people will view your service. Consider investing a few extra dollars in having your flyer professionally designed. For small quantities, printing flyers on your laser or inkjet printer may be an acceptable solution. For larger numbers, you will want to have your flyers photocopied or printed. Either way, be sure the paper stock and colors you use project the image that you want.

Ads Should Win Rewards, Not Awards

Robert W. Bly, www.bly.com

Bob Bly is the author of more than seventy books, including *The Copywriter's Handbook*. Bly advises: "To define what constitutes good print advertising, we begin with what a good print ad is not: It is not creative for the sake of being creative. It is not designed to please copywriters, art directors, agency presidents or even clients. Its main purpose is not to entertain, win awards or shout at the readers, 'I am an *ad*. Don't you admire my fine writing, bold graphics and clever concept?' In other words, ignore most of what you would learn as a student in any basic advertising class or as a trainee in one of the big Madison Avenue consumer ad agencies." Bly explains,

> As for what an ad *should* be, here are some characteristics shared by successful direct response print ads:
>
> 1. They stress a benefit. The main selling proposition is not cleverly hidden but is made immediately clear.
>
> 2. They arouse curiosity and invite readership. The key here is not to be outrageous but to address the strongest interests and concerns of your target audience.
>
> 3. They provide information. Ads that provide information the reader wants get higher readership and better response.
>
> 4. They have a strong free offer. Good ads tell the reader the next step in the buying process and encourage him to take it *now*.
>
> All ads should have an offer, because the offer generates immediate response from prospects who are ready to buy now or at least thinking about buying. Without an offer, these 'urgent' prospects are not encouraged to reach out to you, and you lose many potential clients.

Recipe: Sending Direct Mail by E-mail or Post

There is a significant difference between postal direct mail or unsolicited bulk e-mail and sending *personal* letters or e-mails to prospective clients, which is discussed earlier in this chapter. This difference is marked by both the level of individual attention you give each communication and the volume of marketing pieces you send. And the difference in the impact these two tactics will have is equally significant.

Think of yourself as an example. How much of the mail arriving in your mailbox or e-mail inbox do you actually read? Do marketing letters you get with your name inserted fool you into thinking the letter was written just for you? Who are you more likely to contact—someone who sent you a pitch by mail or e-mail, or someone who was recommended by a friend?

Most people routinely discard mail from senders they don't recognize. If they do hang on to your mailing, it will probably be sitting at the bottom of a to-be-reviewed stack somewhere. This is why calling before you send a personal letter is so important. It may be the only way to save your letter from oblivion. And calling after you send it is the only way to know if it was read.

Sending a generic letter or e-mail to a large mailing list is much better used as a follow-up technique than for filling the pipeline. (See Chapter 8 for more about this.) If despite these warnings, you want to try using direct mail as your first approach to a cold list, use only postal mail for this purpose. Don't even think about sending unsolicited bulk e-mail—that is, spam.

To use postal direct mail, consider working with a marketing communications specialist to design the ad copy and layout for your mailing. Getting professional help to compose your letter, design your mailer, or lay out your postcard can greatly increase its effectiveness.

Try offering a free gift, complimentary consultation, or other time-limited offer as an incentive for the recipient to call you or visit your website. If your mailing is enclosed in envelopes, paying someone to hand-address them is one way to increase the odds of your letters being opened. Printing a teaser on the outside—"Look inside for your free gift"—is another. Just be sure whatever tricks you use to get your mailing piece noticed reflect the professional image you want to present.

Remember, too, as with all forms of written outreach, you will get much better results from direct mail if you couple it with follow-up phone calls.

Recipe: Print and Online Directory Advertising

One of the most popular advertising venues for service businesses is the advertising directory. In print, this category includes the Yellow Pages produced by your local phone company; similar directories produced by competing groups; and membership directories and resource guides printed by associations and unions.

On the Web, directories include local business directories, membership directories for associations and trade groups, and specialized directories for specific market niches. For example, a wedding planner could advertise in WeddingChannel, or an acupuncturist could purchase a listing in Acufinder.

Some directories may offer a basic listing for free, or as a benefit of your membership or paid service. It can be worth your time to create listings in some of these—for example, the local business directories offered by Google Places, Yahoo! Local, or Yelp. Keep in mind that once you do this, you may start to receive online reviews, which are not always positive or accurate.

Most directories will tempt you to upgrade your basic listing to a paid one, or if you are already paying, to add options that cost more. There are really only two reasons to pay to advertise in a particular directory:

1. You expect that potential clients will be looking for your service in that directory at the time they are ready to buy. If you're not sure about this, ask some colleagues what their experience has been with specific directories.
2. It is a standard practice in your industry to be listed in that directory, so it would detract from your credibility if you weren't included.

When advertising solely for the second reason, there's no point in buying a big ad. Just get the basic listing. Even well-established companies often keep this type of ad quite small.

When you are advertising for reason 1, it's important that your ad copy and layout be designed to catch the eye of your best prospects. Study the existing ads in your category carefully. Make yours stand out by using unique graphics or an intriguing headline. If there are many large ads in your category already, recognize that a smaller ad will have a hard time competing.

Rather than packing lots of information into your ad, focus on one key benefit you provide or one problem you solve for your clients. On a page filled with ads for psychotherapy, most of which mention depression, relationship problems, and eating disorders, an ad highlighting "recovery from trauma" could stand out and attract someone for whom this is an issue. If you can't decide which of your services to promote, pick the one no one else is advertising. Remember that the sole purpose of an ad like this is to get prospects to contact you. Once you speak with them to find out about their needs, you may be offering them something different.

Beware of new, untested directories. Just because a vendor prints 50,000 copies or launches a good-looking website doesn't mean anyone will be using this directory to find professionals to work with.

Recipe: Display, Classified, and Calendar Advertising

Placing ads in print or online can take a wide variety of forms. You can place display ads or banner ads in print and online publications and on websites. These highly visible ads, typically in color and with some sort of graphic image, encourage visitors to click on them to visit your website, or in print, they may direct readers to a website or ask them to call. As with any advertising, the most effective ads make a special offer to encourage response.

Classified ads or paid calendar listings are typically text only, or perhaps include a logo, and are shown under headings that collect similar types of ads together.

Some advertising venues will charge you a flat fee to run your ad for a certain period of time, others will charge based on the number of "impressions" your ad receives (i.e., the number of people who view it), and still others will charge for "click-throughs" (i.e., the number of people who click on it). To evaluate using ads for which you pay a flat fee or per-impression fee, review the tips under "Making Advertising Work" above. For ads charging per click, see "Pay-per-Click Advertising" below.

Look for venues where you could be the only advertiser in your category, or offer something completely unique. A career counselor might get a good response from a small ad appearing on a page of job postings for her niche that read, "Looking for something different? Learn to find meaningful work. Call for a free guide."

Use the services of a graphic designer, copywriter, or marketing communications professional to make sure your ad copy and layout will attract attention. Just as with directory advertising, narrow the focus of your ad to one key point that will resonate with your best prospective clients.

The headline of your ad is the most important part of its design. If the headline doesn't attract attention, your ad won't be read. Inexperienced advertisers often make the mistake of headlining their ad with their name or the name of their company. But no one cares who you are unless they need what you have to offer.

Effective headlines directly address a prospect's needs by stating a principal benefit of the service being offered, or mentioning a problem the prospect may have. Here are some examples:

Does Your Computer Give You a Pain in the Neck?

Affordable Bankruptcy

How Safe Are Your Investments?

Help for Adults with Attention Deficit Disorder

Health Care at a Price that Won't Make You Sick

Relationship Troubles?

Remember to track carefully the results of every ad you run. It's the only way you will know what's working for you and what isn't.

Recipe: Pay-per-Click Advertising

Online pay-per-click ads allow you to focus the reach of your advertising and pay only for the response you get. With these text or graphic ads, you pay a fee every time someone clicks on the ad to visit your website. Sometimes these ads appear in a fixed location, such as the top of a designated page on a website. Other pay-per-click ads are context-sensitive (e.g., Google AdWords). This means they are displayed on search engine pages and a wide variety of websites where keywords related to your service are in use.

For example, a security management consulting firm could purchase a pay-per-click ad for the keyword phrase "security consultant" and agree to pay a maximum of $1.50 every time a visitor clicked through to visit the firm's site. When someone searched for "security consultant" using the search engine from whom the firm purchased the ad, the firm's ad would appear on the results page as a sponsored listing. The firm could also opt to have its ad appear on advertising-enabled websites with related content. These could include blogs about security management, security management resource sites, and more.

The key to determining whether pay-per-click advertising is a good choice for you is to know the true value of each click. For example, if 1,000 people currently visit the firm's site each month, this typically results in one new client monthly, and the average profit the firm earns from each new client is $15,000, then the value to the firm of each click is $15. So paying $1.50 per click to get more traffic would be likely worth their while.

But for a business with the same number of current site visitors and monthly new clients which has an average profit from each new client of only $1,000, the value of each click is only $1.00. In this case, paying $1.50 per click for more traffic would make no sense.

Many pay-per-click advertising vendors offer a user guide to help you decide how much you can realistically afford to pay. Be sure to weigh all the factors carefully before agreeing to a contract.

Recipe: Broadcast and Webcast Advertising

Can you afford to advertise in the broadcast or webcast media? Maybe. Is it the best place to spend your advertising dollars? Maybe not.

Broadcast radio and television advertising can bring you name recognition with a wide audience. The Web also offers both live and recorded audio and video programming, often called Internet radio or Web TV. Some of these broadcast or webcast programs are narrowly targeted to a niche audience.

But is there a cheaper way you might produce the same result? Go back and review the "Making Advertising Work" section above, and see if this medium is really worth pursuing. Watch or listen to the stations and shows you might consider as advertising venues. Are there any other businesses like yours advertised? If not, there might be a reason.

With broadcast and webcast media, repeat advertising is the name of the game. Your prospective clients can't tear out your ad and save it, and typically don't want to interrupt their listening or viewing to click through to another site. Unless your ad runs repeatedly, they need to be interested enough in the moment they first hear it to note your phone number or website, or remember your name. That's a pretty long shot.

One of the few valid reasons for a professional services business to use broadcast advertising is if your average sale is so low that you need many, many prospects contacting you. In this situation, you might find it necessary to spend more on advertising than is usual, just to get enough people in the pipeline. But be sure to do your math first. No business is profitable unless it earns more per client than it costs to get each one in the door.

To produce an effective radio or TV ad, professional help with your **ad script** and production is highly recommended. There's no point in spending big bucks to air a second-rate ad. If the station or show you plan to advertise with offers to produce your ad for you, survey the quality of other ads it has produced and make sure they meet your standards. As with all other media, track the results of your ads carefully. If you're not getting the results you want, pull the plug.

The More Things Change, the More They Stay the Same

1. The first time a man looks at an advertisement, he does not see it.
2. The second time, he does not notice it.
3. The third time, he is conscious of its existence.
4. The fourth time, he faintly remembers having seen it before.
5. The fifth time, he reads it.
6. The sixth time, he turns up his nose at it.
7. The seventh time, he reads it through and says, "Oh, brother!"
8. The eighth time, he says, "Here's that confounded thing again!"
9. The ninth time, he wonders if it amounts to anything.
10. The tenth time, he asks his neighbor if he has tried it.

11. The eleventh time, he wonders how the advertiser makes it pay.

12. The twelfth time, he thinks it must be a good thing.

13. The thirteenth time, he thinks perhaps it might be worth something.

14. The fourteenth time, he remembers wanting such a thing a long time.

15. The fifteenth time, he is tantalized because he cannot afford to buy it.

16. The sixteenth time, he thinks he will buy it some day.

17. The seventeenth time, he makes a memorandum to buy it.

18. The eighteenth time, he swears at his poverty.

19. The nineteenth time, he counts his money carefully.

20. The twentieth time he sees the ad, he buys what it is offering.

Written in 1885 by Thomas Smith, London, England

CHAPTER 8

Following Up

When You Know Plenty of People but You're Not Contacting Them

IT'S SIMPLE, BUT NOT ALWAYS EASY

Doing a good job at follow-up is a piece of cake. You just capture every prospect or potential referral partner you run across, then place a call, send the person something, or interact with the person online. If you don't make a sale right away, you put the person on the calendar for the next follow-up and do the same thing again. Pretty straightforward, isn't it? So why is follow-up such a problem? Here are the five most common reasons:

1. **Prioritization.** With an activity that you must initiate, it's easy to let other tasks come first: responding to incoming calls and mail, getting the invoices out, keeping your technology updated, and, oh, yes, doing the client work you get paid for. If you don't set aside reserved time for follow-up, it will never happen.

2. **Disorganization.** Business cards and scraps of paper lying on your desk, numbers in your cell phone, and rosters of social media contacts do not constitute a contact management system. Without accurate records of who you have been in contact with, when, and what your last exchange was about, effective follow-up is impossible.

3. **Lack of Essential Tools.** If you don't know what to say when you call a prospect on the phone, you will probably avoid calling. When you

haven't yet created something to send your website visitors, you won't have a reason to ask them to provide their e-mail address. Simple follow-up tactics become impossible to implement when you are missing basic components.

4. **Resistance.** Do you find yourself saying, "Why do I have to do this? I'm good at what I do. Why aren't the clients coming to me?" You are sabotaging yourself with this line of thinking. Business owners much more established than you are do follow-up every day. It's one of the ways they got established. Regular follow-up does not make people think you don't have enough business; it makes them see you as a professional.

5. **Fear.** "If I follow up that lead, I might be rejected," reasons the voice in your head. "So I'll avoid the pain by not making the call in the first place." Or conversely, you may be thinking, "If I place the call, I might get the business, and then I'll have to do the work, and people will have all these expectations of me." But the reality is that if you don't follow up, you're going to fail even more dramatically than in these two imaginary scenarios.

By working with the Get Clients Now! system to begin with, you are already addressing two of these issues. Using the 28-day program consistently will help you to set better priorities and overcome resistance. Later in this chapter you'll learn more about breaking through fear. So let's tackle disorganization and some essential follow-up tools next.

BASIC INGREDIENTS FOR FOLLOWING UP

SUCCESS INGREDIENTS:

Contact management system   Brochure

30-second commercial   Marketing kit

Ingredient: Contact Management System

Having some kind of **contact management system** is absolutely essential to efficient follow-up. Your chosen method for keeping track of contacts could be as simple as a three-ring binder, but most professionals prefer to manage their contacts electronically. You can choose from desktop software applications like Microsoft Outlook or Sage ACT!, cloud applications like Salesforce.com Contact Manager, Google Contacts, or 37signals Highrise, or apps that run on smartphones and tablets, such as Contapps Contacts or Smartr Contacts. The more sophisticated systems are often referred to as customer relationship management (CRM) systems.

In addition to recording name, company, phone numbers, e-mail, and other essential details, the best systems for follow-up allow you also to document the source of each contact and keep notes about your interaction over time. All cloud apps, most smartphone apps, and some desktop applications can keep your data synchronized between different devices you may use.

Ideally, a contact management system will allow you to sort and select contacts by location, original source, date of last contact, or other helpful characteristics. You can use it to keep track of all the people you know at a certain company, create an e-mail or postal mailing list, or remind you when to call someone back.

To select the best system for your needs, first consider how you work. Do you spend most of the day near your desktop or laptop computer, or are you more likely to have your tablet or smartphone handy? Do you use different devices under different circumstances or do you use the same one most of the time? Is it likely that you will have thousands of contacts to manage or will you be keeping track of only a small number of prospects? Do you work alone or with team members who also need access to your data?

Ask some colleagues or social media contacts what systems they would recommend. Then read some online reviews or message board posts that give pros and cons of systems that might be good candidates. Some of the most popular systems are free to use, and many others offer a free trial, so when you have narrowed your choice to only two or three, see if you can try them out to find out how well they will work for you.

Once you have chosen a system to adopt, you'll need to remember to use it! Each time you follow up with a prospect or referral source, or they follow up with you, make a note of when it was, what happened, and when you plan to follow up next. With many systems, once you enter the next follow-up date, you can receive an automatic reminder when it's due. If your system doesn't have this feature, put important follow-up dates in your calendar so you don't forget about them.

Your contact management system should hold all your prospects, potential referral sources, and clients (past and present). If you've been collecting contacts for a while before you start using a new system, it may seem like an overwhelming task to learn the software and get all your data organized. Just take it a bit at a time, and hire help if you need to. Start working with the system slowly and work on organizing data for a few names at a time. Once you see how much easier a good system can make your follow-up activities, you'll be motivated to use it more fully.

Help, I'm Drowning in Details!

Sylva Leduc, M.Ed., MPEC; www.sageleaders.com

Sylva Leduc is a business and executive coach and the co-founder and former owner of Client Compass, a client information management system for coaches and consultants. Leduc points out: "If you are doing a good job at meeting new people, you'll quickly amass a large number of business cards. It's not too challenging to remember the details about ten or twenty people. If you have a phenomenal memory, you might even recall the specifics about a hundred folks you've met. But beyond that, you'd better have a contact management system in place, or you'll soon be drowning in details." She suggests:

> A simple paper-based system can work for a while, but to be truly efficient and effective, consider one of the many contact management systems available. They save you time; instead of shuffling through piles and files of paper, you can instantly put your fingers on information. And contact managers make you look like a genius when you remember those tiny little details about someone.

> You can find the best system for your own type of business by conducting an Internet search for "contact management system" or "client information management." Be sure to use quotation marks to keep the search targeted. Then, evaluate some of the many different systems available. If you can find a review from one of the computing magazines, that's even better because they will have done all the research for you. Ask your colleagues for the name of the program they use, their likes and dislikes, how easy it is to use, if training and technical support is available, and the costs.

> Then buy and learn how to use the system. Don't let it sit around gathering dust. Every time you speak with someone, enter notes in your "virtual filing cabinet." In a short time you'll become trusted as the person who cares enough to remember the details about everyone.

Ingredient: 30-Second Commercial

A **30-second commercial**, also called an "elevator speech," is typically used when leaving your first voice mail message with a prospect or referral source, beginning a presentation, or formally introducing yourself to a group. It's an ideal tool for one-way communication, and delivering a message in a setting where people may not have a chance to respond to you.

This is different from the 10-second introduction described in Chapter 7, which is designed for two-way communication and facilitating dialogue.

When you are calling someone for the first time and get voice mail, use a 30-second commercial to introduce yourself. You often will not get a return call, but it is a golden opportunity to deliver your marketing message directly into a prospect's ear. A 30-second commercial is also useful in networking situations where you have a chance to stand up and announce to a gathering of interested people more about what you do.

What you don't want to do with your commercial is use it to answer the question, "What do you do?" in conversation. Nor do you want to launch into it when you get a prospect live on the phone. Thirty seconds of you talking without pause is too long for either of those purposes. You can, however, use pieces of your commercial as the basis of an interactive exchange. Developing a strong 30-second commercial will provide you with useful material on which to base a telemarketing call, sales conversation, or dialogue with a potential referral partner.

Begin your commercial with your 10-second introduction; then continue on with a few details about the services you offer. Always include benefits or results to the client rather than just a list of what you provide. Here are two examples:

> "My name is Chris Winston. I help human resource departments keep track of employees, salaries, and benefits. I'm an HR information systems consultant. If your current system isn't keeping up with your needs, I can fix inaccurate reports, install software upgrades, help you meet regulatory requirements, and make the system easier to use. When your system needs replacing, I'll make sure you avoid expensive mistakes, and work with your staff step-by-step to manage a system replacement on time and under budget. Since I specialize in HR, you can be sure I under-

stand all of your unique needs, and stay current on what's essential for you to know."

"I'm Mai Nguyen, and I help my clients maintain healthy lifestyles despite daily stress and chronic medical conditions. I'm a lifestyle coach. If you or your patients are suffering from stress, overwork, or ongoing health problems, I can help with maintaining a healthy diet, staying on an exercise program, and applying stress management techniques to support increased wellness. I work with individuals and health practitioners to make sure people with health challenges don't just talk about lifestyle changes; they make them. I'm a stress management instructor and certified fitness counselor, so you can be confident that I have the training and experience to help my clients live healthier lives."

Ingredient: Brochure

The first thing you should consider about creating a **brochure** is whether you need one at all. Many successful consultants, professionals, and coaches never develop a brochure. When they communicate in writing, they rely instead on personal letters and a few supplemental items, such as a professional biography or résumé and a client list. The rest of the time they refer prospective clients to their website instead of using print materials. When you are just starting out, paying for the design and printing of a brochure can be an expensive mistake if the nature of your services, or profile of your target market, is still in flux.

Look at what your successful competitors are doing. If they all seem to have brochures, you may need one also. If they don't, or there seem to be mixed opinions on this subject in your field, ask yourself whether having a brochure will make a positive difference with your prospective clients. If you think it will, how much brochure can you afford?

The simplest and most inexpensive brochure is a standard tri-fold that you or a graphic designer lays out, and prints or photocopies on standard paper stock or preprinted paper designed just for brochures. For marketing personal or household services to consumers, this may be all you need. For business-to-business marketing, a professionally designed and commercially printed brochure will be much more effective. As a general rule, the more expensive your service is, the more expensive your marketing materials should be. Hire a graphic designer, copywriter, or marketing communications specialist to help you, and be sure to work out a budget in advance.

The best way to decide what will go into your brochure is to review many examples of what others have included. Here are some of the typical elements of a tri-fold brochure:

- ▶ Attention-getting cover design, perhaps with a logo or photo
- ▶ Tag line, positioning statement, or competitive advantage
- ▶ Description of the services you offer
- ▶ Details about your target market or professional specialty (e.g., "We work with health care companies" or "My specialty is intellectual property law")
- ▶ Benefits and results of working with you
- ▶ Brief biography of you, your company, or both
- ▶ Client list, testimonials, or endorsement quotes
- ▶ Photographs or illustrations of you or your work
- ▶ Address, phone, e-mail, website, and social media profiles

Remember that your brochure should be designed primarily for use in follow-up rather than for filling the pipeline. If you are sending it by mail, it will typically be accompanied by a personal letter or note, and in most other situations, you will be giving your brochure to someone you have had some contact with already. So don't feel your brochure has to communicate everything there is to know about your business. A brochure's best use is to support your marketing activities rather than replacing them.

Ingredient: Marketing Kit

When marketing to businesses and organizations, a **marketing kit** is more common than a brochure. Follow the same guidelines suggested above for brochures to determine if you really need a marketing kit.

A typical kit begins with a two-pocket $8\frac{1}{2}$ x 11-inch folder with a cut-out to hold your business card. The contents of your kit are similar to the elements of a tri-fold brochure, with each item laid out on a separate page. Other ingredients might be:

- ▶ Fact sheet about your business or your field (e.g., "How to work with an interior designer" or "Our unique approach to team-building")

➤ Articles written by you, about you, or about the kind of work you do

➤ Testimonial letters from clients

➤ Case study of a successful project

➤ Actual samples of work you have produced, excerpts from it, or photographs of it

A significant advantage of using a kit like this is that you can customize its contents for each recipient. Because you may be assembling kits only as you need them, this can be much more affordable than printing several hundred brochures. You can also easily update individual sheets.

Don't overload clients with information, especially on the first contact. Hold back some of what you have, and use it in further follow-up, or as leave-behinds after a presentation.

What's Different About You?

Ellen Looyen, www.ellen4branding.com

Personal branding expert Ellen Looyen has helped thousands of businesses and professionals to brand and package their businesses. Looyen has discovered that, "In any successful marketing piece, everything works together to support your brand identity and unique message. The copywriting should be persuasive, and the design compelling. An effective brochure, marketing kit, or website needs to exude confidence and convey a sense of quality, honesty, and knowledge to your prospects. It also needs to be written in your prospect's language; generic language is not very effective in the relational marketplace." She advises,

> Tell your prospects what you do, how you do it, who can benefit from what you're offering, and what's different about you. It works best to bullet point as much of this information as possible, so readers can scan for what interests them, instead of having to read every word. Be sure to also include a list of several tangible benefits your clients will receive. The most important information in any marketing piece answers the question, "What's in it for the client?"

> Endorsements and testimonials work well, because people tend to do what their peers do. Be sure your testimonials point to specific results and are not just fluff. If you can get a testimonial from a well-respected expert in your field, highlight it with a compelling graphic, so it gets the notice it deserves.

> Include a biography that instills confidence in your prospects and brands you as an expert in your field. Tell readers what motivated you to get into this business, and why you are the ideal person to be doing this. Highlight your

education, credentials and accomplishments. Give a success story that illustrates the benefits you have achieved for other clients. Make your marketing piece convey your personal brand and value with passion, integrity, and believability.

STRATEGY: DIRECT CONTACT AND FOLLOW-UP AND NETWORKING AND REFERRAL BUILDING

SUCCESS INGREDIENTS:

Model marketing letter   Broadcast e-mail system

In-house mailing list   Bonus for online subscribers

Postcard or mailer   Personal connections

Newsletter or e-zine

In the follow-up stage of marketing, you are primarily using only two strategies: direct contact and follow-up, and networking and referral building. It's important to notice that the activities involved in pursuing these two different strategies are identical: calling and mailing, follow-up meetings, follow-up mailings, and following up online. The difference is in the targets of these activities. Direct contact and follow-up is aimed at prospects, and networking and referral building can be aimed at either prospects or referral partners.

In professions where directly soliciting business is inappropriate, you may be using the strategies in this chapter more for networking to increase referrals than for making contact with prospects. Nevertheless, don't neglect to follow up with prospects as much as you can without crossing the line. Sending a nice-to-meet-you note, interesting article, or informational newsletter is almost always appropriate, whether you are selling to organizations or to individuals.

Recipe: Calling and Mailing

When you are contacting someone directly for the first time, whether it is a potential client or a possible referral partner, the most effective approach is to call, mail, and call, as described in Chapter 7. In other words, call before you mail or e-mail, and call again after you mail.

If you find you are talking to someone both interested and qualified (for example, able to pay), you may be able to set up a sales conversation or networking meeting on your first call. It's more likely, though, you will reach voice mail, an assistant, or someone with "no time to talk." This is why being organized and persistent about follow-up is so important. Once you have made an initial contact, even if only through voice mail or a receptionist, you must follow up with an e-mail, a postal mailing, another call, a text message, or other follow-up approaches—and you will probably have to do this more than once.

Never assume that someone you are calling is going to call you back. Often, they won't. Busy people simply don't have the time to return unsolicited phone calls or, in fact, any call that isn't their top priority that day. If you are of the opinion that not returning a phone call is rude, get over it. Even people you are in the final stages of negotiating a sale with will often not return calls for days or weeks. If you are willing to accept this as a normal business practice and not interpret it as personal rejection, your marketing life will be much less stressful.

It's not a good idea to rely on e-mail as your only method of follow-up communication. For one thing, it's too easy to hide behind—for both you and your prospects. You will find that interactive conversations will be much more productive in determining people's interest level in your offer and handling any objections they have to meeting or working with you. Unless you are absolutely sure that e-mail is the preferred method of communication for a particular prospect, alternate your e-mails with phone calls, and try different phone numbers, if you have them. You might also use text messages as a substitute for e-mail once you have made initial contact.

Also, don't make the assumption that just because you sent an e-mail or text that it was either received or read. E-mail addresses and phone numbers change, messages get lost in transmission, spam filters block e-mails, texts get deleted, and some people receive far too many messages daily to ever read them all.

When sending postal mail or e-mail to someone you have not yet spoken to, keep it simple. Until you know whether the person is interested, don't mail more than a personalized letter, perhaps with a brochure, fact sheet, or announcement enclosed. If you are e-mailing, reference your website, but don't send any attached files. Only if your initial conversation with this person clearly showed some interest should you send any more information than this to encourage him to meet with you. If you use a marketing kit, this is typically when you would send it.

To make this process easier, it is helpful to have a **model marketing letter**, a standard letter sent by mail or e-mail that you can personalize to fit a specific situation. Your letter's first paragraphs typically introduce you or your company, but that shouldn't be your opening line. The best lead sentence will be one that establishes a personal connection between you and the recipient. For example: "I heard you speak at the Iowa Manufacturer's conference," "Rafael Santos suggested I contact you," or "I'm a fellow member of the Northside Community Alliance."

When writing to a prospect with whom you have no connection, a good second choice can be to lead with an attention-getting question, such as, "Would you like to save more on your taxes?" or "Is your relocation company meeting your needs?" Keep the tone of your letter helpful, informative, and professional. Avoid overly promotional copy and hard-sell techniques. Remember that this is a personal letter from you to someone you want to build a relationship with. It's not a direct mail piece aimed at an anonymous buyer.

Next, highlight the benefits of what you offer. Don't just repeat what is listed in your brochure or on your website; expand on it or talk about some actual client results. If you have enough information to do so, suggest specifically how you can help the prospect you are writing to by describing a problem or goal that person has and your proposed solution. Then, describe briefly what qualifies you to provide the service you are offering.

You might create a model letter for each different service that you offer, one for prospects and another for referral partners, or one for warm contacts and another for people who don't know you. One to one-and-a-half pages is a good length. Once you have created a model, all you will have to customize each time is the opening sentence where you state your connection, plus any specific offer of help. See Figures 8-1 and 8-2 for some examples.

Figure 8-1: Model Marketing Letter—Warm Contact

Dear Dave,

It was a pleasure meeting you yesterday, and I enjoyed learning more about you. During our conversation you said many things that sparked my interest in how we may be able to work together. You have very good ideas and I really appreciate your enthusiasm in moving them forward. I would like to help.

While we couldn't share everything during the event, I would like to learn more about your ideas. I help many entrepreneurs to move their ideas to fruition. The experiences I have gained in doing this would be very beneficial for you along your path. I would love to share more with you.

Like we discussed, all business owners know they have to market. Many times, though, they don't know where to start, how to put one foot in front of another, or what path to follow to keep marketing consistently.

That is exactly the premise behind the book, *Guerrilla Marketing in 30 Days*, which I co-authored with Jay Levinson, the father of Guerrilla Marketing. That information is the starting point I use to help businesses like yours reach new levels.

Just laying out the marketing calendar and scheduling marketing activity can get you started and on your way. Planning what networking events you attend, brainstorming positioning statements and taglines, and thinking about getting the right message to the right target are also key components in what I help business owners with. Let's take this to the next step and meet again, one on one, to see how we best do this for your business.

How about we meet for lunch next Tuesday? If you have a more preferable time, let me know and we can schedule accordingly.

Thanks again for your time and I look forward to our next contact.

Sincerely,
Al Lautenslager
Author, Speaker, Consultant
www.marketforprofits.com

A week to ten days after sending your information, place a follow-up call. Don't make the mistake of thinking that if your prospects were truly interested, they would call you. Think about how many days or weeks a low-priority task can languish on your own to-do list. And many people never return calls to a caller they don't recognize.

Figure 8-2: Model Marketing Letter—Cold Contact

Dear Consuela:

I'm a fellow member of the Women in Business Network, and I saw your catering business listed in our directory. Are you looking for more clients right now? I help women business owners and self-employed professionals build their client base quickly without spending all their time at work. I'm a business coach.

Many of my clients find that working with me has doubled their bottom line in a relatively short time. We focus together on identifying practical, affordable business-building strategies that fit your professional image and personal style. I've helped other women in the catering business land more clients and bigger jobs without increasing their advertising budget or working longer hours.

I can assist you with business planning, marketing strategy, time management issues, and balancing work with your personal life, all at a rate you can afford.

I've been doing this work since 2008 and have a number of references I could share with you. I teach marketing at the Hilltop Career Center and write articles on entrepreneurship for their newsletter.

I look forward to finding out if I could be of service to you, and I'll give you a call next week.

Regards,
Tomiko Mifune
(732) 555-1212

When you get a prospect on the phone, try again to schedule a sales conversation. If it doesn't happen this time either, ask if you can follow up at some later date, and determine what an appropriate interval would be: next month, next quarter, or even next year. Then make the entry in your contact management system and move on to the next prospect.

What if you keep getting voice mail? While it is true that some people let all their calls roll to voice mail, especially when they don't recognize the caller, you can sometimes get through to a business prospect by calling off hours, say before 8:30 or after 5:00. After 5:00 or during the lunch hour can also be a good time to try a cell phone number. When calling individuals at home, early evening or Saturday is often the best time. But should you keep calling or leave a message? Actually, you should do both. Since you are assuming that most people won't call you back, keep right on calling them.

Whether you reach your contacts or not, never make them wrong for not returning your calls. Rather than saying a bit peevishly, "I haven't heard from you," instead let them know you are eager to speak with them and wanted to try again while you were in your office. As a general rule, leaving three voice mail messages over ten to thirty days is sufficient (ten for a hot prospect; thirty for a cooler one). If you get no response, wait a month or two and try again.

When you do leave a message, use your 30-second commercial on the first call. In later messages, leave a new and interesting piece of information each time. When calling a prospect, make it a benefit of doing business with you—for example, "I can help you reduce your training costs." Keep your messages to no more than 30 seconds; no one likes to receive lengthy voice mails, and the delete key is at their fingertips.

If you have called, left messages, and still can't get through to the person you want, send a follow-up e-mail. Some people will quickly respond to e-mail because it is easy. If you can interest them in what you have to offer, they may be willing to set up a phone appointment with you to discuss it further.

If you are new at persistent follow-up, it's likely that at some point you will begin to feel you are pestering people. Keep in mind that you have much more awareness about these calls and messages than the person receiving them does. Part of the reason you need to keep contacting people is that they will often forget about you almost immediately. Be pleasant, helpful, and upbeat in your messages, and most recipients will respect your profession- alism. If a prospect really doesn't want to hear from you again, he or she will tell you so, usually quite politely.

So when should you give up on contacting a prospect? That depends on the value of the potential sale. A $1,000 sale might only be worth five attempts by letter, call, or e-mail, but a $10,000 sale would certainly pay you back for many more. Every salesperson has a story about a client who finally said yes after the seventeenth phone call, so if the sale seems worth it, don't quit.

Recipe: Follow-Up Meetings

Your first live meeting with a prospect after your initial contact is typically some sort of sales conversation, whether it takes place in person or by phone. Even if this is primarily a fact-finding meeting, you will be spending some time talking about your services and qualifications. If a second meeting is necessary, it might be a formal presentation to a larger group, an informal meeting where you discuss a proposal you have prepared, or simply a conversation about the details of the proposed work. After this, you may find yourself following up mostly by phone messages, e-mail, letter, or text. The same is also true for referral partners. After an initial meeting in person or by phone, you might not speak to them again in person for some time.

When following up over a long period of time, try to find ways to connect with your prospects, referral partners, and past clients person to person to keep the relationship alive. If they live or work near you, take them to lunch, meet for coffee, stop by their offices (if this would be appropriate), or seek them out at live networking events. For those not in your area, make a date for a phone conversation to talk about their current needs, new projects, personal news, or other topics you have in common. You'll find that a periodic live conversation will keep their awareness of your name and business high, and will ultimately result in more referrals and more sales.

Recipe: Follow-Up Mailings

Whenever you meet someone at a live networking event or elsewhere who is not an immediate prospect, an easy and inexpensive way to follow up immediately is to send a nice-to-meet-you note by postal mail or e-mail. Depending on the nature of the contact, you might include an interesting article or your brochure or fact sheet, or point the person to your website. Then add the person to your contact management system for later follow-up.

In addition, if you are actively engaged in social media, you might also add people you meet to your network by requesting to connect or following them. And, when you have their permission, you might also add them to your broadcast e-mail system, if you have one. See the following sections on "Following Up by E-mail" and "Following Up with Social Media and Online Communities" for more on these topics.

As you work to fill the pipeline, you will constantly be collecting names and addresses of people you have met or spoken with, which you will be capturing in your contact management system and/or your broadcast e-mail system. These people will make up your **in-house mailing list**. When your list reaches about 300 names, consider sending your list some kind of mail or e-mail on a regular basis. This mail to your in-house list is for the purpose of following up with people you already know to remind them of your services and continue building your relationship with them. It's very different from direct mail or bulk e-mail sent to strangers on a prospect list that you bought or compiled.

With hot prospects, frequent referrers, and current clients, you will want to be in contact often, perhaps even monthly. In addition to phone calls, meetings, and interacting online, you might send these special people personal notes or cards by e-mail or mail, as well as articles of interest, links to useful websites, or invitations to upcoming events.

With your larger list of warm or cool prospects, referral partners, and past clients, sending a mailing three to four times per year is often sufficient to keep your name visible. You could opt for a simple postal mail piece like a **postcard or mailer**, or put more effort into publishing your own **newsletter or e-zine**.

Postcards, self-mailers, and other small pieces sent by postal mail often take the form of reminders or announcements with an attention-getting tag line and graphic. Here are some examples:

Overloaded with year-end work? Time to call Rodney Chen.

Sales in a slump? Take Charge Marketing can help.

January special—bring a friend and your next appointment is free!

Now serving Sonoma County! Call for an appointment today.

Keep the amount of text to a minimum. A mailer is not intended to do the job of a brochure. What you want is for the recipients to contact you with their questions, not get all the information they need from your mailer.

Producing a print newsletter can be a sizeable job, requiring skills on several levels: how-to writing for articles, copywriting for promotional sections, and graphic design for art and layout. If your skills in these areas are limited, get some professional help, especially with design. Homemade newsletters usually look it, and there's no point putting in this much time and money if your prospects won't be impressed.

A print newsletter can be as few as two pages or as many as eight. Typical contents include one or more informative articles aimed at your market niche, interspersed with several shorter items sharing news, resources, or inspiration. Be sure your newsletter contains more useful information than it does promotional copy. Ideally, you want the people on your mailing list not only to read your newsletter but to pass it along to friends as a helpful resource.

Instead of a print newsletter, you might choose to use an e-zine, and there's more about that in the next section. But despite its higher expense, a print newsletter can be an effective choice with prospects who will pay more attention to postal mail than to e-mail. This can include both people who don't use e-mail much and those who get far too much e-mail already. A print newsletter can also be used as a marketing piece that you distribute at speaking engagements or networking events, hand out at trade shows, or include in your marketing kit.

The Power of Postcards

Tessa Stowe, www.salesconversation.com

"Once you've met someone, you want to build a relationship with them," advises Tessa Stowe, an expert on how to sell by building relationships. "Most fall into the trap of relying totally on the virtual world to build relationships, with their main tool being e-mails. To check how effective e-mails are for being remembered, look in your own e-mail folders. How many 'nice to meet you' or 'happy birthday' e-mails have you kept? Or did you delete them and forget about them as soon as they came in?" Stowe adds,

> If you are serious about building relationships, then "get real." Connect with potential prospects in the real world with something tangible. A great way to do this is to send postcards in the mail. Cards to say "let's keep in touch," holiday cards, birthday cards. If you make the focus of the cards about them, versus trying to make a sale, people will start to know, like, and trust you.

> If you really want your cards to make an impact, put a photo of them in the card. You will find people will keep these cards (and your contact details) for weeks, months, and sometimes even years. And they will contact you when they are ready to buy.

> Sending postcards like this is easier and quicker than you think. You can do it all over the Internet so there is no need to go to a store, a printer, or the post office. The online system I use enables you to send a personalized postcard to an individual or to everyone on your list in the same amount of time.

> Consider implementing a postcard-based relationship building strategy. You'll then discover they are not only powerful in building relationships, but also your sales.

Recipe: Following Up by E-mail

Following up with your contacts online can take many different forms. You might publish an e-zine, send broadcast e-mail, write a blog, or interact via social media.

If you plan to use an e-zine or broadcast e-mail for online follow-up, you'll need a **broadcast e-mail system**. Instead of sending your e-zine or e-mail broadcasts to subscribers the same way you currently send personal e-mail, you will want to use an automated system to deliver your e-zine and maintain your e-mail list.

Broadcast e-mail systems allow your website visitors to add themselves to your mailing list, update their own e-mail address when it changes, and unsubscribe themselves automatically if they wish. Popular choices for this function are Constant Contact, AWeber, and MailChimp. If you search the Web for "e-mail marketing," you'll find many systems available to choose from, and plenty of online reviews listing their pros and cons. There are also some systems that combine broadcast e-mail capabilities with contact management functions, for example, Infusionsoft. These integrated systems can be considerably more expensive.

With a broadcast e-mail system you can send the same e-mail—such as an e-zine or a promotional message—to thousands of subscribers, or send a sequential series of informational messages to any one person who signs up for your e-mail list.

Publishing an e-zine can be much more affordable than a print newsletter because there is no printing or postage to pay for, and less design work. If you make a habit of asking all your prospects and referral sources to opt in to your e-zine, you will build a substantial subscriber list over time.

The most popular e-zine format is a monthly e-mail publication that mimics the contents of a typical print newsletter, including an article or two, some promotional copy, and perhaps some shorter items. But many other formats are possible. You can send an e-zine quarterly, weekly, or even daily. Instead of articles, your e-zine can consist of brief tips, either one tip per issue or a collection of tips each time. Subscribe to some other e-zines published in your market niche and see what formats appeal to you and are a good match for your professional image, personal style, and the time you have available to commit to publication.

You'll Sell More If You Don't Sell Anything

Michael Katz, www.bluepenguindevelopment.com

"An e-newsletter is the next best thing to having lunch with every one of your clients and prospects once each month," declares Michael Katz, author of *E-Newsletters That Work*. "But what do you think would happen if every time you got together for lunch, you tried to sell those people something? My guess is they would stop having lunch with you." Katz says,

> The reason I bring up this lunchtime scenario is that when it comes to how you develop and manage your e-newsletter, there are a number of similarities. Your e-newsletter functions as kind of an electronic proxy for all those face-to-face interactions that can't possibly happen in the physical world. It puts you in front of your target audience on a regular schedule, and in a nonthreatening context.
>
> There are tangible, measurable, undeniable business benefits associated with relationship building. All those lunches, as nonlinear and unstructured as they may be, have results. But focusing on the desired result (i.e., more sales) at the expense of the relationship, eliminates both. If you use a relationship building opportunity to make a sales pitch, not only do you eat a lot of lunches by yourself, you also eliminate one of the easiest, most efficient means for growing your business. It's certainly fine to talk about what you do, but you can't make it the center of the conversation. As far as your e-newsletter goes, if it becomes nothing more than a telemarketing call in disguise, people will unsubscribe, putting an end to both the conversation and any related future opportunities.
>
> Effective e-newsletters require that you turn the selling machine off. Like a cherished lunchtime companion, a good e-newsletter focuses on offering relevant, useful, interesting information to readers, with an emphasis on providing—not extracting—value.

You can also use your e-mail system to send pre-written e-mail messages automatically. For example, you can provide an instant reply to someone who requests more information while visiting your website. The advantage of using an autoresponse e-mail instead of displaying the same details on your site is that once someone makes a request via an autoresponder, you have her e-mail address and can follow up with her later.

The same autoresponder that provides an immediate reply to an inquiry like this can also be used to send a series of messages at pre-timed intervals after the initial inquiry. For example, if a prospective home buyer makes a request on a real estate agent's site for additional details about some current listings, an autoresponder could send her three more messages after seven, fourteen, and thirty days, each one offering a new tip about home buying and another reason to choose that agent to help with her home purchase.

It's a good idea to include a notice at the beginning of the series that lets prospects know you'll be sending additional informational messages, and gives them a chance to unsubscribe immediately if they don't wish to receive them. That way your prospects will be opting in to the series and you won't offend anyone. You can send these same people occasional broadcast e-mails after your pre-programmed series ends. Just as with an e-zine, you'll find that messages with useful content for readers will keep subscribers longer than those that simply deliver promotional messages.

Another type of broadcast e-mail you might send is posts from your blog, if you have one. As discussed in Chapter 7, you should provide a way for readers to stay up-to-date on your blog posts. This may be an automated system that e-mails them each post as soon as it is made, or you might choose to combine blog posts with other items and send them out as a broadcast.

To encourage people to subscribe to your e-mail list, you can offer a **bonus for online subscribers**. On your website, blog, or social media profile, or at networking events, speaking engagements, or trade shows, you can offer a bonus to people who agree to sign up for your e-mail list and receive your e-zine or broadcasts. Your bonus could be:

▶ An e-book, special report, case study, or white paper
▶ A tip sheet, online assessment, or survey
▶ Access to an audio, video, online resource center, or e-course
▶ Invitation to an upcoming teleseminar or webinar

You should never subscribe someone to your e-mail list without his or her permission. First, an e-zine and e-mail broadcasts are most appropriately used as relationship-building follow-up tools, not as vehicles for filling the pipeline. The people you send your e-mails to should already know who you are. Second, the sending of unsolicited bulk e-mail is governed by various government regulations, most of which can be translated as "don't send bulk e-mail to people who haven't asked for it." Third, subscribing your prospects to e-mail that they never asked for and have expressed no interest in is more likely to be considered an annoyance than a courtesy.

A much better approach to gaining subscribers is to routinely ask clients and prospects if they would like to subscribe to your list when you first make contact with them. When you first publish an e-zine or start sending e-mail broadcasts, most people on your pre-existing in-house mailing list will not be offended if you send a sample copy asking if they would like to become subscribers. But don't subscribe them first, and ask them to unsubscribe if they don't want it.

Turn Your Visitors into Subscribers

Roger C. Parker, www.publishedandprofitable.com

"Your success as a self-employed professional depends on your ability to use e-mail to keep in touch with your prospects and website visitors," claims Roger C. Parker. Parker is a book coach, marketing consultant, and the author of over forty books. "Unless you obtain your blog or website visitor's name and e-mail address on their first visit, you may never get another opportunity to convert their visit into a long and profitable client relationship!" He continues,

> The best way to build your e-mail list is to offer helpful, relevant information—information that helps your visitors solve a problem or achieve a desired goal. Quality counts! The quality of the information you share is more important than its length or the number of words included. You must also choose a title for your incentive that effectively communicates the benefits of the information you're sharing.
>
> Tip sheets make great sign-up incentives. Tip sheets consist of seven to ten numbered ideas, each accompanied by a short paragraph. Rarely are more than two or three sentences needed for each tip. Examples include:
>
> ► Top 10 Tips for. . . (Buying a New Home, Losing Weight, Preparing a Résumé, etc.)
>
> ► 10 Things to Look for. . . (When Job Hunting, Redecorating, Waterproofing your Basement, etc.)
>
> ► 10 Biggest Mistakes to Avoid . . . (When Choosing a Lawyer, Preparing a Will; Buying a Home Theater System, etc.)
>
> ► 10 Questions to Ask . . . (When. . . .)
>
> ► 10 Ways to Save Time . . . (When. . . .)
>
> The advantage of the above tip sheet titles is that the titles not only promise concise, helpful, relevant information, but they also target the keywords and keyword phrases that may have brought your visitors to your blog or website. Once created, your tip sheets can be used for years without change.

Recipe: Following Up with Social Media and Online Communities

If you have decided to make the commitment to actively engage with one or more social media networks or online communities (see Chapter 7 for more on making this decision), this can be one more avenue for following up with your contacts. Regular participation in an online network made up of people in your market niche allows you to stay visible, and build relationships and trust with other network members.

Keep in mind that participating in an online network isn't a substitute for personal follow-up with current hot prospects and active referral partners. You should still reach out to those people directly. But if you can identify, or build, an online network that contains many people in your niche, your regular participation in it can convert cool prospects to warm ones and stimulate referrals.

Here are the types of online networks that can be useful for following up with contacts, and suggestions for how to use them:

▶ **Social media networks.** You'll need to build your personal network on a social media channel before it starts being useful for follow up. See Chapter 7 for suggestions on how to do this. Remember also to add new people to your network when you make contact with them elsewhere. Post updates regularly, and make sure to provide educational, inspiring, or entertaining content, not just promotional messages. Forward, share, and comment on the updates posted by other members as well. It's fine to include some personal information in your updates, but keep the majority of them relevant to your expertise and the needs of your market niche.

▶ **Message boards and discussion groups.** When you can identify an online community specific to your niche that is maintained by a membership organization, media outlet, vendor, or volunteer moderator, you don't have to invest the time and effort to build your own network. By posting questions, answers, and comments on topics related to the group's theme, you can raise your visibility and demonstrate your expertise to other members. Stick to providing relevant, helpful information, and don't promote your services directly (unless the group encourages this). Let your signature box tell people what you do and how to reach you.

▶ **Blogs.** If you publish your own blog or guest blog for someone else, be sure to respond to comments posted by your readers, letting them know you are interested in what they have to say. You can also identify other blogs aimed at your market niche that have an active readership. When you comment on the posts of popular blogs, you make a connection with the blog's author and all of his readers as well.

Because active participation is the key to getting results from using online networks for follow-up, don't try to become active in multiple networks simultaneously. It's recommended that you choose only one new network to engage in during the twenty-eight days of the Get Clients Now! Program.

Recipe: Strengthening Personal Connections

One of the biggest challenges during the follow-up stage of the Universal Marketing Cycle is getting people to respond to your calls and e-mails. When prospects enter your marketing pipeline as a the result of your cold call, their casual visit to your website, or your finding their name on a list, you are essentially a stranger. Unless they have a compelling need for the service you are offering at the exact moment you contact them, they have no real incentive to take your call or answer your e-mail.

You can't make a prospect need you. But what you can do is identify and strengthen the **personal connections** you have with your prospects to increase the likelihood that they will be open to speaking with you.

When you have a particular prospect you can't seem to get through to, one useful tactic is to ask for an introduction from someone you already know. Ask your colleagues, others in your market niche, or members of the business and personal networks you belong to if they know this person. If so, would they be willing to serve as your connection? You might request that your connection call or e-mail your prospect suggesting he speak with you, or simply ask if you can use your connection's name as someone who referred you.

A more helpful approach overall, though, is to focus on filling your marketing pipeline with prospects you are already connected to in the first place. The people you are personally acquainted with in your market niche will probably already be on your prospect list. But your personal connections go far beyond those people you have actually met. Here are some suggestions for people you have a connection with that may not have occurred to you:

- ▶ Members of any association, club, affinity group, or online community you belong to
- ▶ People who share a connection with you on a social media network—for example, friends of your Facebook friends, or people who follow the same people you do on Twitter
- ▶ Other employees of any company you have worked for (as an employee or consultant)
- ▶ Vendors or salespeople who serve your current clients

- ▶ Alumni and faculty of any university or training school you went to
- ▶ Speakers at any meeting or conference you attended
- ▶ Parents of other children at the schools your children attend
- ▶ Current and former co-workers of your family members and close friends
- ▶ Your neighbors and neighborhood merchants
- ▶ Your local political representatives

When you look at how many names could be added to your prospect list from these sources, your circle of connections is probably much more extensive than you thought. Consider approaching prospects who fall into any of these categories instead of those with whom you can't find a connection. When writing a letter or placing a call, name the specific connection you have with each prospect in your opening. You may be surprised to see how many more people will start responding to your outreach.

ANOTHER WORD ABOUT FEAR

The thought of making follow-up calls may be even more paralyzing than cold calling. After all, this is someone you already believe needs your services. Maybe you've already talked or sent information. You've invested some time or made a personal connection, so now if you hear no, the rejection really feels personal.

What you have to remember is that rejection is not about you. This is a business transaction. Your prospects are deciding whether and how to spend their time and money. They are choosing to work on achieving their goals and fixing their problems, or not. They are choosing to hire a qualified person who truly cares whether they get what they want and need (that's you), or not. They are choosing to spend their limited resources on the priorities you can help them with, or on something else. These choices are about *them*, not about you.

The factors that go into your prospects' decision making are innumerable. And frequently, what you are told about why prospects don't want to go forward isn't the full story. Here are some actual reasons that people with a strong need for the service being offered have decided not to buy or have bought from a competitor.

What you were told . . .	*What's really going on . . .*
It's too expensive.	I decided to take a Hawaiian vacation instead.
We don't think you're right for the job.	We got a competing bid from my cousin's boyfriend.
I changed my mind.	I'm getting a divorce and can't think about anything else now.
We have other priorities right now.	The company is going bankrupt.
I can't afford it.	I don't want to take money out of a mutual fund to pay for it.
We're not ready to make a change.	My boss doesn't want headquarters to know there's a problem.
We found someone more qualified.	We liked the competitor's tag line.
Don't call us; we'll call you.	The project was tabled until next year.

When a prospect tells you a competitor was chosen because he or she "has more experience," the message is that the company hires only people with strong experience in its own industry. This is not about you. If you are told the competition "came well recommended," the prospect is choosing to do business with the friend of a friend. It's not about you. When you hear that the other guy's bid was lower, it means the buyer values price over quality. Also, not about you.

The real secret to vanquishing fear of follow-up is to have so many prospects in the pipeline that any one "no" becomes much less important.

Find a Fix for Your Discomfort

Carol Costello, www.soulofselling.com

"The Discomfort Dilemma is that perilous moment when you stand poised between doing whatever is the next step in the selling process—or doing something to avoid it," describes Carol Costello, author of *The Soul of Selling*. "That next step might be making a cold call, calling back the person you agreed to call last week, promising results, or anything that involves discomfort, the possibility of failure, or any potential for rejection." According to Costello,

> In the midst of the Discomfort Dilemma, almost anywhere seems better than where you are. And there are so many more comfortable things to do! You could call a friend. You need to keep up those relationships, after all. You could play with the cat. The poor thing needs exercise. You could e-mail your aunt, or even pay the bills. Hey, you could shampoo the rug!

> Bills do need to be paid. Rugs need to be shampooed. But not during the time when you said you'd make calls.

> For each of your own most likely Discomfort Dilemmas, you need to devise a fix that gets you moving past that paralyzing moment of indecision and takes you into action. One of my clients hated to make the first call of the day. Her fix was to spend a moment before she picked up the phone remembering a recent call that had been particularly pleasant. Another client's Dilemma was that when things were going well and she was ahead of the game, she felt an irresistible desire to shop. She learned to say to herself, "Just do what you promised yourself. When you've done it, you can spend the whole rest of the month in the stores if you want."

> Be imaginative. One client got a tube of glitter glue, and saved it for Discomfort Dilemmas. When she completed the task she had been resisting, she ran a line of glue over it on her to do list. That may sound strange, but when it comes to the Discomfort Dilemma, you want whatever gets you through the night. That woman made more than $350,000 last year, and I, for one, don't laugh at her glitter glue.

"Consider the postage stamp. . . . It secures success through its
ability to stick to one thing until it gets there."

—Josh Billings, nineteenth-century Yankee humorist

CHAPTER 9

Having Sales Conversations

When You're Contacting People but Not Getting
a Chance to Sell

WHAT'S IN THE WAY?

At this stage in the Universal Marketing Cycle, you are more than halfway home. With a full pipeline and consistent follow-up, you are bound to make plenty of sales, right? Well, usually that's true. Finding the right people to contact, and persistently reaching out to them, will produce results in most cases. But sometimes, it's not quite enough.

A sales conversation, whether it takes place in person, by phone, or even by e-mail, is a two-way exchange you have with a prospect to find out what he needs and describe to him what you can do. It's a necessary step in almost every sale of professional services. If you're not having sales conversations, it's pretty likely that you're not getting clients.

When you find yourself making lots of contacts but rarely getting to have an interactive conversation, there's something in the way. Assuming that you have a service your target market needs in the first place, and it's priced within the range your market can pay, what else might be preventing people from wanting to hear what you have to offer? Here are some possibilities:

1. **You're not using the right words.** When you send a letter or call on the phone, or prospects contact you or visit your website, they don't understand how you can help them.

2. **Your telemarketing skills aren't up to the task.** You are nervous or unprepared when you get on the phone, and aren't able to engage people in conversation.

3. **The prospects you are talking to aren't qualified enough.** They don't have a need, can't pay, or are otherwise not ready to take action.

4. **You aren't well-known enough, or haven't been recommended**, so prospects are hesitant to take their time to talk with you.

5. **Your competition seems to have the market locked up.** No one wants to talk to you because they're already being served by someone else.

6. **You are offering what you think your prospects need instead of what they think they need.** They don't see how your service fits into their plans.

7. **The way your services are packaged doesn't make sense to your prospects.** For example, they want to pay a flat fee, and you are charging by the hour.

8. **You are offering so many services that your prospects can't quite figure out what you actually do** and how it matches up with their needs.

In the next two sections, you will find solutions to many of these problems. Suggestions for doing a better job at making contact with your prospects appear first, followed by some ideas for improving your strategic market position.

STRATEGY: DIRECT CONTACT AND FOLLOW-UP AND NETWORKING AND REFERRAL BUILDING

SUCCESS INGREDIENTS:

Telemarketing script/skills   Higher quality leads and referrals
Qualifying questions

Recipe: Making the Pitch

One of the quickest fixes to your selling approach can be to change the words you use. An effective **telemarketing script** positions what you are offering in such a way that prospects grasp what's in it for them. A common mistake is to call prospects with the intent of introducing yourself and telling them what you do. But that's all about you. Why should they care?

Instead, introduce yourself by giving simply your name and any personal connection between you. Then immediately ask about their needs and get permission to talk further. "Do you have a moment to talk about your concerns with the reliability of your network?" is a sample opening question. Try leading with a benefit: "I help companies increase employee retention without added costs. Could we spend a few minutes discussing any issues you're having with employee turnover?" Or ask a qualifying question as your first step: "Are you looking for a new job opportunity right now? I'd like to see if I can help you with that, if you have a couple of minutes."

This is also what you should do when prospects call you. You don't need to ask permission in this case, but you do need to find out what prompted them to call you. Before launching into a description of how you work and what it costs, ask about their situation.

Engaging your prospects in conversation will both establish rapport and provide you with valuable information. Whenever you can, ask open-ended questions rather than prompting yes or no answers. "How much use do you expect to make of outside trainers this year?" can get you much more information than asking, "Does your company use contract trainers?" Include a series of possible questions like this in your script.

The word *script* is not meant to imply that you are reading prepared lines. You don't want to sound as if you are selling magazine subscriptions. Design your script as a list of talking points that you refer to as needed during an interactive conversation.

When you feel that you have both established some rapport and collected enough information from your prospects, tell them briefly and specifically how you can help them, and in their words. If the prospect says "our employee turnover is out of control," you might respond with, "I can really help you with that out-of-control turnover situation. The incentive plan I implemented for Althea Chemical reduced their turnover by 20 percent."

As soon as you know you've got the person's interest, ask for a meeting or turn the call into an immediate sales conversation. Don't wait for her to suggest the next step or back away from making it a direct question. "It sounds as if my services might be just what you're looking for. Would you like to get together and talk about it?" Expect to encounter objections, and have a ready answer for each predictable stumbling block already in your script.

If you have trouble remembering what's in your script, get nervous once you're on the phone, or just can't seem to think quickly enough to deliver the right responses, you need to work on your **telemarketing skills**. Take a class, work with a coach, or practice with friends. Learning your script more thoroughly will enable you to give a better performance under stress.

Prospects Are Also People

Jill Konrath, www.jillkonrath.com

"Treat the person you contact like a human being, not a prospect," recommends Jill Konrath, author of *SNAP Selling: Speed Up Sales and Win More Business with Today's Frazzled Customers*. "In calling a friend, you'd automatically ask if you were interrupting: 'Is it a bad time?' You would notice if they sounded distracted and address it head on: 'Hey, if you're swamped right now, I don't want to interrupt. I'd rather catch you when you have a few minutes to talk.' And you'd immediately suggest a future contact: 'When is a good time to call you back?'" Konrath elaborates:

> Prepare for the common obstacles prior to the call—and eliminate them if at all possible. For example, they say, "We already use XYZ." You respond: "Well, I assume a company of your size would be working with another firm. (pause) And that's why we need to meet . . ."

> Or they say, "We're really busy right now. We couldn't possibly take time to look at options." You respond: "You and I know that six months from now your workload isn't going to be any lighter. And that's exactly why we need to get together . . ."

> Please note that the second sentence in these examples starts with and, not but! Because the "and" doesn't negate your prospect's perspective, they will be interested in learning more.

> Then, reel off two to three valid business reasons that this prospect should get together with you. They need to flow out of your mouth without hesitation, so prepare them ahead of time. These are true statements, not slippery manipulations, so make sure you state them with quiet confidence.

> Sounding like a sleazy, well-oiled seller will not get you an appointment in today's market. Think of your phone calls as business-to-business conversations with peers. That may be a hard mind shift to make, but it's where you need to be.

Recipe: Qualifying Your Prospects

One of the common barriers to having sales conversations is pursuing the wrong prospects. You may have done a good job at defining your target market, but not everyone in your market needs your service now or can afford to pay. When you approach prospects who aren't qualified buyers, your requests to explore their needs and your services may fall on deaf ears, and your efforts will be wasted. **Qualifying questions** are intended to determine whether a prospect is hot, warm, or cold, so you can gauge your level of effort accordingly. Typical qualifiers are:

- ▶ Asking if they have a particular problem your service solves or a goal it aids
- ▶ Finding out how much they are expecting to pay or have paid in the past
- ▶ Determining if they have a budget set aside to get the work done
- ▶ Asking how soon they are expecting to get started or have their project completed
- ▶ Discovering what priority they have attached to addressing their issues
- ▶ Knowing if the person you are talking to is a decision maker
- ▶ Learning how far along they are in making a decision

When you speak to a prospect by phone or in person, you can ask questions like these directly. If you receive inquiries by e-mail, encourage prospects to tell you more when they write. The "contact us" page on your website might suggest a few questions you'd like them to answer, or you can provide a contact form for them to complete.

If you find that once you start asking these questions, your prospect list starts looking pretty chilly, you need some **higher-quality leads and referrals**. What is the profile of the client most likely to buy? Where can you get more leads that fit that profile? If you don't know the answers to these questions, you may need to do more research on your target market. (See the next section for some suggestions.)

Another solution is getting more referral-based leads, rather than working from prospect lists or relying on tips from your networking contacts. A client who is personally referred to you by someone they trust will almost always move forward to the sales conversation stage immediately because they have pre-qualified *you*.

If You Don't Ask, You're Selling in the Dark

Josiane Chriqui Feigon, www.tele-smart.com

"Questioning is your first chance to get inside a company and look around," says Josiane Chriqui Feigon, author of *Smart Selling on the Phone and Online*. "Your questions act as your eyes on every phone call. Questioning is still a skill that is best accomplished by phone and not via e-mail, and technique is critical to uncovering customer needs and opportunities." Feigon explains:

> Does your questioning style create comfort and trust? Do your questions sound relevant and insightful, or do your prospects feel as though they are being interrogated with rapid-fire questioning?

> Skillful questioning habits build rapport and trust. If you ask good questions and listen to the responses to hear your prospects' needs, you will guide them straight to their comfort zone, hold the focus through all their confusion, and very likely close a sale.

> With so much automation in selling now, there is a greater need than ever for the high-touch aspect of effective questioning and listening skills. These critical skills cannot be managed online, because they require a dynamic dialogue, a conversation, a discussion—a direct human interchange best served by the immediacy of live voices over the phone. Think about it: Will a busy prospect really want to spend time responding to a long e-mail string filled with qualification questions they must answer?

STRATEGY: DIRECT CONTACT AND FOLLOW-UP AND ADVERTISING

SUCCESS INGREDIENTS:

Better website conversion

Recipe: Making Your Website a Better Sales Tool

An ongoing challenge with marketing professional services on the Web is the lack of personal, ongoing contact with visitors to your website. If a prospect only visits your site once and never gets past glancing at your home page, it has no more impact than seeing a one-time ad for your service in a magazine. In order to convert site visitors into interested prospects who are open to a conversation about what you can do for them, you need to keep them on your site longer, encourage them to return for future visits, provide a vehicle for following up with them over time, and provide a clear path to taking the next step toward a sale. What you need is **better website conversion**.

Converting more visitors into interested prospects can involve any or all of four different approaches:

➤ **Provide useful information that first-time visitors will want to explore.** This will begin to build the know-like-and-trust factor, keep them on your site longer, and increase the likelihood that they will inquire about working with you. Helpful articles, case studies, videos, or facts about your profession or industry will keep them engaged and acquaint them with more of what you have to offer.

➤ **Offer fresh content or interactive features that will encourage people to return to your site again.** Post new content regularly, such as a blog, articles, videos, tutorials, an event calendar, or links to items of interest for your niche. Encourage visitors to interact with you (or each other) by enabling comments on your blog, providing assessments or quizzes, or hosting a message board. The more value you provide, the more likely it is that visitors will return.

➤ **Capture the e-mail address of your visitors by offering them a subscription bonus.** This will enable you to follow up with them to provide additional information, continue to build their trust, and determine their level of interest in working with you. See Chapter 8 for more about offering a bonus to online subscribers.

➤ **Provide a clear path to visitors for taking the next step to explore working with you.** The core purpose of a professional services website is not to do all your selling for you, but to get prospects to tell you they are interested so you can have a sales conversation. Tell visitors exactly what you want them to do, and make it easy for them to do it. You might point them to your contact page, include your phone number in multiple places, provide a contact form for them to fill out, allow them to make an appointment on your calendar, or even offer a live chat feature.

Actively maintaining a website with many different features can be a significant undertaking. Be careful that you are not investing more time and money in your Web presence than the resulting sales are worth. Remember to ask yourself the essential question needed to evaluate any marketing tactic—is there a cheaper and easier way you could generate the same amount of revenue? If most clients find you online, investing more in your presence there can be worthwhile. But if your best clients all came to you via referrals, putting too much effort into your website could be an expensive mistake.

BASIC INGREDIENTS FOR HAVING SALES CONVERSATIONS

SUCCESS INGREDIENTS:

Professional visibility	**New market position**
Competitive research	**Better service package**
Target market research	**Narrower focus of services**

Ingredient: Professional Visibility

If the first time that prospective clients hear your name is when you call them to have a sales conversation, you will find it much harder to get their attention than if they already know you or know of you. Increasing your **professional visibility** is not just a tactic for filling the pipeline; it's also a way to influence buying decisions.

Networking and referral building activities will help you become more visible in your market niche and build trust. Attend networking events frequented by your clients and prospects or network with them online. Volunteer in a high-profile position, such as the program committee of an association your clients belong to, or as chairperson of a project likely to get good coverage in the trade press or generate buzz online.

The strategies of writing and publicity and public speaking will help you to become more visible professionally, while simultaneously building your credibility. When prospects type your name into a search engine, and see that you are regularly writing articles and giving presentations about your specialty, they will be more likely to take your call or return it. Promotional events like free teleclasses, workshops, or demonstrations give you a reason to send out invitations and press releases, or post about your activities online, which will increase your exposure.

All of these strategies have a higher effectiveness rating than advertising in bringing you more visibility with your target audience. They will allow you to establish the personal connections and trust that result in having more sales conversations and easier sales.

Connecting with the Invisible

Harry Beckwith, www.beckwithpartners.com

"Products are made; services are delivered," asserts Harry Beckwith, author of *Selling the Invisible*, *The Invisible Touch*, and *What Clients Love*. "Products are used; services are experienced. Products possess physical characteristics we can evaluate before we buy; services do not even exist before we buy them. We request them, often paying in advance. Then we receive them." Beckwith adds,

> And finally, products are impersonal: bricks, mortar, pens, car seats, fruit— things with no human connection to us. Services, by contrast, are personal— often frighteningly so. A service relationship touches our essence and reveals the people involved: provider and customer. For that reason, a service marketing course belongs in the school of the humanities. Service marketers, like humanities scholars, strive to answer this question: "What does it mean to be a human being?"

> . . . Our lives seem increasingly disconnected. Our grown children move farther from home; technology reduces direct contact with people. Our drive for connection grows more intense. Making genuine, human connections becomes more important everywhere—not least of all in our businesses every day.

Ingredient: Competitive Research

The position that you occupy in the minds of your prospective clients can be a critical factor in their decision to speak with you or not. If you find that prospects are choosing to work with your competitors, you may need to reposition yourself against the competition.

Start by conducting some **competitive research** to find out what it is that clients like about the people you are competing with. Are those qualities you can emulate? In what areas are clients not as satisfied with them? Could you offer them more satisfaction there?

Ask your current or former clients about their experience with the competition. They may be quite candid with you about what they liked and didn't like, and also give you some valuable insight into why they chose you. To expand your competitive research to prospective clients, spend some time sleuthing online. Testimonials and reviews posted by your competitors' clients can be quite revealing about how they see your competition. Or, consider hiring a market researcher to survey some prospective clients for you. Prospects may be much more willing to speak with a third party.

To learn more about how your competitors are positioning themselves, visit their websites. Read their mission statements or tag lines, review their lists of features and benefits, notice how they headline their Web copy. Consider how you might position your services more positively when compared to theirs.

Ingredients: Target Market Research and New Market Position

Target market research is another direction to look if prospects are telling you they don't need what you are offering. If you think a company needs a team-building retreat, but they think their problem can be solved with more skills training, you won't make a sale.

What are the hot topics in your market's trade press? What blog posts in your niche stimulate the most comments? What themes are being addressed at industry conferences? What issues seem to surface frequently in social media exchanges?

When you learn more about how prospects view their own challenges, you can develop a **new market position** to match their mental, or real-life, purchase order better. Often just a change in language can alter how prospects view your offer. Your retreat might turn into a sale if you described it as "an intensive three-day training program in the critical skills needed for effective teamwork."

Ask current and former clients to help you position your services more positively. One way to discover how your market perceives the value in your work is to ask satisfied clients for a testimonial letter. The way they describe the work you do and benefits they received from it can give you valuable clues in how to sell it to others. An evaluation questionnaire can be used for the same purpose. Try asking, "How would you describe my service to someone else who could use it?"

It's also possible you will discover that you've chosen the wrong market; the perceived need for what you offer just isn't strong enough, they aren't willing to pay what you need to charge, or the size of the market is too limited. In this case, it's time to position yourself for an entirely different market. Make sure you do your homework on any possible new markets in advance, so you won't make the same mistake a second time.

A career counselor who is having a hard time finding individuals who will pay her fee can market herself to companies in need of outplacement services. A computer software trainer who discovers that large companies prefer working with training firms that can serve them on a national scale might find a better market in small to midsize organizations. Keep asking the question, "Who is most likely to hire me?" until you find the right fit.

Ingredients: Better Service Package and Narrower Focus of Services

Another problem your research might uncover is that your service isn't packaged in a way that prospects want to buy it. Developing a **better service package** could make what you offer more attractive. A marketing consultant who has been working on a project basis might find clients more receptive to a monthly retainer they can budget for. An interior designer encountering resistance to paying an hourly fee might instead raise his markup or commission on furnishings, and no longer charge by the hour at all.

Sometimes just naming your service package can make a difference. An image consultant might be much more successful selling the "One-Day Makeover" than suggesting to clients they buy six hours of her time to revamp their whole look. When doing your market research, try asking your prospects how they prefer to buy services like yours, and tailor your offering to their preferences.

One final roadblock you may be putting in your own way is offering too much. When someone asks exactly what it is that you do or specifically how you can help them, it really doesn't work to say, "I can do pretty much anything in the area of [fill in the blank]. What do you need?" It may be absolutely true that you can do almost anything in your field of expertise, but people don't buy "anything," they buy something specific. It's a rare prospect who will agree to meet with you just to share his problems and goals without knowing exactly what you are selling.

A **narrower focus of services** will allow prospects to have a better sense of how much they need you. It will also help them remember who you are. Having people know that you do "anything with computers" will not lead to many inquiries or referrals. If they think of you instead as the expert in accounting and financial management software, you could find a place in their contact database.

Just as with choosing a market niche, don't worry that you are limiting yourself with this narrower focus. Once you are in conversation with a prospect, you can propose other services that are within your range of expertise. But you need the narrower focus to get their attention so you can have the conversation in the first place.

Know Yourself and You'll Know Your Clients

Allison Bliss, www.allisonbliss.com

"All the tips and tricks in the world don't work unless a business has a good service or product for which there is a market," contends Allison Bliss, director of a marketing communications agency that serves many small, growing companies. "It also saves time and cost to conduct some basic market research to define your target market (it may not be what you first expect), to position, package, and promote your business effectively." Bliss points out,

> There are many easier ways to do research now than even five or ten years ago: Using search engines, social media, and Meetup groups discussing your business topic. In these groups, you can listen to what they need or value and work that into your business plan. By adding a new option or variation that your research reveals, your sales could skyrocket. For example, if there are dozens of piano teachers in your market area, perhaps you could stand out by teaching jazz instead of just the typical classical standards.

> Market research doesn't have to force you into an uncomfortable box. When businesses position their company based on their own unique spirit or passion, they feel more comfortable in their marketing efforts and generate better results. Instead of trying to find a market that could afford your services, it's far smarter and easier to find a market that you really want to help, or those you truly care about. Use your uniqueness in positioning to promote your business, so you gain a better market share, and attract the clients with whom you want to conduct business.

MORE WORDS ABOUT FEAR

It's inevitable during the stage of Having Sales Conversations that you will experience some fear. Throughout this chapter, you have been encouraged to initiate live conversations with prospective clients. In most cases, this will require you to pick up the phone and call people you don't know well, which many people find to be challenging. When you ask prospects to take the time to speak with you about your services, you expose yourself to the possibility of rejection. It's likely that more people will say no to you than will say yes. Knowing this, you may feel quite apprehensive about putting yourself in this situation. Under those circumstances, you may avoid and delay reaching out to prospects, often without acknowledging to yourself that fear is at work.

If you notice that you are putting off contacting your prospects, calling when you're sure they won't be there, e-mailing when you know you should call, or any other signs of avoidant behavior, take some time to read through the section on self-confidence skills in Chapter 7. Choose one of the approaches described there and dedicate some time to working with it.

You can do this.

> *"When you get into a tight place and everything goes against you,*
> *till it seems as though you could not hold on a minute longer, never give*
> *up then, for that is just the place and time that the tide will turn."*
>
> —Harriet Beecher Stowe

CHAPTER 10

Closing Sales

When You're Having Sales Conversations but Not Getting Sales

THE FINAL FRONTIER

To make your way to this final stage of the Universal Marketing Cycle, you've already done a lot of things right. You've identified good prospects, gotten up the nerve to follow up with them, and convinced them to speak with you. Getting stuck at this point, after investing a great deal of time and effort, can be really frustrating.

Understand first that some sales can't be made—or at least can't be made now. The vast majority of reasons that a prospect may choose to say no are completely out of your control. In fact, most consultants, professionals, and coaches find that only one out of three prospects they present to will become a client. This means at least two out of three are saying no.

Many of the reasons prospects decide not to buy are standard objections you can attempt to handle, some of which are covered near the end of this chapter under "Making the Sale." Others, however, have more to do with how you are presenting and selling yourself. Since this *is* under your control, some suggestions for improvement follow. First we'll look at issues of credibility and then move on to specific techniques that you can use for your sales conversations.

BASIC INGREDIENTS FOR CLOSING SALES

SUCCESS INGREDIENTS:

Professional credibility

Testimonials or references

Ingredient: Professional Credibility

If you find that prospects tend to ask a lot of questions about your background and experience, increasing your **professional credibility** may help to make the sale go through. Using the marketing strategies of public speaking and writing and publicity are one way to do this. Networking or volunteering in a professional association (yours or the prospect's) is another. Referral-building activities focused on prominent center-of-influence people is a third.

Take a hard look at your credentials: work experience, formal education, speaking and publication credits, professional affiliations, and visible achievements. Based on what you see, would you hire yourself? Without a strong recommendation, prospects may be hesitant to do business with you if your credentials are light.

If it's experience you lack, consider donating your professional services to a community organization. If it's education, it might be time to earn a certificate in your specialty or take some more classes. Find other opportunities to add to your list of accomplishments and affiliations. Teach a class, record an audio or video tutorial, organize a community or professional event, enter a contest, or seek out an award.

Then make sure you broadcast your credentials in all your marketing efforts. Cite the key accomplishments that make you credible in your Web copy, social media profiles, marketing materials, article bylines, or advertisements. Mention them in social media posts, or when you speak or host a promotional event. It won't help you to acquire more credentials if people don't know about them.

Ingredient: Testimonials or References

A solid portfolio of **testimonials or references** can also convince prospects of your credibility. Include testimonial quotes or videos on your website, quote them in your brochure, or include testimonial letters in your marketing kit.

The best testimonial letters are written directly to you ("Dear Karl, Thank you so much for the contribution you have made to my success . . ."), rather than "To Whom It May Concern." Whenever clients tell you how happy they are with the service you are providing, ask if you can quote them. If your service needs to remain confidential, ask for an anonymous testimonial, and identify the client only by first name and job title or city.

Testimonials or your client list are good to include in your marketing materials, but references should be available only by request. You don't want prospects calling your references before they decide to meet with you. Have a list of references ready, though, to offer after your sales conversation, if prospects ask. The more current your references are, the better, and be sure all the contact information is up to date.

Whether you let your references know who will be calling them is up to you, but definitely stay in touch with references as long as you continue to give out their names. When choosing who to use as a reference from many possibilities, focus on who can give the best confirmation of your capabilities. If those turn out to be the smaller or lesser-known clients, that's okay. You can still use any big names to head up your client list.

Boost Credibility and You'll Boost Sales

Nancy Marmolejo, www.vivavisibilityblog.com

"The Latin root of 'credibility' is 'credo,' meaning 'I believe.' It's about the truth of you, reflected in your actions and experience, your know-how, and your belief that yes, you are an expert!" That's the view of Nancy Marmolejo, who teaches entrepreneurs how to stand out and make more money as experts in their field. She explains,

> When you establish a firm base of credibility around your business, then sales come in with ease. People trust you, the key component of a transaction.

> Here are some tips to boost your credibility so you can enjoy increased sales and more opportunities:

1. Believe in your own expertise. View your expertise as the gap between what your target market doesn't know and what you know. They're paying you to fill that gap. Own the fact that you are an expert.

2. Get others to back you up. You can't be the only one to toot your horn. You need third party verification that you're the expert you say you are. Collect case studies, testimonials, media spots, and other outside sources who can honestly attest to your talents, skills, and abilities.

3. Make "provide value" your mantra. Instead of opening up Facebook and saying, "Hmm, how am I going to make money off these people today?" shift your approach to "How can I add value to my network?" Think of things you can share, say, or do that will show people your contributions are worth paying attention to.

4. Trust sells. When we ground our actions in credibility and provide value, we create trust. Constantly pitching your business doesn't build trust, it builds resistance. Find a balance between letting people know how they can buy from you while providing them with valuable information that will make them want to know you.

STRATEGY: DIRECT CONTACT AND FOLLOW-UP AND NETWORKING AND REFERRAL BUILDING

SUCCESS INGREDIENTS:

Better-qualified prospects

Stronger relationships

Presentation script/visuals

Presentation skills

Portfolio

Leave-behind

Selling script

Selling skills

Recipe: Changing Whom You Have Sales Conversations With

One of the ways to have more sales conversations turn into closed sales is to have fewer sales conversations—fewer, that is, with people who aren't qualified buyers. It's tempting to have a sales conversation with anyone who will listen, but that just takes up time you could have spent finding **better-qualified prospects**. Review the suggestions in Chapter 9 for asking qualifying questions and finding higher quality leads and referrals to help with this goal.

Remember that the more people you can get to contact you, instead of you contacting them, the easier your selling task will be. Focusing more effort on professional visibility, generating referrals, and better website conversion can help just as much in closing sales as it does in filling the pipeline and having sales conversations.

Sometimes the main reason that sales conversations don't result in closed sales is that your prospects don't know you well enough yet. Consider spending more time building **stronger relationships** up front with the people you wish to have sales conversations with. Here are some ways you might do this:

- ▶ Attend networking meetings, conferences, or social events that your prospects frequent.
- ▶ Invite prospects to events you plan to attend.
- ▶ Schedule coffee, lunch, or a date to play tennis or golf to get better acquainted.
- ▶ Send your prospects articles and other information that will help them do their jobs better or achieve their personal goals.
- ▶ Interact with prospects in social media networks or online communities.
- ▶ Ask prospects to subscribe to your newsletter or blog.
- ▶ Follow some of the suggestions in Chapter 9 to identify personal connections that already exist between you and your prospects.
- ▶ Find a mutual contact to put in a good word with prospects on your behalf.

A primary reason that people hire a professional services provider is to serve as an expert resource. Look for ways to serve your prospects before selling to them. Give them tastes of your expertise and the resources at your disposal in all your marketing materials, on your website, in your social media posts, at speaking engagements, in your newsletter or blog, and any other way they come in contact with you. Often this will result in prospects becoming clients without either of you having to work at it.

Recipe: Scripting Your Sales Conversations

It can aid your sales conversations considerably to be prepared with a **presentation script**. The term "presentation" means simply that you are presenting your services to a prospect, not that you are giving a prepared speech. Like a telemarketing script, this is actually a series of talking points, rather than something you memorize and repeat. Here's a general outline:

1. **Establish rapport.** Introduce yourself, make sure you know with whom you are speaking and who else is in the room or listening in. When meeting in person, chat about whatever sequence of events got you there or something else you all have in common.

2. **Determine their needs.** Begin by repeating what you already know, and then start asking questions. Your script should include all the questions you must have an answer to in order to write a proposal or close the deal on the spot. Open-ended questions will elicit more information than those that can be answered with a yes or no. Many questions will be specific to your line of business, but here are some typical ones:

- What is your current situation?
- How important or urgent is it that you solve this problem?
- What have you already tried?
- When do you need this done, or when were you thinking about getting started?
- What resources do you already have lined up?
- What other solutions are you considering?
- What would the perfect solution look like?
- What kind of budget do you have, or what were you expecting to pay?

3. **Explain how you can meet their needs.** Using the information you have just gathered, respond to each problem or goal they mentioned by describing how you can help. Use specific examples to illustrate your expla-

nation—for example, "My last client had exactly the same challenge, and what I did for her was . . ."

4. **Answer their questions.** Find out how you are doing by asking, "What else do you need to know?" Keep asking for and answering questions until they seem satisfied. Address any concerns that come up, one by one. Reassure them that you are the right solution to their problem by responding specifically with how you can help.

5. **Ask for the business.** Don't leave this step out. Even if you know they will want to see a proposal first, are talking to other people, or aren't ready to make a decision, ask anyway. It's the only way you will find out how close you are to making a sale. Whatever they say in response to this question will tell you exactly what you need to resolve before your prospects will buy.

6. **Decide on a next step.** Whether or not you have closed the sale, be absolutely certain that both you and the prospect know what happens next. Is she ready to get started? When? Will there be a contract or purchase order involved? Who has to sign off on it? Does she need a written proposal? Does she want to check your references? Can you call back in a week? If you don't already know, find out if she will be talking to other people before making a decision. And be sure to ask if there is anything you can do to help move things forward.

If you use a free sample of your services as a sales strategy, such as a complimentary consultation or sample session, don't allow the sample to completely replace your sales conversation. Although many of the questions you might normally ask during a sales conversation may be covered during the course of your complimentary session, you will still need to connect the dots for your prospect between what he needs and what you do. Don't assume he will figure that out by himself just from his brief experience of working with you. You will also still need to ask for the sale. Be sure to leave enough time at the conclusion of your session for these important aspects of selling.

Once you have developed and mastered the content of your sales conversations, consider whether your **presentation skills** may also need some improvement. For one-on-one conversations, work on your questioning and listening abilities. When you present your business to groups of people, your speaking skills become more important. Take a workshop, hire a coach, or join a group to gain more practice.

These suggestions for sales conversations assume that they are taking place interactively, in person or by phone. But it is sometimes possible to have a "conversation" by e-mail or online chat. While this is not typically the most effective approach, some prospects may lead you into an e-mail conversation by e-mailing you with detailed questions about how you work and what you charge before they are willing to speak with you live. Or they may catch you while you're on social media site with a chat feature, and initiate a chat to ask questions.

When you find yourself in this situation, take care that you have learned enough about your prospect's needs to adequately explain how you can meet them. You may need to ask additional questions of your own before responding with all the details your prospect has requested. If you don't take this step, your generic response may be a poor match for her requirements and you won't get a second chance to present what you can do.

Recipe: Adding Tangibility to Your Sales Conversations

Services are intangible; they can't be seen or touched like a product can. Consider supporting your talking points with some **presentation visuals**. In person, topics outlined on a flipchart or laptop screen, or diagrams, illustrations, and photographs can help give what you have to say more weight. When having a sales conversation by phone, the same material can be displayed on the Web or e-mailed to your prospect in advance, so the two of you can review it together.

Another solution is to provide a **portfolio** of your best work. Artists, designers, and other professionals who create tangible objects routinely do this, but in fact, anyone can. Your portfolio could be available online, or you can bring a portfolio with you to an in-person meeting. You might include samples of your writing, reports you have prepared, program outlines, photos of your past projects, or a video of you at work. Going through your portfolio with a prospect, or flipping to a certain page as questions arise, can further establish your expertise.

While a portfolio is something you and a prospect often review together, the purpose of a **leave-behind** is to give your prospects a sample of your work they can hang on to or a gift to remember you by. A leave-behind that serves as a sample could be a case study, special report, before-and-after photos, demonstration DVD, or a collection of testimonials. Gift leave-behinds include books, CDs, DVDs, promotional products with your logo (coffee cups or notepads, for example), or even candy. You can also mail or e-mail your leave-behind after a sales conversation by phone. The idea is to give your prospect a present they will use or refer to, and therefore continue to think of you.

Make a Connection and You'll Make the Sale

Patricia Haddock, www.patriciahaddock.com

"Pay attention to what others say as they say it. Don't formulate your response while they are speaking. Just listen." That's the advice of communications consultant Patricia Haddock, author of eleven books and over 600 magazine articles. Here are some of her tips for more powerful presentations.

1. Use stories and anecdotes to illustrate your points and involve your listeners. People relate to other people; storytelling captures the imagination and the memory.

2. Rehearse. Each time you rehearse your presentation—whether physically or going over it in your mind—you program it into your brain and body. The more familiar you are with the material, the more natural you will sound.

3. Make continuous eye contact to draw your listeners to you and keep their attention. Express interest by nodding, making eye contact, and smiling.

4. Read audience body language to make sure you are keeping their attention. If you see glazed looks, crossed arms, or blank stares, pick up the pace, move around, ask questions, tell a story, or cut to a key benefit that will wake them up.

5. Ask open-ended questions that require more than simple yes or no answers. Require straightforward answers to your questions. Rephrase your question until the person responds appropriately.

6. Paraphrase what the other person says, and ask if you are interpreting his or her comments correctly.

7. Ask for what you want, and if you hear no, start negotiating.

Recipe: Making the Sale

If you're doing your job right, the selling begins as soon as the sales conversation does. The moment you begin explaining exactly how your services can solve the prospect's problems, you are starting to sell. So what's the difference between a **selling script** and a presentation script? Not too much. But if you find yourself doing fine until it's time to ask for the business and then you start floundering, a better selling script is what you need.

Asking for the business can feel confronting. This is the moment in your sales conversation when you are most likely to be rejected, so you may find yourself resisting asking a direct question to find out whether you have the sale. Keep in mind that your prospect is expecting this question. He knows this is a sales situation and at some point you are going to request his agreement to go forward. So don't back away from asking directly. You will leave your prospect hanging, and the future of your sale uncertain.

Up until this point in the conversation, the questions you have been asking have been mostly open-ended to gather as much information as possible and keep all possibilities open. Now you should switch to a yes or no question. What this form of question will do is elicit three possible answers: yes, no, or the reason why not. The good news is that prospects almost never say no. Instead, they respond with a specific reason why they aren't saying yes just yet. And this is exactly the information you need to make the sale.

There are many different ways to ask your prospects for their business. Here are some sample questions that might be in your selling script:

"Are you ready to get started?"

"Would you like to schedule an appointment?"

"Shall I draw up a contract?"

"Would you like to sign up?"

"Is my proposal acceptable?"

"Shall I finalize the details?"

"Do we have a deal?"

The most important element of asking for the business is to ask your closing question and then shut up! Don't talk yourself out of a sale by saying, "Is my proposal acceptable or is the price too high? I know you had some concerns about the budget and. . . ." Wait to hear whether your prospect has any objections, and if so, what they are. Even if the silence starts to get uncomfortable, don't speak until your prospect answers you.

The next words out of your prospect's mouth will tell you exactly what you need to hear. It's likely to be an objection. This doesn't mean you have lost the sale. In fact, it may mean you have made it. "Well, it's a lot of money to spend," is not a real objection; it's probably a statement of fact. An appropriate response might be, "You're right, it's quite an investment. What do you think, are you ready to take the plunge?"

Real objections, though, need to be overcome—or to reframe this in a way you might find more helpful, they are "considerations that need to be resolved," or "points that need to be handled," in order for the sale to go through. Include in your selling script all the typical objections people in your line of work encounter, and some possible responses to each one.

Never disagree with a prospect's objections or try to argue with her. Instead, validate what your prospect is saying and reassure her that the two of you will work together to find a solution that serves you both. Once your prospect hires you, you will be working together on many solutions, and what better time to start? Maintain a friendly, helpful, service-oriented attitude, and you will find selling conversations to be much more comfortable than if you become defensive or adversarial.

Remember, too, that once you leave the room or hang up the phone, you may find yourself back in voice mail limbo. For that reason, it's wise to make every possible use of this opportunity to deal with your prospect's considerations person to person.

The best way to respond to an objection is to agree completely with what your prospect is saying, then ask another open-ended question that leads the conversation back to how your service can be of value. Here are some examples:

The prospect says . . .	You respond . . .
We can't afford to spend that much.	Yes, I know the price is significant. For comparison, though, what is it costing you not to fix it?
I need to think about it.	It's a big decision, and I'm sure you do. Tell me, what are some of your concerns?
I'm not sure it will help.	Yes, I understand you can't know for sure until we get started. If it did help, though, what might you gain?
We're too busy right now.	I know how busy you are. Tell me, if you don't deal with the situation now, when will you be less busy?
It's too expensive.	Yes, it's a big investment. What results would make that kind of investment worthwhile?
We're not ready.	I understand that you have a lot going on. What will need to change in order for you to be ready?

I'm not sure you're right for the job.	Yes, I know that you may have concerns about that. What would you need to feel more confident about in order to hire me?

When your prospect replies to the new question you have asked, treat his response as one more need he has expressed, and explain how you can meet it. If you still believe that your service is the best solution your prospect could find, keep asking questions until you have uncovered and responded to as many objections as you can. Then ask for the business again and see what happens.

If at any point in the sales conversation, you discover some concrete reasons why your service would not be a good fit for your prospect's needs, tell him so, and gracefully end the conversation. Recommend another provider who might be a better solution, if you know one. There's no value to either of you in trying to close a sale that will ultimately end in you taking a job you won't enjoy, or your client not being satisfied.

If every sales conversation seems to get bogged down with objections at the end, you are probably asking for the business too soon. Try asking, "What concerns do you have?" before introducing a closing question. That way you can work to resolve those concerns while you are still in the more comfortable phase of open conversation, and don't yet feel so pressured to sell.

Learning to do a good job at this kind of high-stakes verbal exchange may require improving your **selling skills**. Books, audio programs, and videos can help, but significant improvement will take practice. Workshops and other group environments are one way to practice, or you can role-play with a friend or coach. One of the biggest obstacles to successful selling is lack of self-confidence, and that's what practice in a safe environment will help you to build.

To Win More Sales, Try Being Yourself

Rochelle Togo-Figa, www.salesbreakthroughs.com

"Do you have to be like the pushy used car salesman to be successful in sales? Absolutely not!" asserts Rochelle Togo-Figa, creator of the Sales Breakthrough System. "Have you ever watched someone speak and found yourself listening to every word they say? You don't know the person, yet there's something about them that draws you to them. It happens because they're being genuine and real. They're being themselves." She continues,

> Being successful in sales doesn't come from being slick or pushy, or copying someone else's selling style. That never works because people can sense you're not yourself. The key is to let go of trying to be what you're not and to trust yourself.
>
> Let's define what selling really is:
>
> 1. Selling is no longer being the slick, aggressive, and pushy salesperson.
> 2. Selling is being more interested in the prospect than in what you have to say.
> 3. Selling is creating a trusting and honest relationship with the prospect.
> 4. Selling is being a keen listener and listening for what's most important to the prospect.
> 5. Selling is thinking of ways of helping the prospect.
> 6. Selling is going the extra mile and doing the unexpected for the prospect.
> 7. Selling is showing you genuinely want to help them get to where they want to go.
> 8. Selling is making yourself easily accessible to your prospects either by phone or e-mail.
> 9. Selling is trusting who you are and being yourself. You are unique and special just as you are, so let that shine through!
>
> Sales success begins with being yourself. It really is as simple as that. The prospect will come to you because they're attracted to your authenticity. When you're being real, your honesty and trust shines through, and people are drawn to you.

Recipe: Following Up

When you don't close the sale at the time of the sales conversation, you haven't yet lost it. But if you don't follow up, you probably will. Everyone who has been in business for any length of time has a story about a sale that finally went through eighteen months after the first sales conversation or after the eleventh follow-up call. Once you have made contact with a prospect who needs you, can pay you, and already knows what you can do for them, don't let them go!

Contact your prospects at regular intervals, using all the methods described in Chapter 8. Be friendly, considerate, and professional, but be persistent. If they really don't want to hear from you, they will tell you. Until then, keep following up.

A FINAL WORD ABOUT FEAR

The moment of truth in a sales conversation is when you ask for the business. As soon as you ask the question, you run the risk of being turned down. The thought of that can be so scary that you stop yourself from asking, maybe not even consciously. You walk out of the meeting or hang up the phone, and realize that you still don't know whether the prospect will buy.

To become successful at selling, you must overcome this last self-imposed obstacle. Try a memory jogger first. When having sales conversations by phone, post a sign bearing your favorite closing question where you can't avoid seeing it. For in-person conversations, you may need to be more subtle. Stick a reminder wherever you will be taking notes—on your laptop or tablet's desktop, or inside your note pad.

If you still find yourself choking on the closing question, start by asking something more indirect. At the point in the sales conversation where the prospect has no more questions, ask, "Where are we?" or "What's our next step?" This may give you all the information you need to uncover any objections before moving forward. Then it may feel safe enough to ask a more direct question to see if you have the sale.

Practice asking closing questions with a friend or coach. Trust that the more you ask, the more confident you will become. And remember that the only way you are likely to get anything you want in life is to ask for it.

The Doorway to Freedom

Rhonda Britten, www.fearlessliving.org

"Fear is the gatekeeper of your comfort zone," counsels Rhonda Britten, Emmy Award-winning life coach and author of four bestsellers including *Fearless Living*. Britten says,

> Your comfort zone is whatever is familiar to you. As a little child, your comfort zone was your mother's lap. You ventured away out of curiosity but scurried back to safety when you felt threatened. Now your comfort zone is the people you already know, the routines you're used to, the places where you feel at home. Whether these are bad, good, happy, or sad is immaterial. As the old saying goes, 'Better the devil you know than the devil you don't know.'

But how satisfying is safe? Fear keeps us from feeling alive when there's a danger of not being accepted, approved, or understood. Therefore we deny our essential nature. Fear doesn't know you are an adult who craves adventure and love and fulfillment. It doesn't know that you could handle it from here. That is why a crisis is sometimes what's necessary to shake up your world and give you the courage you need to show your fear who's boss.

There is almost certainly some level of crisis manifesting itself in your life right now. Maybe you are simply sick of letting yourself down or listening to your own excuses. Perhaps you've had enough of never finding the courage to stand up for yourself. Maybe you are tired of not earning what you're worth just because you can't bring yourself to put a real value on your contribution. You may not even be able to pinpoint what's going on but you know something isn't quite working. Your soul yearns for more. That's all you need to get started on the journey from fear to freedom.

Index